LIVES OF THE NUNS

LIVES
OF THE
NUNS

Biographies of Chinese
Buddhist Nuns from the
Fourth to Sixth Centuries

A translation of the
Pi-ch'iu-ni chuan,
compiled by Shih Pao-ch'ang

Translated by
Kathryn Ann Tsai

University of Hawaii Press
Honolulu

© 1972 Kathryn Ann Adelsperger Cissell

© 1994 University of Hawaii Press

Printed in the United States of America

94 95 96 97 98 99   5 4 3 2 1

Library of Congress Cataloging-in-Publication Data

Pao-ch'ang, 6th cent.

[Pi ch'iu ni chuan. English]

Lives of the nuns : biographies of Chinese Buddhist nuns from the

fourth to sixth centuries : a translation of the Pi-ch'iu-ni chuan /

compiled by Shih Pao-ch'ang ; translated by Kathryn Ann Tsai.

p.   cm.

Includes bibliographical references and index.

ISBN 0–8248–1541–6

1. Buddhist nuns—China—Biography—Early works to 1800.

I. Tsai, Kathryn Ann.   II. Title.

BQ634.P3713   1994

294.3'657'092251—dc20   93–50627

[B]   CIP

University of Hawaii Press books are printed on
acid-free paper and meet the guidelines for permanence and
durability of the Council on Library Resources

Designed by Paula Newcomb

for Anna-la
1938–1991

CONTENTS

PREFACE

A millennium and a half ago there lived in China some remarkable women who cast aside the fetters of the world to become Buddhist nuns. *Lives of the Nuns* preserves the memory of their lives and deeds and gives us a look into a world that is foreign, exotic, and now vanished; yet, that world is far less alien than we might first think, for it is peopled with men and women who express the same emotions—the same desires, aspirations, or longings for spiritual enlightenment—as those found at all times and in all places. Furthermore, the character of these nuns who lived during dangerous and chaotic times can instruct us who also live in such times. We need not be Chinese Buddhists of the sixth century to be charmed by the nun Hui-chan's insouciant bravery (no. 7), or to be moved by Chih-hsien's fearless integrity (no. 3), or to smile at Ching-ch'eng's clever ruse (no. 28). And we who have in this generation seen Buddhist monastics offer their bodies as a sacrifice by fire will feel kinship with the religious and laity of long ago who, when they learned that T'an-chien (no. 46) had offered her body by fire to the Buddha, "lamented, their cries reverberating through the mountains and valleys."

This translation of *Lives of the Nuns,* a major revision of an original translation done as part of my doctoral dissertation for the University of Wisconsin, was prepared with both the general reader and the scholar in mind in the hope that those who have no special background in the subject may take up the material and read with pleasure and understanding, while the scholars in the field may also enjoy the *Lives.*

The Translation

Because the biographies are often concise to the point of obscurity, and because allusions, references, names, and places familiar to the Chinese reader of nearly fifteen hundred years ago are simply not going to be clear to the present-day English-speaking reader, the translator has taken the liberty of adding to the text of the biographies bracketed phrases or even sentences necessary to provide a smoother narrative. Any material that cannot be worked into the biography itself is found in the notes.

To provide a sense of geographic direction, place-names are supplemented with brief phrases indicating where they were in China or where they were in relation to the southern capital, which, as the major city of the southern dynasties, makes an obvious reference point. A map of China, showing many of the places mentioned in the biographies, is also included. It should be kept in mind that, whenever a biography mentions the place where the woman's family came from, it frequently means the place from which the family had emigrated several generations previously. When a place-name cannot be located with reasonable certainty, no attempt is made to locate it.

To clarify relationships or to bring out more clearly the point of a nun's connection with particular individuals, named persons, whenever possible, are identified by a brief phrase in the translation. Additional information, if any, appears in the notes. Those individuals who are otherwise unknown will not be annotated.

To help readers fix the events in time, dates of birth and death are given when known and, for emperors, dates of birth, beginning of reign, and death.

The bibliography of sources, reference works, and readings describes the books mentioned in the notes, those used as sources and references for the preparation of the translation, and those that readers might find of further interest.

Appendix A is a more technical discussion of the history, sources, and literary prototypes for the text of the *Lives*.

The romanization system used for transcribing the Chinese characters is a modification of the Wade-Giles system, chosen because the English-language references and suggested further readings also use this system, thereby creating a consistency that the reader might find helpful.

Words of Sanskrit origin are transcribed using the long marks (macrons) over the vowels but not the retroflex marks under certain consonants. The letter combination *sh* represents both the consonant often transcribed as an *s* with the acute accent and the consonant *s* often transcribed with the retroflex dot underneath. The letter combination *ch* represents what is often written only as the letter *c*. The letter *n* before *g, k,* or *h* represents what is often written as an *m*. These differences should be noted when trying to find in other readings the words or titles of Sanskrit origin used in the *Lives of the Nuns*.

The nuns' personal names have been transliterated, with a translation of the name appearing only in the glosses that begin the individual biographies. Names of convents and monasteries have been translated to provide the reader with a respite from the many Chinese names and in some instances to make clear the point a biography is trying to make concerning the choice of a name for the convent, as for example, biography 5. Place-names have been transliterated, except for some names of mountains that can be straightforwardly translated into English. The names of the two most famous rivers in China are given in the form familiar to English-speaking readers—that is, the Yellow and the Yangtze rather than the Ho and the Chiang.

Thanks are due to the late Arthur E. Link for having introduced me, many years ago, not only to the *Pi-ch'iu-ni chuan* but also to the world of medieval China, to the late Richard H. Robinson for having supervised my initial work, and to the late Holmes Welch for having provided opportunities for further study and research.

I must also thank a colleague whom I have never met, Li Jung-hsi, of the Chinese Buddhist Association in Peking, whose own English translation of the *Pi-ch'iu-ni chuan* I reviewed in 1985. Although I would have preferred speaking with him personally, having his translation at hand meant that I was able, in a sense, to ask his opinion about any phrase or sentence in the text. Because we are working with difficult and often ambiguous material, it is to be expected that we will not always agree.

A heartfelt thank you I offer to Sharon Yamamoto of University of Hawaii Press not only for her initial interest but also for her encouragement and for her well-chosen suggestions for improving the book.

To my husband, Tsai Hsiang-jen, I owe deep and deserved thanks in recognition of his patient endurance as well as his very concrete help in more ways than I can count.

To the late Anna Katharina Seidel of the Institut du Hōbōgirin in Kyoto, for her help, criticism, and especially for her unfailingly kind generosity, I owe a debt of gratitude that can never be adequately repaid. Whatever is good in this work is hers, and to her I dedicate *Lives of the Nuns*.

KATHRYN ANN TSAI

Introduction

The Chinese Buddhist canon of scripture includes a unique and remarkable text, the *Pi-ch'iu-ni chuan,* or *Lives of the Nuns* (hereafter *Lives*), a collection of chronologically organized biographies of sixty-five Chinese Buddhist nuns.[1] More than a mere collection of biographies, their dates cover the period of the founding and establishing of the Buddhist monastic order for women from the early fourth century to the early sixth century. The *Lives* allows us to see the development of monastic life for women in China from its beginnings.

Shih Pao-ch'ang,[2] who compiled the book in or about A.D. 516, selected his subjects with careful discrimination and produced a document of interest for his readership, whom he presumably had hoped to spur on to greater efforts in the Buddhist life (see Pao-ch'ang's preface).[3] Fifteen hundred years later the biographies are of interest to us for very different reasons. We see in hindsight many features of the early history of Buddhism in China and many reasons why women of that time might take up the life of a Buddhist nun.

Buddhist Texts

Although many of the Buddhist texts, both Disciples' Vehicle and Mahāyāna, or Great Vehicle,[4] contain virulent misogynistic sections, there were in fact no doctrinal reasons that denied enlightenment and, later, Buddhahood to women.[5]

The women of China ardently embraced Mahāyāna Buddhism and its large number of texts, although only a small number of these scriptures became extremely popular—such as the *Flower of the Law, Vimalakīrti, Perfection of Wisdom,* and the Amita or Pure Land texts. The most significant obstacle to a woman's entering the Assembly of Nuns was men rather than doctrine. The Assembly of Nuns was dependent on the Assembly of Monks for several of their required rites and rituals. The reverse was not the case.[6]

Of the three types of Buddhist writings—the Buddha's own word *(sūtra),* the commentaries *(shāstra),* and the monastic code *(vinaya)* that tied the Assembly of Nuns to the Assembly of Monks—the Buddha's word and the commentaries were eagerly translated; however a lack of adequate *vinaya* texts in the early history of Buddhism in China hindered the establishment and development of the monastic order for women.

Buddhism in China: Beginnings

The Buddha Shākyamuni lived from about 560 B.C. to 480 B.C. in northern India.[7] The way of life that he founded was from the first both a monastic and a missionary religion. Spreading far beyond its homeland, about five hundred years after the death of the Buddha, Buddhism traveled quietly along the Silk Road into China.

The first positive evidence for Buddhism in China dates to A.D. 65 in the Latter Han dynasty (25–220). There is a brief reference in the *Hou han shu* (History of the Latter Han dynasty)[8] to Buddhism together with Taoism in the city of P'eng-ch'eng, a city that may be considered the easternmost terminus of the Silk Road (see map).[9] The next positive reference to Buddhism in China dates to the middle of the second century, in the northern city of Lo-yang, where foreign missionary monks and their Chinese followers set up a translation center.[10]

Unfortunately, by the middle of the second century the Latter Han dynasty had begun the decline that ended with its collapse in A.D. 220. Rebellions, contenders for the throne, and nomadic tribes riding down from the north pressed the agrarian Chinese and created great social upheaval: families were separated; many became refugees; famine and disease were widespread; and there was general social and political chaos. The Great Wall had been built as a bulwark against the nomads, but it was only as strong as the defending dynasty.

Undaunted by all the difficulties in China, Buddhist missionaries continued to arrive and continued to translate scriptures.[11] They brought a religion that offered consolation for a very uncertain world. The Buddhist emphasis on the world's illusory quality attracted many more followers than perhaps it would have in a time of peace and tranquility. In a time of social tranquility it could have ended up as a sect of Taoism, with which it was often associated during its early years in China.[12]

The wars, however, continued. A trio of ill-starred dynasties tried to restore the old Han empire, but none could prevail over another or

over the nomads until the Chin dynasty (265–317/317–420) briefly
united the country in A.D. 280.[13] But that unity was neither long nor
peaceful. The nomadic tribes sacked the two major northern capital
cities of Lo-yang in 311 and Ch'ang-an in 316. In 317 the court of the
Chin dynasty, along with many others, fled to the south. The loss of
northern China to the barbarians began the division of the country
into the Northern and Southern dynasties. A relatively stable, non-
Chinese dynasty fringed with many, often ephemeral barbarian kingdoms controlled the north, while a series of short-lived Chinese dynasties controlled the south. This division would last for several centuries
until one ruler reunited the country in 589, long after the *Lives* was
completed.

Because the Confucianism that had been the philosophical foundation of the Han dynasty had failed to prevent the disintegration of the
empire, it lost the allegiance of many of the educated elite. Men began
to look elsewhere for a way to order their lives and their land. The old
loyalties were loosened, giving both Buddhism and Taoism a greater
scope for development and expansion. Buddhism held its own and
gradually became a less exotic sight and in addition became separated
more and more from Taoism, with which, in the early days, it had
often been confused and mingled.

In both north and south, Buddhism gradually became a part of
upper-class life, but, after the shock of losing the heart of the empire
to barbarians and the flight to the south in 317, the Chinese embraced
Buddhism with a positive passion that continued throughout the time
of the Northern and Southern dynasties. The Buddhist institutions
that both immigrant and native worked to establish in the lower
Yangtze River valley were planted so deeply that, despite the vicissitudes of decline, rebellion, and persecution over the centuries, these
institutions always revived to regain their vitality.[14]

Buddhism, Taoism, and Confucianism

Not everyone during the Northern and Southern dynasties in China
welcomed the new religion. Despite many superficial similarities
between Buddhism and Taoism, and despite much mutual influence in
their development, Taoists saw the foreign religion as a direct rival.

Buddhism and Taoism appealed to the same people: those wanting
metaphysical stability or a sense of permanence in a turbulent age,

those wanting very long life or immortality, those seeking a way of life different from, or at the least a respite in private life from, the Confucian ideal of social and familial obligations and public service. Furthermore, Buddhists and Taoists practiced similar arts. Magic, for example, played an important role in the initial acceptance of Buddhism, and Taoist practitioners found themselves facing tough adversaries.[15] The biography of Tao-jung (no. 10) illustrates one such encounter.

For the most part, any hostilities that arose were expressed verbally, but once in a great while partisans felt compelled to take stronger action. The biography of Tao-hsing (no. 9) clearly shows the rivalry when a Taoist woman poisoned a Buddhist nun because "the people of the region had respected the Taoist woman and her activities very much until Tao-hsing's Way of Buddhism eclipsed her arts." The rivalry did not go in one direction only. In a collection of biographies of Taoist women, we learn that a Taoist nun was accosted by knife-wielding Buddhist monks.[16]

Confucianism was the far more serious threat to Buddhism, however, because it had shaped the institutions at the heart of Chinese life: the imperial government and the family. Buddhism ran directly counter to Confucian norms in many aspects of life, one of the most important being that the monastic life required celibacy. In traditional China a good son had the duty to marry and produce male offspring to continue the family line. Shaving the head, also a requirement of Buddhist monastic life, ran contrary to Confucian principles because one's hair was a gift from one's parents and so was not to be cut off. In death, too, there was conflict. Cremation, the deliberate destruction of the body, was abhorrent to those Chinese who considered the body to be a gift from one's father and mother. Buddhists had to try to convince the population at large, as well as individual distraught parents, that a child's entering the Buddhist monastic life not only was not at all unfilial but also was a superior kind of filial piety. The discussion in the biography of An Ling-shou (no. 2) illustrates this well.

Another argument against Buddhism was that it was foreign. This accusation drew forth forged books, such as the *Chou-shu i-chi* (Records of the strange in the Book of Chou) and *Han fa-pen nei-chuan* (Hidden account of the origin of the [Buddhist] law in the Han dynasty), that said that the Buddha was born before Lao-tzu. The Taoists responded in kind, forging their own works, especially the

Hua hu ching (The scripture on the conversion of the barbarians), which said that Buddhism was simply Taoism in exotic dress. Many other forged texts, and their fantastic claims, issued forth from both the Buddhists and the Taoists, each trying to outdo the other to establish the antiquity of the Buddha or Lao-tzu.[17]

Despite clever but less than convincing Buddhist apologetics, the government, an institution fundamentally built on Confucianism, began to take measures against Buddhism, especially as the number of monastics greatly increased. The question was not merely one of Confucian principle, however. Monastic life removed able-bodied men and women from production and therefore from liability for payment of taxes.[18] The monasteries, as they grew wealthy, became centers of power rivaling the various offices of the government. Occasionally, therefore, during the time of the Northern and Southern dynasties, local administrators carried out what was called sifting and weeding of the monastic institutions. This meant an investigation to try to determine those who had a genuine calling to the monastic life from those who were merely slackers, having entered that life to avoid laboring in the world. One such local sifting and weeding is recorded in the biography of Hui-hsü (no. 48). In the Southern dynasties, as compared to the Northern dynasties, the government almost always actively favored Buddhism and often gave such lavish support that corruption became widespread.

Throughout the time of the political and social turmoil, Buddhist missionaries and their disciples continued to work. Not only did translations of doctrinal texts spread more and more rapidly through Chinese society, but also the monastic life began, even though it was for men only.[19] The rules for monastic living, the *vinaya* texts, were not so quickly translated as the texts of doctrine and meditation, however, and the monastic life was set on a more firm foundation only during the fourth century,[20] thanks to the efforts of the monk Tao-an[21] and his pupil Hui-yüan.[22]

The Monastic Institution in China

Monasticism as an institution was as foreign to China as Buddhism itself. The earliest time for which we have a positive record of a monastery is the late second century.[23] For the convent, it is reasonable to consider the convent founded by Ching-chien (no. 1) in 317 to be the first, even though a sixth-century work, the *Lo-yang ch'ieh-lan chi* (A record of monasteries and convents in Lo-yang) suggests that there were some convents in Lo-yang prior to the sacking of the city.[24] Ching-chien (no. 1) founded her convent in Ch'ang-an one year after the sacking of that city by the nomads.

The monastery and convent, on the positive side, provided an alternate family, a significant refuge during social upheaval. The *Kao seng chuan* (Lives of eminent monks) records that many boys entered the Assembly of Monks as orphans or as children of impoverished families.[25] These reasons also appear in the *Lives*. Convents provided shelter for women who had no protection from father, husband, or son. Both the monastery and the convent served as social institutions of great importance in a time of necessity.

On the negative side was the conflict between the monasteries and the state. Hui-yüan had made it a principle that a monk does not bow to the emperor, meaning that the monastery was to be free from state jurisdiction.[26] For the time being, Hui-yüan's view prevailed.

The convents, quite the contrary, had no independent status because of their bonds to the Assembly of Monks. Furthermore, when we compare the two assemblies as pictured in the two major biographical collections, the *Lives* and the *Kao seng chuan,* we find a major difference: both assemblies, when in the capital, were not free from the constant interference of the imperial state and of the nobility and aristocratic families. The Assembly of Nuns, however, was also subject to the monks. More important, monks were able to set up monasteries in the wilderness and in the seclusion of the mountains. Those who did so developed important centers of learning and monastic discipline. The assemblies of monks and nuns that stayed within the reach of the meddlesome aristocratic families and nobility often suffered a surfeit of donations and activities that could have disrupted and corrupted even the strictest of monasteries or convents. Nevertheless, even in the midst of social activities and interference, many nuns demonstrated holy lives and holy deaths.

Becoming a Nun

The biographies record that women entered the monastic life anywhere from a very young age of five or six to the age of seventy. Those who took up that life as children would have remained novices until the proper age for receiving the full obligation, which was ordinarily age 20. Anyone entering the monastic life also had to have permission from the person who had authority over her, whether father, husband, or son.[27] On occasion permission was given by the local governor (no. 54) or even by the Buddha (no. 24).

There were probably as many reasons to become a nun as there were nuns, but general motives can be identified.[28] Ideally, one joined because of religious aspirations. One felt a desire to live in an environment within which to observe the precepts of Buddhism, disciplining oneself in the rigors of convent life, which provided the best place to cultivate meditation with the hope of enlightenment. Many nuns certainly followed such hopes into the convent.

For women, however, the convent also provided a refuge from such vicissitudes of life as unwelcome marriage, flight from war, homelessness, lack of protection, or frustrated intellectual ambitions.

The most dramatic example, perhaps, of a woman fleeing marriage is T'an-hui (no. 54), who threatened a spectacular suicide if forced to marry. The threat of suicide, although by less bizarre means, was a part of Chinese tradition. The woman of virtue and principle does not shy away from taking her own life if necessary.

For women who had been left without a family and without protection during the years of warfare and turmoil, the convent provided a haven and a refuge, a home and a family. The most poignant case is that of Fa-sheng (no. 15), who became a nun at age 70: "She still longed for her old home. Only by delving deep into the mysteries of Buddhism was she able to leave behind sorrow and forget old age."

Fifty-three of the sixty-five biographies mention the woman's ability to read and write. Traditional Chinese society did not encourage literacy among women, and education for girls was ordinarily restricted to the domestic arts. Therefore, the very high rate of literacy among our select group of nuns is noteworthy. The biographies suggest that some women may have gone into the monastic life to be able to follow scholarly pursuits, a vocation that might otherwise have been denied them. The repeated claim that a nun was very intelligent is not necessarily mere convention.

The Convent: Social Life

The general level of education among the subjects of the biographies suggests an upper-class origin for many of them, and for some the biography explicitly states that the women had received their education at home, such as Tao-ch'iung (no. 17), of whom it is written, "When she was a little more than ten years old she was already well educated in the classics and history, and after her full admission to the monastic assembly she became learned in the Buddhist writings as well. . . ."

Another indication of upper-class background is that frequently the woman's family name and original place of residence, and at times even the official positions of male ancestors, are known. The woman's easy concourse with high government officials, nobility, and members of the royal family, including the emperors themselves, also suggests that they were moving among their own kind. Very frequently ladies of high social standing visited the nuns or were visited by them. Those who could afford it often held a vegetarian feast in honor of the nun. This contrasts vividly with the *Kao seng chuan,* wherein the origin of the monks is very frequently unknown.[29] Many boys of obscure background are to be found reaping honors and fame that they could scarcely have imagined, thanks to the preservation of the record of their lives.

The influence of the teaching and preaching nuns spread the word of the Buddha far and wide (no. 35), their sincerity bringing forth a response from hundreds. One nun often wept as she implored her listeners to take up the religion of the Buddha (no. 4). Nuns who dared to chastise laymen in a public place (no. 4) were honored. This indicates that nuns taught and preached effectively. Some nuns were so famous that the world came to them to hear the word (no. 61).

Eight major convents in the capital account for over half the biographies, and the lineages can be traced through several generations. Pao-ch'ang probably knew some of the women in person, or he had access to very recent records and memories because of his own presence in the capital.

With famous nuns as the subjects of the biographies, we are not able to find a picture of an ordinary nun living an ordinary life in the convent, without noble visitors, without doing anything to bring attention to herelf. This is a pity because our picture of the religious heroines becomes the image we remember, and we forget that for every famous nun there was an unknown number of unknown nuns of ordinary standing. We cannot see them.

The Convent: Religious Life

In the middle of the fifth century, a matter of great concern to the nuns themselves was the proper transmission of the monastic rules. Several of the biographies (nos. 14, 27, and 34) deal with the question of whether the Chinese nuns were truly nuns, whether the proper ritual had been carried out in the proper way. This question was important because the lineage—that is, the transmission of the teaching from master to disciple—defined where one belonged and whether one belonged. An authentic lineage established legitimacy. The problem of the transmission of the monastic precepts was solved to everyone's satisfaction, but it must be pointed out that it was the foreign monks and nuns who pressed for resolution on behalf of the Chinese nuns. Chinese monks are conspicuously absent.

The monastic precepts were designed to serve as a guide for living the Buddhist life of self-discipline and nonharm as well as to keep harmony and order within the religious community. The biographer's frequent emphasis on a woman's strict observance of the monastic precepts suggests, however, not only that the woman was fulfilling her monastic duties to perfection but also that she perhaps stood in contrast to other nuns who did not live up to the monastic code. Furthermore, the strict observance of the precepts, as described in the biographies, looks very much as though it had become a religious ritual in and of itself rather than merely the means to self-discipline and harmony.

The women engaged in many cult practices, among which were devotion to Kuan-yin in particular, a bodhisattva (Buddha to be); to Amita Buddha who presides over the Western Paradise; to Maitreya who is the next Buddha and presides over the Tushita Heaven; and to Pindola, an arhat (enlightened one), who showed off his magic powers and was required by the Buddha to remain in the world to serve as a field of merit until the last person attains enlightenment. Worshipping, making vows, or sincere requests to these four divine figures brought responses that pointed out the holiness or sincerity of the petitioner. In the *Kuan-yin Scripture* boons such as safety from brigands are promised to one who chants the scripture with all her heart and mind. Hui-chan (no. 7) is an excellent example. Faith brings response and provides the proof of the truth of the Buddhist claims.

Amita Buddha, also called Amitāyus (infinite life) or Amitābha (infinite light), honors the believer with supernal signs, indicating that the woman will be reborn in the Western Paradise. Maitreya, the next Buddha, presiding over the Tushita Heaven, welcomes to his heaven those who hope to be reborn on earth when he himself is born there as the Buddha. Ching-hsiu (no. 52) was a devotee of Maitreya.

Connected at times with the Maitreya cult is the cult of Pindola. The nun prays and petitions for the presence of Pindola. If she is sufficiently worthy, he will let his presence be known. Because Pindola is never seen, one must listen carefully to hear him should he accept the invitaton and come to bathe. Or if a fresh flower is placed under the mat where Pindola is invited to sit, the flower will not be faded or crushed. The nun Ching-hsiu (no. 52) was also a devotee of Pindola.

Another very important Chinese Buddhist practice was vegetarianism. In the earliest days of Buddhism in India, monks and nuns ate whatever was put into their begging bowls—be it vegetable or meat, fresh or spoiled. They were to eat all with equanimity, so long as they had no reason to suspect that an animal had been harmed or killed specifically for their use. Yet, in China, vegetarianism, although it derives logically from the first Buddhist precept of nonharm to living creatures, received other influences, too. Beyond merely strict vegetarianism, when we read of women giving up all cereals (nos. 25, 28, and 34) or eating any part of the pine tree (no. 25), we have crossed over the line into Taoist practices designed to lead to immortality.[30] This is yet more evidence found in the early Chinese Buddhist biographies, whether of monks or of nuns, that indicates the lack of clear separation between the practices of the two religions in the first years of Buddhism in China.

A third type of dietary regimen is the eating of fragrant oil or incense (no. 36), a practice connected with preparations for self-immolation by fire. Finally, some women forgot about food altogether (no. 47).

Another very important monastic activity was the reading, studying, and chanting of the Buddhist scriptures and the texts of monastic rules. Traditional Chinese reverence for the written word worked favorably for Buddhism, which is not a laconic religion, and this attitude focused not only on the meaning of the contents but also on the actual materials, the written characters, and even the physical volume embodying those contents.[31] Preservation and transmission of the texts was very important. Monastics strove to memorize vast amounts of scripture, their success measuring, to a certain degree, their sanctity. Another mark of sanctity was the ability to chant these texts very rapidly. The chanting itself may also be seen as a kind of incantation or magic spell.

Meditation was the heart of Buddhist monastic life. The biographer lauds many women for their ability to enter the meditative state, but, in those biographies where a physical description of the meditating woman is given, we find that the woman has entered a trance state of which other Buddhists of the time disapproved.[32] The body of the woman in a trance was like wood or stone, rigid and inflexible, and her companions easily mistook her trance for death (no. 29). This kind of trance points away from Buddhism and toward the Taoist belief in a seeming death as a doorway to immortality.[33] Once again Buddhism and Taoism are intermingled.

A nun's manner of death is as important as her way of life because an auspicious death identifies holiness. Omens such as fragrance or lights may appear (no. 25) The Buddha himself may come to receive the dying woman (no. 15). The biographer in his preface singles out for special mention those women who commit suicide by fire as having "achieved the epitome of the ascetic life" (nos. 26 and 47). This practice, always carried out at night so that the nun, in effect, made of herself a lamp, finds authority in the Buddhist scripture, *The Flower of the Wonderful Law.*[34] This scripture specifically and graphically describes the practice of burning a finger, an arm, or the whole body as an offering in honor of the Buddha, an exhortation to fervor and zeal that was not necessarily meant to be observed literally. In China, nevertheless, not a few monks and nuns chose to offer themselves by fire to the Buddha.

Under the right circumstances Chinese tradition accepted suicide as the proper thing to do. Taoists generally cherished life, seeking elixirs of immortality, but a certain Taoist precedent could have contributed to the state of mind that found burning oneself up for the sake of the Buddha an acceptable practice. According to traditional accounts, some Taoist practitioners, after years of carrying out particular rituals and eating special diets, used fire to transform themselves into immortals, their souls rising up to heaven on the smoke.[35]

Ambivalence about the practice of burning one's body in honor of the Buddha is illustrated in the biography of Hui-yao (no. 36). She sought and received permission from the governor of the province to carry out self-immolation, but he later withdrew his approval.

The nuns carried out their suicides by fire on the nights of the changing phases of the moon, either the half-moon on the eighth day of the lunar month or the full moon on the fifteenth day.

Women who rise bodily up to heaven (no. 1), or who simply disappear (no. 10), are dying in a Taoist rather than a Buddhist manner, such deaths signifying that the person has become an immortal.[36] The body of the nun Shih Hui-ch'iung (no. 20) remained incorrupt—a proof, for Taoists, of immortality.[37] Buddhists in China accepted the phenomenon of the incorrupt body as a mark of holiness, and throughout the centuries many incorrupt bodies of holy monastics have edified the faithful.

Conclusions

Monasticism in China, although originally foreign, was a successful institution for both men and women. Besides being the best place for Chinese Buddhists to live and to practice their newly found religion, it was also a refuge and home in a deeply troubled and perilous time.

Women themselves were also successful, living holy lives—learned lives, lives bound to obligations of their own choice—and dying holy deaths. Their lives and actions demonstrated the truth of the promises in the Buddhist texts. We do not know anything about ordinary Buddhist nuns that would allow us to compare them with our paragons. We could derive a very similar picture of Buddhism in early medieval China from the *Kao seng chuan,* probably even much more than from the *Lives* because it is a much longer and detailed document. Nevertheless, without the *Lives* a very important dimension would have been missing.

Buddhism in China came at a fortunate time when it was needed to help restore meaning to life for many who had been disillusioned and who suffered from political and social troubles. Buddhist thought fit in with an intellectual elite, accustomed to metaphysical talk based especially on Lao-tzu and Chuang-tzu and unaccustomed to the loss of their homeland to nomadic barbarians. Buddhist piety attracted both the elite and the commoner.

For women in particular, not only Buddhist thought and piety but also the monastic institution itself was a beneficial import. The religion, seen as not so very different from native Taoism, proved attractive to many levels of society, and even as the differences with Taoism became more and more apparent, Buddhism still continued to grow ever more popular. The religion had enemies, but it had fewer during the Northern and Southern dynasties than it had later in more settled times when the central government could exercise greater jurisdiction and power.

We cannot know whether Pao-ch'ang achieved his purpose of encouraging Buddhists to greater efforts, but the text of the *Lives* circulated through the south, one of the many Buddhist biographical texts. The *Lives* provides us with a small but privileged view of the early stages of Buddhist monasticism for women. The sixty-five nuns who are the subject of this work would no doubt be surprised to find that their lives are still edifying readers.

Table of Dynasties and Kingdoms

SOUTHERN DYNASTIES	NORTHERN DYNASTIES	
Eastern Chin (317–420)	Northern Wei (386–534)	
Sung (420–479)	Western Wei (535–557)	Eastern Wei (534–550)
Ch'i (479–502)	Northern Chou (557–581)	Northern Ch'i (550–577)
Liang (502–557)		

SIXTEEN KINGDOMS		
Ch'eng Han (304–347)	Latter Chao (319–350)	Western Liang (400–420)
Former Liang (320–376)	Former Yen (337–370)	Northern Liang (397–439)
Former Ch'in (351–394)	Southern Yen (398–410)	Southern Liang (397–414)
Latter Ch'in (384–417)	Latter Yen (384–407)	Western Ch'in (385–431)
Latter Liang (386–403)	Northern Yen (407–436)	Hsia (407–431)
Former Chao (304–329)		

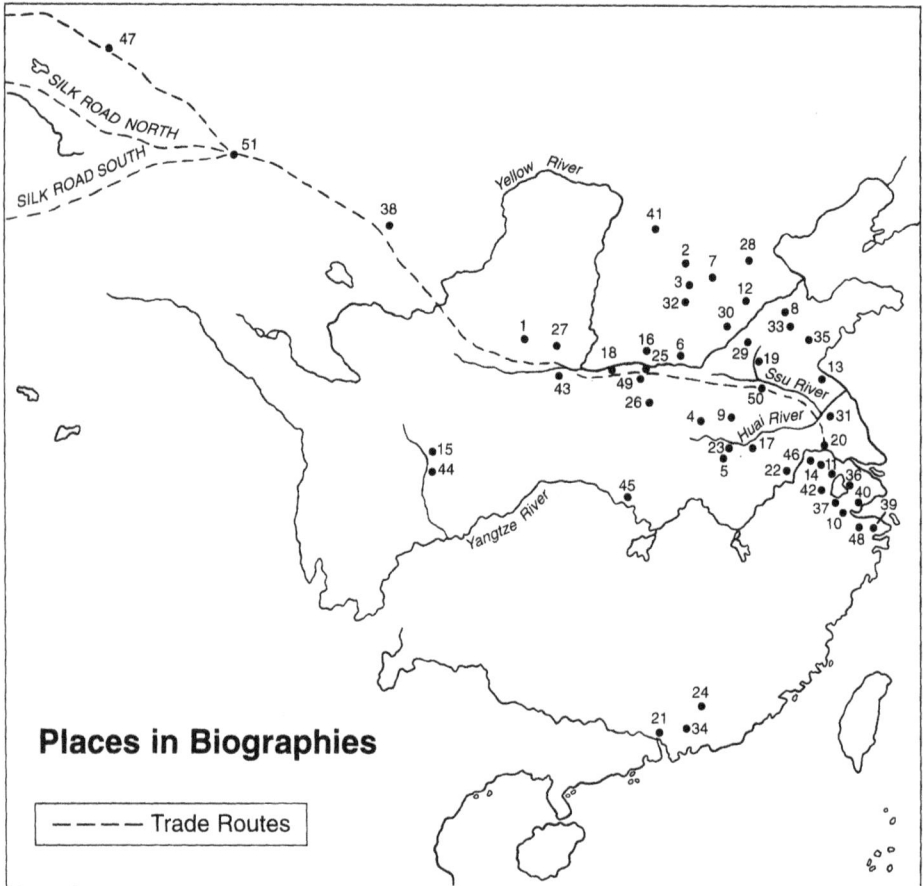

Places in Biographies

---- Trade Routes

47
SILK ROAD NORTH
SILK ROAD SOUTH
51
38
Yellow River
41
2 7 28
3 12
32 30
1 27 33 8
16 6 35
18 25 29 19 13
43 49 Ssu River 50 31
26 4 9
23 17 20
5 22 46 14 36
45 42 40
37 39
Yangtze River 10 48
24
21 34

An-ting	1	Kuang Province	21	Wu Commandery	36
Ch'ang-shan	2	Li-yang	22	Wu County	35
Chao	3	Liang Commandery	23	(see Wu Commandery)	
Ch'en Commandery	4	Lung-ch'uan County	24	Wu-hsing Commandery	37
Ch'en-liu	5	Meng Ford	25	Wu-wei Commandery	38
Chi Commandery	6	Mo-ling (see Chien-k'ang)		Yen	39
Chi Province	7	Nan-yang Commandery	26	Yen-kuan County	40
Chi-nan	8	P'an-yü (see Kuang Province)		Yen-men	41
Ch'iao Commandery	9	Pei-ti	27	Yung-shih	42
Ch'ien-t'ang	10	P'o-hai	28		
Chin-lung	11	Po-p'ing	29 or 30	IMPORTANT CENTERS	
Ch'ing-ho	12	Shan-yang Commandery	31	Ch'ang-an	43
Ch'ing Province	13	Shan-yin (see Kuei-chi)		Ch'eng-tu	44
Chü-jung	14	Shu Commandery		Chiang-ling	45
Fan County	15	(see Ch'eng-tu)	31	Chien-k'ang	46
Ho-nei	16	Ssu Province	32	Kao-ch'ang	47
Huai-nan	17	T'ai-shan	33	Kuei-chi	48
Hung-nung	18	Tan-Yang (see Chien-k'ang)		Lo-yang	49
Kao-p'ing	19	Tseng-ch'eng	34	P'eng-ch'eng	50
Kuang-ling	20	Tung-huan	35	Tun-huang	51

Shih Pao-ch'ang's Preface to
Lives of the Nuns

Is it not fundamental, as regards pure mind, lofty purpose, unusual virtue, and extraordinary integrity, that these qualities do not come simply through natural means but are encouraged by respect for noble character? Therefore, it is said, "The man who emulates a paragon will become a paragon himself," and "The horse who emulates a thoroughbred is a thoroughbred as well."[1] These nuns then, whom I hereby offer as models, are women of excellent reputation, paragons of ardent morals, whose virtues are a stream of fragrance that flows without end.

That is why I take up my ink brush and cleave to my stylus to record the women's biographies to hand on to later chroniclers, that they in turn might use the material I provide to encourage and admonish generations to come. Therefore, although I might wish to teach wordlessly [as the sages do], in this case I cannot refrain from using words.[2]

In the past, when the Great Awakened One came to birth in the town of Kapilavastu, the Buddha sun appeared in India. The three realms [of the desire, form, and formless worlds] took refuge [in the spiritual power of the Three Treasures—the Buddha, his teaching, and the monastic assemblies]; and those beings of the four types of birth [—from egg, womb, moisture, and metamorphosis—] offered obeisance [to the Three Treasures].

The first Buddhist nun in the world was Mahāprajāpatī, [the Buddha's own stepmother]. [From the time of Mahāprajāpatī] nuns throughout the succeeding generations have ascended the stages of the Buddhist path and realized the fruits of spiritual practice. These illustrious examples of the religious life are like the sun passing through the sky, shedding light and warmth on all.

Since [the Buddha] lay down between two [shāla] trees in the village of Kushinagara [and there entered final nirvana], the passing years have brought degeneracy and chaos, and men of our times confound faith and falsehood; they confuse what to preserve and what to discard, not knowing where the truth may be. That the Profound Word wastes away is because the wicked confuse it; that the True Religion flourishes again is because the wise support it.

When, during the second age of the Buddhist religion [which began five hundred years after the death of the Buddha], the faith spread east to China, the nun Chu Ching-chien (no. 1) became the first [Chinese Buddhist nun], and for several hundred years nuns of great virtue appeared in China one after another.[3] Of these nuns, Shan-miao (no. 26) and Ching-kuei (no. 47) achieved the epitome of the ascetic life; Fa-pien (no. 31) and Seng-kuo (no. 27) consummately excelled in meditation and contemplation. Individuals such as Seng-tuan (no. 24) and Seng-chi (no. 8), who were steadfast in their resolution to maintain chastity, and Miao-hsiang (no. 4) and Fa-ch'üan (no. 44), who were teachers of great influence, appeared very frequently. Such virtue as theirs is like the deep ocean or the lofty peak—like the harmonious music of bronze and jade bells. Indeed, they are models of virtue in an autumnal age, reliable guides in a decadent time.

Even though as the years go by the pure monastic rules are gradually forsaken, nevertheless the nuns' excellent tradition will be a pattern for a millenium.

I frequently deplored that a record of their achievements had not been made, and therefore, for a long time, I have been examining epitaphs and eulogies and searching in collections of writings. Sometimes I inquired among the well informed; sometimes I interviewed the aged. Putting this material in order from beginning to end I compiled the biographies of the nuns. Starting with the *sheng-p'ing* reign period (357–361) of the Eastern Chin dynasty and ending with the *t'ien-chien* reign period (502–519) of the Liang dynasty, there are altogether sixty-five women.

I did not embellish the material; rather, I worked to preserve the essentials, hoping that those who seek freedom from the world of suffering will emulate the nuns' virtue. And yet, because my researches are limited and perhaps incomplete, I ask my discerning readers to advise me of any deficiencies.

1. The Chin Dynasty

(265–317 / 317–420)

1. CHU CHING-CHIEN

竺淨檢

The nun Chu Ching-chien (Pure Example) (in the lineage of an
Indian monk) (ca. 292–ca. 361)[1] of Bamboo Grove Convent of
Lo-yang in the Chin dynasty[2]

Ching-chien's secular surname was Chung and her given name was
Ling-i. Her family was originally from P'eng-ch'eng in northeastern
China.[3] Her father, Chung Tan, served as administrator of Wu-wei
Commandery [in far northwestern China].[4] As a small child Ching-
chien had been very fond of learning. She was still quite young when
the death of her husband left the family impoverished, and to earn a
living she often taught lute and calligraphy to the children of noble
families.

When Ching-chien first heard about the Buddhist teaching she felt
faith and joy, but there was no one from whom to receive detailed
instruction. Later she met the Buddhist monk Fa-shih who was thoroughly versed in scripture and practice. In the *chien-hsing* reign period
(313–317) of Western Chin he established a monastery at the West
Gate of the imperial city [of Lo-yang].[5] When Ching-chien visited
there, Fa-shih explained the teachings to her. As a result she had a
great awakening and grew firm in her resolve to seek the benefits of
the religion of the Buddha. Borrowing a scriptural text from Fa-shih to
study, she proceeded to master its contents.

On another day she said to Fa-shih, "In the scriptures it says, '*Bhikshu* and *bhikshunī* aspire to deliverance.' [What are *bhikshu* and *bhikshunī*?]"

Fa-shih replied, "In the western regions there are two monastic assemblies, that of *bhikshu,* or monks, for men and that of *bhikshunī,* or nuns, for women; but in this country the books of rules for the monastic life are not complete."

Ching-chien asked, "Because the scripture speaks of the two terms, *monk* and *nun,* can it be that the rules for each group are different?"

Fa-shih said, "Foreign Buddhists say that nuns have five hundred rules to follow as compared to fewer for monks, and that must be the difference.[6] I asked the instructor about this, and he said that the rules for nuns are highly similar and only slightly different from the monks' regulations, but, if I cannot get the complete texts of these rules, then I certainly cannot bestow on women the obligation to observe them. A woman aspiring eventually to become a nun may, however, receive the ten fundamental precepts from the Assembly of Monks only, but, without a [female] monastic instructor to train her in the practice of all the rules, a woman has no one on whom to rely [for that training which prepares her to accept the obligation to observe all the rules of monastic life]."[7]

Ching-chien, nevertheless, received the tonsure [required of all who leave the household life], cast off secular garb and accepted the ten fundamental precepts from the instructor. There were twenty-four other women of like mind, and together they established Bamboo Grove Convent at the West Gate of the imperial city. They had as yet no female teacher, so they all consulted Ching-chien, whose instruction and advice were superior to those already recognized as accomplished [in religious thought and practice].

The instructor [who had bestowed the ten fundamental precepts] was the Buddhist monk Chih-shan from Kashmir [in the western regions of central Asia].[8] Gentle in wisdom and elegant in thought, he cultivated both meditation and chanting. He supported himself by begging for alms, and his preaching surely spread the Buddhist Way. At that time in China, however, faith was shallow, and no one knew enough to request instruction from him. Therefore, in the first year of *chien-wu* (317) he returned to Kashmir.[9] Later, when [the Buddhist magician monk from Kucha, Chu] Fo-t'u-teng, returned [to the Lo-yang region], he recounted Chih-shan's virtues; everyone felt great remorse [for having lost the opportunity to learn from the monk of Kashmir].[10]

Ching-chien supported and cared for her community of disciples; she observed the monastic rules with purity and distinction. The influence of her preaching of the Buddhist teaching was [in Mencius' words], like wind moving grass.[11]

In the *hsien-k'ang* reign period (335–342) of Eastern Chin the Buddhist monk Seng-chien,[12] when in the land of the Scythians in central Asia, got hold of a nuns' rites and rules book of the Mahāsānghika Buddhist sect.[13] In the first year of the *sheng-p'ing* reign period (357), the translation of the text was completed in Lo-yang[14] on the eighth day of the second month [in honor of the Buddha's entry into final nirvana].[15] The foreign Buddhist monk T'an-mo-chieh-to set up a ceremonial dais [on which Ching-chien and her disciples were to accept all of the monastic rules for women as found in the newly translated text]. The Chinese monk Shih Tao-ch'ang objected to this action, however, on the basis of scriptures on the origins of monastic rules that said that, because there was no Assembly of Nuns in China to bestow the rules on the women as the scriptures required, the ritual should not be carried out.[16] His objections were not acknowledged and, as a result, [Shih Tao-ch'ang] took a boat down the Ssu River to the south.[17] Ching-chien and the others, four altogether, became Buddhist nuns by accepting, from the Assembly of Monks only, the obligation to observe all the monastic rules. Ching-chien is thus the first of the Buddhist nuns in China.

On the day of that ritual, remarkable fragrance and perfume [filled the air]. Everyone smelled it, and there was none who did not rejoice and marvel; respect for her increased all the more. Ching-chien well cultivated the monastic rules and resolutely studied without ceasing. Although the gifts of the faithful were many, she distributed everything she received, always putting herself last and others first.

At the end of the *sheng-p'ing* reign period (357–361) Ching-chien once again smelled the same fragrance [that had graced the ritual of her becoming a nun], and she saw a red, misty cloud. Out of that cloud a woman holding a five-colored flower in her hands descended from the sky. Ching-chien was delighted to see her and said to the nuns, "Manage your affairs well in the future. I am taking leave of you now." Clasping their hands she bid them farewell and then rose up into the air.[18] The path she traveled looked like a rainbow going straight up to heaven. At that time she was seventy years old.[19]

2. AN LING-SHOU
安令首

The nun An Ling-shou (Esteemed Leader) (in the lineage of a
Parthian monk) of Founding of Wisdom Convent of the
Northern, non-Chinese dynasty of Chao[20]

An Ling-shou's secular surname was Hsü. Her family was originally
from Tung-huan [in northeastern China]. Her father Hsü Ch'ung
served the non-Chinese dynasty of Latter Chao (319–350) as an
undersecretary of the provincial forces.[21]

When she was young, Ling-shou was intelligent and fond of study.
Her speech was clear and beautiful; her nature modest and unassum-
ing. Taking no pleasure in worldly affairs, she was at ease in secluded
quiet. She delighted in the Buddhist teachings and did not wish for her
parents to arrange her betrothal.

Her father said, "You ought to marry. How can you be so unfilial?"

Ling-shou said, "My mind is concentrated on the work of religion,
and my thought dwells exclusively on spiritual matters. Neither blame
nor praise moves me; purity and uprightness are sufficient in themselves. Why must I submit thrice [to father, husband, and son], before
I am considered a woman of propriety?"[22]

Her father said, "You want to benefit only one person—yourself.
How can you help your father and mother at the same time?"

Ling-shou said, "I am setting myself to cultivate the Way exactly
because I want to free all living beings from suffering. How much
more, then, do I want to free my two parents!"[23]

Hsü Ch'ung consulted the Buddhist magician monk from Kucha,[24]
Fo-t'u-teng, who said, "You return home and keep a vegetarian fast,
and after three days you may come back to see me again."[25] Hsü
Ch'ung obeyed him. At the end of the three days, Fo-t'u-teng spread
Hsü Ch'ung's palm with the oil of sesame ground together with saf-
flower.[26] When he ordered Hsü Ch'ung to look at it, Ch'ung saw a
person who resembled his daughter dressed in Buddhist monastic
robes preaching the Buddhist teachings in the midst of a large
assembly.

When he told all of this to Fo-t'u-teng, the monk said, "This is a former incarnation of your daughter, in which she left the household life
and benefited living beings—such were her deeds. If you consent to
her plan, she indeed shall raise her family to glory and bring you bless-

ings and honor; and she shall guide you [to nirvana] on the far shore of the great ocean of suffering known as the incessant round of birth and death."

Hsü Ch'ung returned home and permitted his daughter to become a nun. Ling-shou thereupon cut off her hair, discarded secular ornaments, and received the rules of monastic life from Fo-t'u-teng and the nun Ching-chien. She established Founding of Wisdom Convent, and Fo-t'u-teng presented her with a cut-flower embroidered vestment, a seven-strip monastic robe,[27] and an elephant-trunk-shaped water ewer[28] that Shih Lo (274–319–333),[29] first emperor of the Latter Chao dynasty, had given him.[30]

Ling-shou widely perused all kinds of books, and, having read a book through only once, she was always able to chant it by heart. Her thought extended to the depths of the profound; her spirit intuited the subtle and divine. In the religious communities of that time there was no one who did not honor her. Those who left the household life because of her numbered more than two hundred. Furthermore, she built five or six monastic retreats.[31] She had no fear of hard work and brought her projects to completion.

The Emperor Shih Hu (?–335–349),[32] nephew of the late Emperor Shih Lo, honored her and promoted her father Hsü Ch'ung to the official court position of undersecretary of the Yellow Gate and administrator of Ch'ing-ho Commandery.[33]

3. CHIH-HSIEN
智賢

The nun Chih-hsien (Wise Virtue) (ca. 300–ca. 370+) of West Convent of Ssu Province in north China

Chih-hsien's secular surname was Chao. Her family was originally from Ch'ang-shan Commandery [in north China, north of the Yellow River].[34] Her father Chao Chen was the magistrate of Fu-liu County in the same territory.[35]

While still a child, Chih-hsien was both principled and virtuous, and, after she grew up and put on the dark robe [of a Buddhist nun], her observance of the monastic rules was perfect. Her spirit was concentrated and far-reaching, encompassing all things without being confused by any particular matter.

The administrator of the commandery, Tu Pa, staunchly believed in the Taoist system known as the Way of the Yellow Emperor and Lao-tzu.[36] He detested the Buddhist monks and nuns. Because of his hatred, he issued an order that the assemblies of both monks and nuns were to be investigated [with regard to the quality of their practice, and those found unworthy] were to be sifted out.[37] The standards used in the investigation were very severe and could scarcely be met by ordinary persons. The younger [monks and nuns] quaked in fear; anticipating the administrator's hostility, they fled. Chih-hsien alone was unafraid and remained at ease. Only the elderly nuns dared to gather outside the city walls at the archers' practice hall where the investigation was to be held. On the day of the examination, of the able-bodied nuns, only Chih-hsien remained.

The administrator first examined Chih-hsien with regard to the monastic regulations and found that her practice was more than adequate. Because of her refined beauty and eloquent speech the administrator harbored depraved intentions, and he forced her to remain alone [with him]. Chih-hsien, recognizing his intentions, vowed not to break any of the monastic rules concerning relations between the sexes. Disregarding her own safety, she protested and resisted strongly. Angered by her rejection of his advances, the administrator stabbed her over twenty times with his dagger. She fell unconscious to the ground, not reviving until after the administrator had left.

This event behind her, Chih-hsien redoubled her zeal in the practice of vegetarian fasts and austerities. She and her disciples, who numbered more than a hundred, always dwelt in accord.

When Fu Chien (339–357–385) took the throne of the non-Chinese dynasty of the Former Ch'in (351–394), he heard of her reputation and showed her great respect.[38] He had made for her finely embroidered outer robes, whose preparation required three years and whose value was one million in cash.

Later she lived in West Convent of Ssu Province [in north China], where she propagated the true teaching and spread the belief and practice of Buddhism.[39] During the *t'ai-ho* reign period (366–371) of the [southern, Chinese] dynasty of Chin she was seventy-some years old.

Chih-hsien had made a specialty of chanting the *Flower of the True Law Scripture*.[40] Even in her advanced age, she could still chant it in its entirety in only one day and one night.[41] [Another sign of her spiritual accomplishments was that] the many birds that roosted in the area where she lived would follow her,[42] chirping and twittering, whenever she engaged in the [ritualized] walking exercise [between periods of meditation.][43]

4. Miao-hsiang
妙相

The nun Miao-hsiang (Subtle Characteristic) of North Peak
Convent of Hung-nung [Commandery in north China, west of
Lo-yang along the Yellow River]

Miao-hsiang's secular surname was Chang, and her given name was P'ai-hua. She was from Hung-nung,[44] and the family of her father, Chang Mao, was very wealthy.[45] While yet very young, Miao-hsiang became well versed in the teachings of the [Confucian] classics, and this set the tone of her character. She was married at age 15 to Huang-fu Ta of Pei-ti in northwest China,[46] who was a secretary in the crown prince's grand secretariat of the right.[47] When her husband was mourning for his parents, he did not behave according to [Confucian propriety].[48] [Because of his lack of filial piety] Miao-hsiang disliked him and sought to end the relationship and subsequently to become a Buddhist nun. Her father consented to both requests.

Miao-hsiang assiduously kept to a vegetarian diet. Her mind roamed in the scholarly explanations of the Buddha's discourses; she clearly understood the difficult Buddhist doctrine and analysis of the characteristics of existence.

She lived on North Peak in Hung-nung in a shady forest facing the open countryside, where she and her many disciples led a life of joyful resolve in the quiet retreat. [In this manner she withdrew from the world for] over twenty years, strengthening her ascetic practice more and more as the years passed by.

Whenever she preached the [Buddhist] teaching, she saved people. Because she often feared that those listening to her would be unable to concentrate their resolve to attain freedom from birth and death, she would at times weep to exhort them to greater efforts. Thus her preaching always brought about great benefits.

During the *yung-ho* reign period (345–356) of the Chin dynasty the administrator of Hung-nung Commandery requested her to carry out a seven-day vegetarian religious feast. A lay guest sitting on the dais for honored guests asked a question about the Buddha's teaching, but his words were presumptuous and his attitude disrespectful. Miao-hsiang, very serious, said, "Not only do you treat me arrogantly, but also you are showing contempt for an official of the country. How can you be so rude when appearing in public?" Thereupon, the man feigned illness and withdrew; both religious and laity marveled in admiration of her.

Later she was seriously ill for many days. As she neared death, she was in a joyful mood, and she advised her disciples, "Regardless of poverty or success, anyone who is born must also die. This very day I am leaving you." Having spoken, she died.

5. K'ANG MING-KAN
康明感

The nun K'ang Ming-kan (Bright Influence) (in the lineage of a
Sogdian monk) of Establishing Blessings Convent

Ming-kan's secular surname was Chu, and her family was from Kao-p'ing [in northeast China].[49] For generations the family had venerated the [Buddhist] teachings known as the Great Vehicle.[50]

A bandit who wanted to make her his wife abducted her, but, even though she suffered increasing torment, she vowed not to give in to him. She was forced to serve as a shepherdess far from her native home. Ten years went by and her longing for her home and family grew more and more intense, but there seemed to be no way back. During all this she kept her mind fixed on the Three Treasures, and she herself wished to become a nun.[51]

One day she happened to meet a Buddhist monk, and she asked him to bestow on her the five fundamental precepts [of a Buddhist house-holder].[52] He granted her request and also presented her with a copy of the *Bodhisattva Kuan-shih-yin Scripture,* which she then practiced chanting day and night without pause.[53]

Deciding to return home to build a five-story pagoda, she fled to the east in great anxiety and distress. At first she did not know the road but kept traveling both day and night. When crossing over a mountain she saw a tiger lying only a few steps away from her. After momentary terror she composed her mind, and her hopes were more than met, for the tiger led the way for her, and, after the days had grown into weeks, she finally arrived in her home territory of Ch'ing Province [in the northeast]. As she was about to enter the village, the tiger disappeared, but at that moment, having arrived in the province, Ming-kan was again abducted, this time by Ming Po-lien. When word reached her family, her husband and son ransomed her, but the family did not let her carry out her wishes [to enter the life of a Buddhist nun]. Only after three years of cultivating stringent religious practices was she able to follow her intention. As a nun, she especially concentrated on the cultivation of meditation, and she kept all the regulations of a monastic life without any transgressions. If she happened to commit a minor fault, she would confess it several mornings in a row, ceasing only after she received a sign or a good omen. Sometimes as a good omen she saw flowers rain down from the sky or she heard a voice in the sky or she saw a Buddha image or she had auspicious dreams.

As Ming-kan approached old age, her moral cultivation was even more strict and lofty. All the men and women north of the Yangtze River honored her as their spiritual teacher in whom they could take refuge.

In the spring of the fourth year of the *yung-ho* reign period (348) of the Chin dynasty,[54] she, together with Hui-chan (no. 7) and others— ten in all—traveled south, crossed the Yangtze River, and went to see the minister of public works, Ho Ch'ung (292–346), in the capital of the Eastern Chin dynasty.[55] As soon as he met them, he showed them great respect. Because at that time there were no convents in the capital region Ho Ch'ung converted one of his private residences into a convent for them.

He asked Ming-kan, "What should the convent be named?"

She replied, "In the great realm of the Chin dynasty all the four Buddhist assemblies of monks, nuns, and male and female householders are now established for the first time.[56] Furthermore, that which you as donor have established will bestow blessings and merit. Therefore, let us call the convent Establishing Blessings Convent." Ho Ch'ung agreed to her suggestion. Not long afterward Ming-kan took sick and died.

6. T'AN-PEI

譽備

The nun T'an-pei (Perfection of the Dharma) (324–396) of
Northern Everlasting Peace Convent[57]

T'an-pei's secular surname was T'ao, and she was a native of Tan-
yang in the city of Chien-k'ang [the capital of the Eastern Chin
dynasty located on the south bank of the Yangtze River].[58] When she
was a young child, she already had pure faith and wished to cultivate
the true teaching of Buddhism. She was an only child and lived with
her widowed mother, whom she served with such filial devotion that
her clan commended her behavior. When T'an-pei grew to marriage-
able age, she would not accede to any betrothal plans, and her mother,
unable to go against her daughter's wishes, allowed her to leave
worldly life [and become a Buddhist nun]. With great zeal, T'an-pei
practiced the monastic rules day and night without remiss.

Emperor Mu (343–345–361) of Chin respectfully received her in
audience, and he often praised her, saying, "The more I see her, the
more excellent she seems."[59] To Empress Chang—that is, Madame Ho
[niece of Ho Ch'ung]—the emperor said, "Among the Buddhist nuns
here in the capital there is rarely one who can compare with
T'an-pei."[60]

In the tenth year of the *yung-ho* reign period (354) the Empress
built a convent for T'an-pei in the Ting-yin Neighborhood, calling it
[Northern] Everlasting Peace Convent (which I, Pao-ch'ang, the compiler, note is now known as Empress Ho Convent).[61]

Modestly and selflessly T'an-pei guided others and never once gave
any evidence of haughtiness. Her fame spread daily, and women from
far and near gathered about her as disciples until there was a community of three hundred. T'an-pei was seventy-three years old when she
died in the twenty-first year of the *t'ai-yüan* reign period (396).

Her disciple T'an-lo was well read in the scriptures as well as in the
monastic rules, and her skills and talents in these subjects were broad
and thorough. By imperial command she filled T'an-pei's position as
teaching master of the convent. Furthermore, she had built a four-
story pagoda, a lecture hall, and living quarters; also, she had made an
image of the Buddha reclining [as he entered final nirvana], and a hall
for the images of the seven Buddhas [of the past].[62]

7. HUI-CHAN
慧湛

The nun Hui-chan (Deep Wisdom) of Establishing Blessings
Convent

Hui-chan's secular surname was Jen, and her family was originally
from the city of P'eng-ch'eng [long a home to Buddhists, in northeast
China]. Of extraordinary countenance and high moral standards,
Hui-chan took as her vocation the saving of living beings from the suffering of birth and death. She found great joy in wearing her rough
clothing and eating vegetarian food. Once when she was carrying
rather than wearing her outer robe as she traveled over a mountain,
she encountered a band of robbers. They tried to attack her with
knives, but [as proof of the power of the Bodhisattva Kuan-yin chapter in *The Flower of the Law Scripture,* which promises that help will
be vouchsafed to those who call on Kuan-yin in times of distress] the
robbers' hands were paralyzed.[63]

Foiled in the attempt to kill her, they wanted to take the robe she
was carrying over her shoulder. Hui-chan laughed gaily and said to
them, "You wanted a lot, but what you are going to get is worth very
little," and she handed over not only the robe she was carrying but also
her new lower skirt from inside the robe she was wearing. Shamed, the
robbers tried to return both robes to her, but she tossed the clothing
aside and went on.

In the second year of the *chien-yüan* reign period (344), she went
south across the Yangtze River.[64] The minister of public works, Ho
Ch'ung (292–346), respected her greatly and requested her to live in
Establishing Blessings Convent.

8. SENG-CHI
僧基

The nun Seng-chi (Foundation of the Sangha) (ca. 330–397) of
Increasing Joy Convent[65]

Seng-chi's secular surname was Ming, and her family was originally
from Chi-nan [in northeast China].[66]

When Seng-chi was still very young, she had already fixed her mind on the way of Buddhism, holding fast to her wish to leave the household life and become a nun. Her mother, however, would not hear of it and secretly betrothed her, hiding the engagement gifts. Thus the daughter knew nothing about it until the wedding day drew close [but as soon as she found out] she immediately refused to eat or drink a thing. Even though all her relatives tried to get her to change her mind, she would not be moved.

After Seng-chi had fasted seven days her mother summoned the bridegroom, a man of devout faith, who, when he saw that his bride was in danger of death, said to his prospective mother-in-law, "Each person has his own will that cannot be forced." The mother then acceded [to her daughter's wishes], and consequently Seng-chi left the household life. At that time she was twenty-one years old. Relatives from both sides of the family came to express their best wishes, and they vied with one another to give fine banquets and other precious gifts in honor of her becoming a nun. The provincial magistrate presented gifts, and the commandery administrator attended in person. Monastics and householders alike marveled [that this degree of honor given her] was most unusual.

Seng-chi kept the monastic rules in great purity, and she diligently studied the scriptures. When compared to the nun T'an-pei (no. 6), her reputation was nearly equal. Her mental faculties were most concentrated, and she was good at deliberation and decision making.

The Emperor K'ang (322–343–344) often paid respects to her,[67] and, in the second year of the *chien-yüan* reign period (344), the Empress Ch'u (324–384), consort of K'ang, built for her a convent named Increasing Joy in T'ung-kung Lane in Chien-k'ang, the capital of Chin.[68] Seng-chi took up residence there, and more than a hundred disciples came to her.

Because in her management of all affairs she was clear and intelligent, both monastics and householders respected her more and more. She was at least sixty-eight years old when she died in the first year of the *lung-an* reign period (397).[69]

9. CHU TAO-HSING

竺道馨

The nun Chu Tao-hsing (Fragrance of the Way) (in the lineage of
an Indian monk) of the Eastern Convent of Lo-yang[70]

Tao-hsing's secular surname was Yang. Her family was originally
from T'ai-shan [in northeast China].[71]

Tao-hsing was both scrupulous and firm in character, and she was
able to get along with everyone. During her probationary period
before becoming a full-fledged nun, she practiced chanting the scriptures while running errands and performing other duties. Therefore,
by the time she was twenty she could recite from memory the *Flower
of the Law*,[72] the *Vimalakīrti,* and other scriptures.[73] After she had
accepted the full obligation of the monastic rule and become a nun,
she pursued her study of Buddhist teachings while continuing to maintain her vegetarian diet and her practice of austerities. As she grew
older, rather than taking more ease, she intensified her rigorously
ascetic way of life.

Tao-hsing lived in Eastern Convent of the old capital city of Lo-
yang [in north China on the south bank of the Yellow River]. She was
particularly adept in the [intellectual acrobatics of the philosophical
discourse known as] Pure Talk,[74] and she was especially competent in
[the Buddhist scripture known as] the *Smaller Perfection of Wisdom*.[75]
She esteemed the understanding of principles and did not engage in
mere argumentation. All the students of the [Buddhist Way] in the
entire province considered her as their teacher and master. Tao-hsing
was the first of the nuns who specialized in expounding the meaning of
the scriptures.

In the *t'ai-ho* reign period (366–371) of the Chin dynasty there lived
a woman named Yang Ling-pien, who was an ardent follower of the
[Taoist Way] of the Yellow Emperor and Lao-tzu, and she practiced in
particular the breathing exercise known as swallowing the breath
[designed to strengthen the body's vital essence and lead to physical
immortality].[76] The people of the region had respected the Taoist
woman and her activities very much until Tao-hsing's Way of Buddhism eclipsed her own arts. Yang Ling-pien pretended distant kinship
with Tao-hsing on account of their having the same last name and,

using that as a reason, cultivated a friendship with Tao-hsing; [but in reality] she harbored great envy and looked for a chance to poison the Buddhist nun. She eventually succeeded in putting poisonous herbs into Tao-hsing's food, and, despite many medicines, Tao-hsing did not recover. Nevertheless, when her disciples asked her in whose house she had contracted this illness, she answered, "I certainly know who did this, but all is a matter of karmic connections [and was meant to turn out this way], so do not ask me any more about it. Even if telling you who did it would help me, I still would not say; how much less am I likely to say when there is no cure at all." Tao-hsing died without revealing the name of her poisoner.

10. TAO-JUNG
道容

The nun Tao-jung (Look of the Way) of New Grove Convent

Tao-jung originally lived in Black River Convent of Li-yang [southwest of the capital, along the north bank of the Yangtze River], where her practice of the monastic rules was lofty and undefiled.[77] She was good in the arts of divination and could predict fortune and misfortune. People in the surrounding area passed it about that she was a holy person.

The Emperor Ming (300–323–326) of Chin[78] revered her and secretly spread flowers under her sitting mat to verify whether she was an ordinary worldling or really was holy—the flower did not wither [thus her holiness was confirmed].[79]

Many years after that, before the Emperor Chien-wen (320–371–372) ascended the throne,[80] he first honored as teacher the Taoist master of Pure Water.[81] This Taoist master was known in the capital by the name of Wang P'u-yang. The future emperor built a Taoist worship hall in his own mansion, and, although Tao-jung frequently tried to guide him to the Way [of Buddhism], he did not listen to her. Later, however, each time the future emperor entered his Taoist worship hall, he would see spirits in the form of Buddhist monks filling the whole room. He suspected Tao-jung was responsible, but he could not prove it.

After Chien-wen's accession to the throne a flock of crows [an evil omen], nested in the emperor's own palace. He employed a fortune-teller named Ch'ü An-yüan to divine it, and the fortune-teller reported back to him saying, "Southwest of here lives a female master who can destroy this evil omen."[82] Therefore the emperor sent an envoy to Black River Convent to welcome Tao-jung to his presence to consult about the matter.

Tao-jung said, "Your majesty need only hold a pure vegetarian fast for seven days and receive and keep the eight fundamental Buddhist precepts; then of itself the omen will disappear."[83] The emperor, with proper demeanor and concentrated mind, carried out her orders, and, before the seven days were over, the crows all flocked together, moved their nests, and left. The emperor then deeply trusted and respected Tao-jung and built a convent for her, providing all the necessities. The convent was called New Grove [Convent] after the grove of trees in which it stood.

The emperor served Tao-jung with all the rites proper to serving a teacher, and, furthermore, he honored the True Law [of the Buddha]. That the people of the Chin dynasty in subsequent years respected the Way of the Buddha was because of Tao-jung's strong influence. By the time of Emperor Hsiao-wu (362–373–396) [who succeeded Chien-wen to the throne], Tao-jung was even more respected and honored.

In the *t'ai-yüan* reign period (376–396), she suddenly disappeared, and no one knew where she was.[84] The emperor issued an order to bury the robe and begging bowl that she had left behind, and for this reason there is a grave mound next to the convent.

11. LING-TSUNG

令宗

The nun Ling-tsung (Esteemed Lineage) of West Convent of
Ssu Province

Ling-tsung's secular surname was Man. Her [family's] original home was Chin-hsiang in Kao-p'ing Commandery [in northeast China].[85]

While she was yet a child, Ling-tsung had a pure faith [in Buddhism], and the villagers in the area praised her for it. Her family met with disaster, being driven away from their homeland by invading nomadic tribes.[86] Ling-tsung, with utmost sincerity and complete faith, called on the spiritual power of the Three Treasures for help.[87] She also received the Universal Gate chapter [of the *Flower of the Law* in order to ask for help from the bodhisattva Kuan-yin].[88] She plucked out her eyebrows and pretended to her captors that she had a loathsome disease. Pleading thus, she attained her release.

Retracing the road they had traveled, she went back toward the south, but, going through the province of Chi [still far north] of her home, she was pursued once more, this time by bandits.[89] She climbed to the top of a dead tree and concentrated all her faculties [in accordance with the Buddhist Way]. Those seeking to capture her looked all around but never looked up. Having searched and searched without finding her, they suddenly left. Ling-tsung climbed down and went on her way again.

She dared not beg for food and at first did not even feel hungry. One evening she came to Meng Ford [on the Yellow River], but there was no boat to ferry her across.[90] In great trepidation she again called on the Three Treasures. Suddenly Ling-tsung saw a white deer that came from out of nowhere and crossed over the river.[91] Sand and soil rose up behind the animal, and there were no waves at all. Following the deer, she crossed the river without getting wet, walking as easily as on dry land.[92] Thus she was able to return home.

Ling-tsung then entered religious life. With sincere heart and profound scholarship her study and practice were the essence of earnestness; she was widely read in the scriptures, and her deep comprehension entered the realm of the divine. When Emperor Hsiao-wu of Chin (362–373–396) heard of her reputation, he sent a letter from [his capital in the south all the way to her northern home] to communicate his respect for her.[93]

Later on, during a time when the people suffered a plague and the destitute were numerous, Ling-tsung unstintingly helped, begging everywhere for alms. She fled neither obstacles nor distances to do what she could to help the needy; those who relied on her were many. Because she herself also endured hunger and privation, her own appearance became haggard and careworn.

When she was seventy-five years old, she unexpectedly summoned her disciples one morning to tell them about a dream she had had the previous night. She said, "I saw a large mountain, the one called Sumeru, whose unusually beautiful peaks reached as high as the sky. Decorations and embellishments of precious ornaments glowed like the shining sun. The drum of the Buddha's law reverberated; fragrant incense filled the air. When spoken words commanded me to go forward, I was startled awake, but immediately I felt physically quite different from usual. Although I had no pain, it was as though I was in a swoon."[94] Tao-chin, a companion [in the Way of the Buddha], said to her, "This is surely the Western Paradise of Amita Buddha."[95] This conversation had not come to an end when suddenly Ling-tsung's spirit shifted from this world to the next.[96]

12. CHIH MIAO-YIN
支妙音
The nun Chih Miao-yin (Subtle Voice)[97] of Simple Tranquility Convent

No one knows where Miao-yin's family originally came from. Having set her will on the Way [of the Buddha] while yet a child, she lived in the capital city [of the Chin dynasty]. She studied extensively both Buddhist and non-Buddhist writings and was especially good at composing literary essays. Emperor Hsiao-wu (362–373–396) and the grand tutor, Tao-tzu, prince of Kuei-chi (364–402) [who was the emperor's brother], both treated her with great respect.[98] Often she would hold discussions and write compositions in company with the emperor, grand tutor, and court scholars, whereby her considerable talent gained a widespread reputation.

In the tenth year of the *t'ai-yüan* reign period (385) the grand tutor built Simple Tranquility Convent for Miao-yin and appointed her to the position of abbess over her more than one hundred disciples. All those talented people, both within and without monastic circles, who wished to use her influence to advance themselves bestowed gifts on her without end until the convent became the richest in the capital. Both nobles and commoners revered her as their master, and every day outside the convent gate there would be over one hundred chariots of the people who had come to call on her.

At the death of Wang Ch'en (d. 392),[99] who was the governor of Ching Province [in central China to the west of the national capital], the emperor wanted to select Wang Kung (d. 398)[100] to take the vacated position. At the same time, a certain Huan Hsüan (369–404)[101] in Chiang-ling [the provincial capital of Ching], who had always been blocked in his own plans by Wang Ch'en, heard that Wang Kung would be the replacement, and he was already afraid of Kung. Wang

Kung, however, had a partisan named Yin Chung-k'an (d. 399/ 400),[102] an imperial attendant, who, as Huan Hsüan knew, was weak and easy to manage. Therefore Huan Hsüan wanted [Yin Chung-k'an] to be appointed as governor [to replace the deceased Wang Ch'en]. He sent a messenger to the nun Miao-yin to prevail on her to arrange the governorship for Yin Chung-k'an. Before long, the emperor consulted Miao-yin on this very matter.

He said, "The position in Ching Province is vacant. Those outside monastic circles are asking who should fill it."

Miao-yin responded, "How can I, a woman of religion, have the freedom to discuss worldly matters. Nevertheless, I have heard those both within and without talking about it, and all are saying that no one surpasses Yin Chung-k'an. Because he takes a broad view of things, he is the one needed in the territory of Ching and Ch'u."[103] The emperor went along with this and replaced [Wang Ch'en] with [Yin Chung-k'an].[104]

Thus did [the nun Miao-yin's] power overrule the whole court, and her authority extend both within and without Buddhist circles.[105]

13. TAO-I

道儀

The nun Tao-i (Dignity of the Way) of Empress Ho Convent

Tao-i's secular surname was Chia. Her family was originally from the town of Lou-fan in Yen-men Commandery [in north China].[106] She was the paternal aunt of the famous monk Hui-yüan.[107]

Tao-i was married to a certain Hsieh Chih of the same commandery, who died when he was the administrator of Hsün-yang Commandery[108] [on the Yangtze River some distance southwest of the Chin capital of Chien-k'ang]. Tao-i was then twenty-two years old. At that time she cast off secular bonds and donned the robe of religion.

The nun Tao-i was intelligent, bright, quick-witted, and wise; she was widely learned and had an excellent memory, being able to chant by heart the *Flower of the Law Scripture*[109] and to expound the meaning of the *Vimalakīrti*[110] and *Smaller Perfection of Wisdom*.[111] She achieved enlightened understanding of the subtle points and transcendent principles of Buddhist doctrine by means of her own mind [without having to rely on teachers].[112] Her practice of the monastic regulations was eminent; her spiritual nature was profound.

When Tao-i heard that in the region of the capital of Chin the [Buddhist] doctrinal scriptures and the texts of monastic rules were gradually being collected, translated and given explanatory commentaries, she went there at the end of the *t'ai-yüan* reign period (376–396) and took up residence in Empress Ho Convent.[113]

Once there Tao-i devoted herself to the study of the collection of texts of the monastic rules and regulations, investigating in a most marvellous way the subtlest of points. All the while she retained her usual humility and reverence, never relaxing her discipline even in solitude, wearing rough and ragged monastic robes and carrying with her own hands the begging bowl and staff [of a Buddhist religious mendicant].[114] Because of her total lack of arrogance and pride, both monastics and householders highly esteemed the nun.

When Tao-i was seventy-eight years old, she fell seriously ill. She even more fervently concentrated her mind and chanted the scriptures without becoming exhausted, but her disciples requested of her, "We wish that you would try to find a treatment for this disease so that you might overcome your debility."

Tao-i replied, "That is not a proper thing [for a Buddhist disciple] to say." As soon as she had spoken, she died.

2. The Sung Dynasty
(420–479)

14. Hui-kuo
慧果

The nun Hui-kuo (Fruit of Wisdom) (ca. 364–433) of Luminous
Blessings Convent

Hui-kuo's secular surname was P'an. Her family was originally from
Huai-nan [on the south bank of the Huai River to the west and north
of the capital of Sung].[1]

Hui-kuo, never dressing in fine silks, lived an ascetically disciplined
life and took sincere delight in the pure and unsullied observation of
the monastic rules.[2] Her reputation was known far and wide to
monastics and householders, who alike praised and admired her. The
governor of [the northeastern province of] Ch'ing of the Sung dynasty,[3] a certain Chuan Hung-jen whose family had originally come
from Pei-ti [in north China], greatly praised her noble character and
lavishly bestowed on her gift after gift.[4] In the third year of the *yung-
ch'u* reign period (422) (I, the biographer, was told by my fellow monk
T'an-tsung that it was the seventh year of the *yüan-chia* reign period
[430],[5] but the abbess of Luminous Blessings Convent, the nun Hung-
an, let me see the land deed, which shows the date to be the third year
of *yung-ch'u*), the governor donated a plot of land to the east of his
own mansion to build a monastic residence for her, naming it Luminous Blessings, and appointed Hui-kuo to oversee it. Everything that
was donated to Hui-kuo herself she gave to the Assembly of Nuns as a
whole. Her community flourished, and both elite and ordinary happily submitted to her spiritual authority.

In the sixth year of the *yüan-chia* reign period (429), the central
Asian missionary monk Gunavarman (367–431) arrived.[6] [Hui-kuo

questioned him about the validity of the status of Buddhist nuns in China, whether the proper transmission of the rules for women from the time of the Buddha had been carried out in China.][7]

She said, "All the Buddhist nuns here in China who earlier received the obligation to keep the rules did not receive it according to the fundamentals of the rituals. [That is, they accepted the rules, incomplete though the ceremony may have been, from the Assembly of Monks only] and they had as their eminent precedent the Buddha's stepmother, Mahāprajāpatī [who received the rules from the Buddha only; at that time, when the Buddha's stepmother sought to enter the homeless life, there was in fact no Assembly of Nuns from whom to receive the rules because Mahāprajāpatī was the first Buddhist nun in the whole world]. But those first Chinese nuns did not know, and neither do I, whether there is any difference [between Mahāprajāpatī's situation and that of the nuns who came after her]."

Gunavarman replied, "There is no difference."

Hui-kuo continued, "According to the literature of the monastic regulations that I have read, the teacher who administers the rules and the obligation to follow them has committed an offense by permitting women to receive the rules from the Assembly of Monks only. [Therefore, how can there be no difference?"]

Gunavarman replied, "If a nun lives in a monastic community without having first trained in the rules for two years as a novice before accepting the full obligation to keep all the rules, then one may speak of an offence."

Hui-kuo asked again, "Then is it possible that formerly, when there were as yet no nuns here in China, there were certainly some in India?"

Gunavarman replied, "According to the disciplinary regulations [a candidate for the Assembly of Nuns must receive the obligation to observe all the rules from a minimum of] ten members of the assembly who themselves have received the full obligation. [In certain circumstances] such as in a frontier country, only five such members are required. The correct view is that, if there is an established assembly present, one cannot but go along with all the requirements."

Again Hui-kuo asked, "How far away must a place be before it is considered a frontier?"

Gunavarman replied, "Beyond a thousand Chinese miles or where oceans and mountains create a barrier."[8]

In the ninth year (432), Hui-kuo took her disciples Hui-i,[9] Hui-k'ai, and others—five in all—to receive the full monastic obligation from the Indian missionary monk Sanghavarman.[10] They respectfully received this obligation as their most precious possession.

Hui-kuo was seventy-some years old when she died in the tenth year of the *yüan-chia* reign period (433).

Her disciples Hui-i and Hui-k'ai were also well known in their day for their strict practice in keeping the monastic rules.

15. FA-SHENG

法盛

The nun Fa-sheng (Flourishing Law) (368–439) of Establishing
Blessings Convent

Fa-sheng's secular surname was Nieh. Her family was originally from Ch'ing-ho [in north China, north of the Yellow River],[11] but, during the fighting when the [non-Chinese] dynasty of Latter Chao (319–350) was coming to power, the family fled south to Chin-ling [that is, to the southern capital, on the Yangtze River].[12]

In the fourteenth year of the *yüan-chia* reign period (437) of the Sung, Fa-sheng, who was talented, intelligent, and very quick to understand everything, became a nun [at the age of seventy] in Establishing Blessings Convent in the capital city. She had sojourned there in her old age, but, even though once again the imperial capital was peaceful and prosperous, she still longed for her old home. Only by delving deep into the mysteries [of Buddhism] was she able to leave behind sorrow and forget old age.

Fa-sheng accepted responsibility for keeping the vows of a bodhisattva [or Buddha to be] from the master of the law Ou who came from the Site of the Way Monastery [also in the capital].[13] By day, Fa-sheng set forth the profound fundamentals of Buddhism; by night she gave lucid discourses on the flavor of the principles. Continuously immersing herself in these activities she became, despite her old age, radiantly healthy, surpassing those in the prime of life.

Fa-sheng had always expressed the wish to be reborn in the Western Paradise [of Amita Buddha].[14] To her sisters in religion, T'an-ching and T'an-ai, she said, "I have devoted myself to following the [Buddhist] Way, and my will is fixed on the Western Paradise."[15] Thus it happened that in the sixteenth year (439), ninth month, and twenty-seventh day, she worshipped the Buddha at the pagoda, and that evening she became ill. The illness grew worse, and on the evening of the night of the new moon, the last day of the month, as she lay asleep [Amita Buddha] the Tathāgata,[16] appeared in the air together with his two bodhisattva attendants [Kuan-shih-yin on the left and Ta-shih-chih on the right], with whom he discussed the two types of Buddhism [namely, the Mahāyāna, or Great Vehicle, and the Hīnayāna, or Small Vehicle].[17] Suddenly [Amita Buddha] with his entire entourage soared over in a fragrant mist, descending to visit the sick woman. Rays of light gleamed, filling the whole convent for all to see. When everyone came to Fa-sheng to ask about the light, she explained what it was, and as soon as she had finished speaking, she died. She was seventy-two years old.

The governor of Yü-chang,[18] Chang Pien,[19] a native of Wu Commandery [southeast of the capital], who from the first had had high regard for her narrated this account.[20]

16. Hui-yü
慧玉

The nun Hui-yü (Jade of Wisdom) of Cowherd Convent

Hui-yü was from Ch'ang-an [in the old northern heartland of China]. She zealously cultivated and thoroughly perfected the study and practice of Buddhism. She traveled throughout the country preaching and converting people, and, adapting to whatever circumstances, she did not flinch from either cold or heat.

Hui-yü went south to the territory of Ching and Ch'u [in western central China] and then took up residence in Cowherd Convent in the town of Chiang-ling in the province of Ching [on the north bank of the Yangtze River some distance west of the capital].[21] She specialized in the chanting of the *Flower of the Law,*[22] *Shūrangama,*[23] and other scriptures, being able to get through them all in a period of only ten days.[24] Monastics and householders of western Shan honored her, taking refuge in her as their teacher, and, indeed, she never wearied in her study of the scriptures and commentaries.[25]

In the fourteenth year of the *yüan-chia* reign period (437) in the tenth month, Hui-yü first carried out a seven-day austerity fast and then made a vow, saying, "If truly the fast I have just completed has its effect so that after I abandon my body in death I will assuredly see the Buddha in his paradise, then may I see, as proof, the radiant light of the Buddha manifest within seven days." During the night of the fifth day after making the vow, a supernatural light glowed among the trees east of the convent. Hui-yü informed the community of nuns who happily congratulated her and were henceforth even more devoted to her. Afterward, the abbess Fa-hung had a meditation hall built on the spot where the light had appeared.

When Hui-yü was still in Ch'ang-an, she saw a red and white colored light at the family temple of Secretary Hsüeh. It brightly illumined the whole area for ten days before fading. Later, on the eighth day of the fourth month [the Buddha's birthday], a monk of Six Prohibitions Monastery found a one-foot-high gold image of the future Buddha, Maitreya, at the spot where the light had shone.[26]

17. Tao-ch'iung
道瓊

The nun Tao-ch'iung (Rare Jade of the Way) of Establishing Blessings Convent

Tao-ch'iung's secular surname was Chiang. Her family was from Tan-yang [near the capital of the Sung dynasty]. When she was a little more than ten years old, she was already well educated in the classics and history, and after her full admission to the monastic assembly she became learned in the Buddhist writings as well and also diligently cultivated a life of asceticism.[27] In the *t'ai-yüan* reign period (376–396) of the Eastern Chin dynasty, the empress admired her exalted conduct,[28] and, whenever she wished to gain merit by giving gifts or by listening to religious exhortations, she most often depended on the convent where Tao-ch'iung lived for such opportunities. Ladies of noble family vied with one another to associate with Tao-ch'iung.[29]

In the eighth year of the *yüan-chia* reign period (431) [of Sung] she had many Buddhist images made and placed them everywhere: in P'eng-ch'eng Monastery, two gold Buddha images with a curtained dais and all accessories; in Pottery Office Monastery, a processional image of Maitreya, the future Buddha, with a jeweled umbrella and pendants; in Southern Establishing Joy Monastery, two gold images with various articles, banners, and canopies.[30] In Establishing Blessings Convent, she had an image of the reclining Buddha made, as well as a hall to house it.[31] She also had a processional image of the bodhisattva, P'u-hsien [or Samantabhadra], made. Of all these items, there was none that was not extremely beautiful.

Again, in the fifteenth year of the *yüan-chia* reign period (438), Tao-ch'iung commissioned a gold Amitāyus [or Infinite Life] Buddha, and in the fourth month and tenth day of that same year a golden light shone forth from the mark between the eyebrows of the image and filled the entire convent.[32] The news of this event spread among religious and worldly alike, and all came to pay honor, and, gazing at the unearthly brilliance, there was none who was not filled with great happiness.

Further, using the materials bequeathed to her by the Yüan empress consort, she extended the convent to the south to build another meditation hall.[33]

18. TAO-SHOU

道壽

The nun Tao-shou (Longevity of the Way) of Jeta Grove Convent
in Chiang-ling

No one knows where Tao-shou's family originally came from. Of pure and gentle character, she was commended for her reverence and filial piety. When she was yet a child, she accepted the five fundamental precepts of a Buddhist householder, and not once did she commit an offence against them.

In the *yüan-chia* reign period (424–453) of Sung, Tao-shou was in mourning for her father, and as a result she grieved herself sick but felt no pain or discomfort. For several years she remained sickly and skeletal, not responding to any medical treatment. Therefore she vowed that, if she were cured, she would leave the household life to become a nun. After making the vow she gradually recovered, and in fulfillment of her vow she left the household life and became a nun in Jeta Grove Convent, where her practice of austerities was unequaled.[34] She chanted the *Flower of the Law Scripture* three thousand times and frequently saw glorious omens.[35] For example, in the middle of the night on the seventh day, ninth month, of the sixteenth year of the *yüan-chia* reign period (439), a jeweled canopy [such as the kind placed over images of the Buddha] descended and hovered over her.[36]

19. SHIH HSÜAN-TSAO

釋玄藻

The nun Shih Hsüan-tsao (Mysterious Elegance) (in the lineage of
Shākyamuni) of Great Mysterious Terrace Convent of Wu
Commandery

Hsüan-tsao's secular surname was Lu. She was the daughter of Lu An-
hsün of Wu Commandery [southeast of the capital city].[37]

When Hsüan-tsao was a little over ten years old, she contracted a
serious illness, and, despite all the medicines, the days went by with no
improvement. At that time [the nun] Shih Fa-chi of the Great Mysterious Terrace [Convent] said to Hsüan-tsao's father, "This illness is
probably the consequence of deeds done in a former life and therefore
is not something that medicine can cure. I go by the Buddhist scriptures, which say that, if those who walk in danger and suffering are
able to take refuge in the spiritual power of the Three Treasures and
confess their faults, aspiring to attain spiritual accomplishments, then
they will indeed gain freedom from suffering and danger.[38] If you and
your daughter cast aside the corruption of the world, wash away the
dust of secular life and single-mindedly turn for refuge to the [bodhi-
sattva Kuan-yin],[39] then there should be a cure." Lu An-hsün agreed to
this, and in his own house sponsored a vegetarian feast in honor of the
bodhisattva Kuan-shih-yin.

With unsullied intent they worshipped [the bodhisattva], and
Hsüan-tsao, despite her illness, concentrated her thoughts and made
prostrations continuously. After seven days, at the first watch of the
night, there suddenly appeared a gold image slightly more than a foot
high. The image rubbed Hsüan-tsao's body three times from head to
foot, after which the girl felt the illness rapidly disappear.

Because of this miraculous cure she sought to enter the life of a Buddhist nun and so took up residence at Great Mysterious Terrace Convent. Her zealous practice included chanting the *Flower of the Law
Scripture* and maintaining a strict vegetarian diet for thirty-seven
years. With constant longing and concentration she vowed to be
reborn in the Tushita Heaven [of Maitreya, the next Buddha].[40]

In the sixteenth year of the *yüan-chia* reign period (439), she went
to the capital city to copy scriptures, but the circumstances of her
death are unknown.[41]

20. SHIH HUI-CH'IUNG

釋慧瓊

The nun Shih Hui-ch'iung (Rare Jade of Wisdom) (in the lineage
of Shākyamuni) (ca. 368–447) of Southern Eternal Peace
Convent

Hui-ch'iung's secular surname was Chung. Her family was originally
from Kuang Province [in southernmost China].[42]

Hui-ch'iung's practice of religion was both exalted and pure. She
tasted neither fish nor flesh, and, when she reached the advanced age
of eighty, her resolve was even more zealous. Never touching fine
silks, she wore only straw sandals and hempen robes.[43] She was in
charge of administering the convent, and in addition she lectured [on
the Buddhist scriptures]. At that time she lived in Southern Peace Convent in Kuang-ling [which was on the north bank of the Yangtze River,
northeast of the capital of the Sung dynasty].[44]

In the eighteenth year of the *yüan-chia* reign period (441), Madame
Wang [mother of the eldest son, Lang (d. 453),[45] of the prince of
Chiang-hsia (413–465),[46] fifth son of the founder of the Sung dy-
nasty],[47] presented some land to Hui-chiung who used it as the site of
a convent that she named Southern Eternal Peace Convent. In the
twenty-second year of the same reign period (445), a man named
Hsiao Ch'eng-chih,[48] originally of Lan-ling [a town some miles to the
east of the capital], built a foreign-style pagoda for her.[49]

In the fifteenth year of the *yüan-chia* reign period (438), Hui-
ch'iung also had Bodhi Convent built. Because all its halls, shrine
rooms, and living quarters were so beautiful, she moved there and
donated her original convent, Southern Eternal Peace, to the monk
Hui-chih.[50]

In the twenty-fourth year of the *yüan-chia* reign period (447),[51] she
traveled in the party of the [official] Meng I,[52] who was going to Kuei-
chi [Commandery as administrator].[53] They got as far as the P'o-kang
Canal [southwest of the capital near Chü-jung County, when Hui-
ch'iung died]. She had instructed her disciples, "After I die you should
not bury me, but rather give my body to someone to chop it up and
feed it to the animals."[54] When she expired, however, her disciples
could not bear the thought of chopping up her body, so they carried
her to the mountains in Chü-jung County [only a short distance from

P'o-kang], and left her where the birds and beasts themselves could come up and feast on her.[55] After ten-some days, nevertheless, the corpse was undisturbed, and the complexion had not altered.[56] The county magistrate sent nearby villagers to scatter uncooked rice around the body, with the result that the birds ate up all the rice lying at some distance but left untouched the rice near the corpse. When her disciple Hui-lang, who was in the capital, heard about this, she hurried to bring the body back. She buried it on the hill in front of Eminent Dais Monastery,[57] and she had a memorial pagoda erected over the burial mound.[58]

21. P'U-CHAO
普照

The nun P'u-chao (Universal Illumination) (418–442) of
Expanding Nation Convent of Nan-p'i in northeast China

P'u-chao's secular surname was Tung, and her given name was Pei. Her family was from An-ling in the P'o-hai Commandery [in northeast China, in the territory held by the non-Chinese dynasty of Northern Wei.][59]

When she was a young girl, she already adhered to high moral principles, and at the age of seventeen she left the household life to become a nun at Expanding Nation Convent in Nan-p'i [a town to the northwest of An-ling].

Later, P'u-chao accompanied her religious instructor to study at Establishing Splendor Convent in Kuang-ling [a town on the northern bank of the Yangtze River, northeast of the capital].[60]

She upheld her religious faith and practice with all her heart for which the rest of the community praised her; and, when her instructor, Hui-tzu, died, P'u-chao retired from all social occasions and instead practiced austerities even more fervently.

In the twelfth month of the eighteenth year of the *yüan-chia* reign period (441), she became ill from exhaustion. Although the malady was serious, she still held her deep and abiding faith. When at first she did not improve, she concentrated her mind and prayed in utmost sincerity both day and night. Because she could not lower herself to the ground to make prostrations, she would touch her forehead to the pillow while confessing her faults. When she rested from this, she continued her usual practice of chanting the *Flower of the Law Scripture*[61] at the rate of three scrolls a day.[62]

In the second month of the nineteenth year (442), she suddenly expired, but after a short time—about the length of two meals—she revived.[63] She said, "Along the road toward the west there was a pagoda. A monk sat inside, his eyes closed in meditation. Startled by my appearance, he asked where I came from. I answered, and then I asked him, 'How far from here is a certain convent?' He answered, 'Fifty million miles.' The road was grassy and there were many travelers, but no one whom I recognized. At that moment the clouds were piled high, and the whole place was utterly pure. Toward the west everything shone even more brightly, and I wanted to go forward in that direction, but the monk forbid it. So I turned back and suddenly awoke."

Seven days later P'u-chao died at the age of twenty-five [in the year 442].

22. SHIH HUI-MU

釋慧木

The nun Shih Hui-mu (Tree of Wisdom) (in the lineage of
Shākyamuni) of Chu-ko Village Convent in Liang Commandery

Hui-mu's secular surname was Fu. Her family was originally from Pei-ti [in northwest China, north of the old capital of Ch'ang-an].

Hui-mu left the household life at age 11 and undertook the ten obligatory rules [of a novice] under the instruction of Hui-ch'ao, living in Chu-ko Village Convent of Liang Commandery [in the Huai River valley some distance west of the capital of the Sung dynasty].[64]

When she first read the *Larger Perfection of Wisdom*,[65] she was able to chant from memory two chapters a day [each chapter having more than ten thousand words].[66] She was also able to understand the meaning of a variety of other scriptures.

Hui-mu's mother was old and sick. Because her mother had no teeth, Hui-mu first chewed the meat she gave her mother to eat. As a result, however, Hui-mu's mouth was impure.[67] Therefore she did not take on herself the obligation to observe all the monastic rules and become a full-fledged nun [as she would have liked to do] but instead continued her zealous devotions and confession of her faults while still garbed in the dress of a householder.

Unexpectedly one day she saw that the ceremonial platform for the ritual of accepting the monastic rules and the space around it were a golden color. Raising her head and looking toward the south, she saw a man wearing a trimmed robe that was also golden in color. Appearing sometimes near and sometimes far, he said to Hui-mu, "I have already bestowed the monastic obligations on you," and thereafter he disappeared. Hui-mu told no one about this, which was like many of the other unusual things that happened to her.

Because Hui-mu's elder brother heard rumor of some of these experiences and wanted to know more about them, he tricked her, saying, "You have followed the way of religion for a number of years, but in the end it has been of no benefit to you. Because that is the case, you might as well let your hair grow, and I shall find a husband for you." When Hui-mu heard these words her heart was sorely grieved, so she revealed to him what she had seen.

Shortly thereafter Hui-mu received full admission into the Assembly of Nuns. One night not long before the ceremony was to take place she dreamed that she saw a person who recited the book of the monastic rules. After her full admission to the assembly she read that same book only twice before being able to chant it from memory.

During the *yüan-chia* reign period (424–453) of the Sung dynasty she had images of the Buddhas of the ten directions made and presented them together with copies of the *Dharmaguptaka Monastic Rules in Four Divisions*[68] and the *Rituals for Entering Monastic Life*[69] to the four Buddhist assemblies [of monk, nun, male, and female householders].

22a. SHIH HUI-MU

釋慧木

[A second version of Hui-mu's life taken from the sixth-century collection titled *Ming hsiang chi* (Records of mysterious omens)][70]

The nun Hui-mu of the Sung dynasty was surnamed Fu. She entered the religious life at age eleven but accepted only the ten rules [of a novice in the monastic life]. She lived in Chu-ko Village Convent in Liang Commandery.

When Hui-mu first read the *Larger Perfection of Wisdom,* she was able to chant from memory two chapters a day [a total of more than twenty thousand words]. Her teacher, Hui-ch'ao, had built a scripture hall, and once, when Hui-mu went in to offer worship, she saw in the northwest corner of the room a Buddhist monk wearing the gold-colored robe of a Buddhist monastic, and his feet were not touching the ground.

Another time when Hui-mu, in the middle of the night, was lying down and memorizing scriptures, she had a dream in which she traveled to the west, where she saw a pool filled with lotus blossoms, and sitting inside each lotus was a person who had been born there [by metamorphosis]. One large flower, however, was empty. Hui-mu, wanting to climb up onto the flower, grabbed hold of it with all her strength but, without realizing what she was doing, also began to chant scripture in a loud voice. Because her mother, hearing the chanting, thought that Hui-mu was having a nightmare, she woke her daughter up.

Hui-mu's mother was very old, and, because she had lost all her teeth, Hui-mu always thoroughly chewed her mother's food first so that her mother could eat. Doing this, however, meant that Hui-mu had to eat after noon as well as before thereby transgressing the monastic rule of not eating after mid-day. For that reason, even though Hui-mu had grown up and come of age to be able to accept the full obligation of the monastic life, she did not do so.

After her mother died, Hui-mu herself cleaned and prepared the ground for the placing of the ceremonial platform used for receiving the monastic rules, and she asked her teacher to bestow them. Suddenly, the space around the platform glowed with dazzling light, all a golden color. Hui-mu looked toward the southwest, where she saw a heavenly being who wore a trimmed robe of russet-gold color. He seemed now close and now far away, but, when she sought after him, he had disappeared.

The extraordinary things that happened to her she kept secret, but, when her elder brother became a monk, he heard rumors and wanted to find out for sure, so he tricked her, saying, "You have been living the religious life many years now, but with no results. Therefore, you might as well let your hair grow and become a wife."[71] When Hui-mu heard this, she felt great dread and thought she should tell the truth about everything, so she gave a rough description of what she had seen.

When the nun Ching-ch'eng heard of her Way and virtue, she went to Hui-mu for the purpose of becoming well acquainted with her, the more easily to ask about the unusual phenomena Hui-mu had experienced, and Hui-mu told her everything in detail.

Later, Hui-mu and her companions in religion were worshipping the Endless-Life Buddha [Amitāyus]. Because Hui-mu did not get up after a prostration, the others thought she had fallen asleep. Someone kicked her and asked, but Hui-mu said nothing at all. When Ching-ch'eng again begged and entreated her, Hui-mu said, "While I was prostrate on the ground [worshipping the Buddha], I had a vision of going to the Western Paradise and seeing Amita Buddha, who was explaining the *Smaller Perfection of Wisdom* [to me]. He had already gone as far as the fourth chapter when, to my very deep regret, I was kicked awake."

In the fourteenth year of the *yüan-chia* reign period (437), Hui-mu was sixty-nine years old.

23. FA-SHENG
法勝

The nun Fa-sheng (Victory of the Law) of Wu County South Convent

Fa-sheng's [origins are unknown].[72] When young, she left the household life and took up the life of a religious in South Convent of Wu County [some distance to the southeast of the capital of the Sung dynasty].[73] Some sources say it was East Convent. Her piety and zeal were recognized by the assembly.[74]

In the *yüan-chia* reign period (424–453) of the Sung dynasty a certain Ssu-ma Lung, originally of Ho-nei [in the north],[75] who was serving as the county magistrate of P'i-ling [southeast of the capital], met up with an attack and was killed in battle.[76] The parents of his wife, Madame Shan, had already died, and she had no children. Madame Shan was already advanced in years when she went to Wu County to stay with Fa-sheng, who treated her as her own mother. Almost half a year later Madame Shan got sick. The illness grew progressively worse and after three years was at a critical stage. Because Fa-sheng had nothing stored in reserve, she had to beg for all the medicines needed to treat Madame Shan. When begging for the medicines, Fa-sheng feared neither rain nor heat; she fled neither wind nor cold. Madame Shan's condition thereafter improved, and everyone praised and honored Fa-sheng.

Later, Fa-sheng traveled to the capital to further her study of meditation, in the course of which she penetrated the riches of contemplation, and she investigated to the utmost the subtle and hidden fruits of the spiritual life. She instructed her disciples, accomplishing this without undue severity. When acting she did not seek personal gain; when in repose she did not seek fame. In her diligent and complete observation of all her duties, she could not but save living beings.

At age 60 she had been ill for some time, and she herself said she would not recover. When her intimate disciples, puzzled, asked how she knew, Fa-sheng informed them, "Just now I saw two Buddhist monks who told me this is the case." After a brief while she continued, "I see two other monks, different from the ones I saw previously. Their right shoulders are bare as though they are preparing to circumambulate the Buddha in worship, and they are carrying flowers and placing them by my bed.[77] Some distance behind them I see a Buddha sitting on a lotus flower, and his radiance is reflecting on my body." After this she did not go to sleep again that night. Instead, she asked someone to chant the *Flower of the Law* for her, but near the end of the night her breath grew short, so she gave the command, "Stop chanting the scripture and instead repeat the name of the Buddha for me." She herself also repeated the name of the Buddha and at dawn, her countenance unchanged, she suddenly died.

24. SENG-TUAN
僧端

The nun Seng-tuan (Propriety of the Sangha) (ca. 378–448) of Eternal Peace Convent

Seng-tuan was from Kuang-ling [which was on the north bank of the Yangtze River to the northeast of the capital city of the Sung dynasty]. For generations her family had worshipped the Buddha, and she and her sisters were very devout.

Seng-tuan had vowed that she would leave the household life instead of being married off. Nevertheless, her beauty of face and figure was well known in the region, and a wealthy family had already received her mother and elder brother's agreement to a betrothal. Three days before the marriage ceremony was to take place Seng-tuan fled in the middle of the night to a Buddhist convent whose abbess hid her in a separate building and supplied her with everything she needed. Seng-tuan also asked for a copy of the *Bodhisattva Kuan-shih-yin Scripture,* which she was then able to chant from memory in only two days.[78] She rained tears and made prostrations day and night without ceasing. Three days later, during her worship, she saw an image of the Buddha, who announced to her, "Your bridegroom's life span is coming to an end. You need only continue your ardent practice without harboring these sorrowful thoughts." The next day her bridegroom was gored to death by an ox. Thus was Seng-tuan able to leave the household life.

[As a nun] she steadfastly observed all the monastic regulations, and, when she concentrated her mind in the vast realm of Buddhist meditation, she seemed as though she could form no words at all. When, however, she explicated the distinctions between the philosophical concepts of name and reality, she could speak indefatigably. In addition to her other accomplishments she could also chant the entire *Great Nirvāna Scripture* [a total of about three hundred fifty thousand words][79] in only five days.[80]

In the tenth year of the *yüan-chia* reign period (433), she went south to the capital and took up residence in Eternal Peace Convent. In managing the affairs of the community she treated everyone the same with equal affection for all. Great and humble happily submitted to her authority, and, with the passing of time, she was even more respected.

In the twenty-fifth year of the *yüan-chia* reign period (448), when Seng-tuan was more than seventy years old she died. Her disciples P'u-ching and P'u-yao were also well known for their practice of austerities and for their chanting of the *Flower of the Law Scripture.*

25. KUANG-CHING

光靜

The nun Kuang-ching (Shining Peace) (d. 442) of Central
Convent of Kuang-ling

Kuang-ching's secular surname was Hu, and her given name was Tao-pei. She was from Tung-ch'ien in the Wu-hsing Commandery [to the south of Lake T'ai, southeast of the capital].[81]

When Kuang-ching was yet a child, she left the household life and went with her instructor to live in Central Convent of Kuang-ling [on the north bank of the Yangtze River, northeast of the capital of the Sung dynasty].

Kuang-ching cultivated a diligent zeal in her religious practices while still a young girl, and, when she grew up, she undertook in particular the practice of meditation. She ate neither sweet nor fat foods, and, when she was ready to accept the full obligation of the monastic life, she gave up even cereals, eating instead only pine resin, a diet she continued for fifteen years after becoming a full-fledged nun.[82] But, even though her mental faculties were as clear and fresh as ever, her body had no strength left. She prayed ardently, but she was in a constant state of exhaustion from her efforts. The Buddhist monk Shih Fa-ch'eng admonished her, "Eating is not the most important matter in Buddhism."[83] When Kuang-ching heard these words, she gave up her diet of pine resin and went back to eating ordinary rice. Nevertheless, she doubled her heroic efforts, studying single-mindedly without growing weary. Those who practiced contemplation under her tutelage always numbered over one hundred.

In the fifth month of the eighteenth year of the *yüan-chia* reign period (441), Kuang-ching got sick. She said, "I have been wearied and afflicted with this body for a long time." Thereupon, because of her illness, confession of her transgressions was never absent from her thoughts or speech. In mind and expression she was happy and tranquil.

On New Year's Day of the nineteenth year (442), she suddenly gave up all food and drink. Concentrating her thought on the Tushita Heaven of Maitreya [the next Buddha], she kept it constantly in mind, and thus she continued until the night of the fourth month and eighth day [the Buddha's birthday],[84] when, in the presence of unusual fragrance and good omens appearing in the sky, she died.

26. SHAN-MIAO

善妙

The nun Shan-miao (Excellent Subtlety) of Shu Commandery in western China

Shan-miao's secular surname was Ou-yang. She was from Fan County [in western China].[85]

Shan-miao left the household life while still a child. Being amiable in character, she seldom went to either extreme of anger or joy. She neither wore good clothing nor ate fine food. She had a younger sister, a widow, whose husband had died, leaving her no support. Therefore, taking her child with her, she lodged with Shan-miao. Often she heard Shan-miao herself lament that she had not been born while the Buddha was on earth, and every time she said this her tears flowed in uncontrollable sorrow.

They lived together for four or five years, but the younger sister never once saw Shan-miao eating. Whenever the younger sister had cooked a meal, she would call Shan-miao to come join her, but Shan-miao would always say that she had already eaten somewhere else, or she would say that she was not feeling well and therefore could not eat anything. This went on for quite a few years until the sister felt so ashamed that she said, "My unlucky husband has perished, and, further, my child and I have no other relatives and must depend on elder sister, troubling her to no end. She is no doubt tired of us and therefore will not eat with us."

Having spoken, she wished to leave, but Shan-miao took her by the hand and explained to her, "You have misunderstood my intention. Because, fortunately, I am able as a Buddhist nun to receive offerings and donations from others, why should I eat up the food here? Don't be upset any more. Before long, I'll be going away, so you should maintain your household here and by all means do not leave." When the younger sister heard these words she stayed.

Shan-miao herself wove a length of cloth and bought many measures of oil, putting it in various jars and jugs in the courtyard. She cautioned her sister, "This oil is for a work of religious merit. Be careful that you do not use any of it."

At midnight of the eighth day of the fourth month, the [Buddha's birthday], Shan-miao wrapped herself up in the cloth she had woven and had soaked in the oil and set herself on fire. When the flames had reached as high as her head she ordered her sister, "Tell the administrator of the meditation hall to strike the gong to summon all the other nuns that they may come quickly to say farewell because I am now abandoning this life." She had not yet died by the time all the nuns had arrived in great haste and alarm. Shan-miao said to the nuns gathered there, "Each of you must diligently make the effort to perfect your spiritual life because the cycle of birth and death is a fearsome thing. You must seek to escape it, taking heed not to fall into further transmigration. I have previously abandoned this body as a worship offering to the Buddha twenty-seven times, but it is only this time that I shall attain the first fruit [whereby I am no longer liable to rebirth in the woeful destinies of hell, hungry ghosts, or animals]."[86] (I, Pao-ch'ang, the compiler, have consulted with several elderly persons from that region. Some say she set fire to herself in the seventeenth year of the *yüan-chia* reign period (440); some say it was the *hsiao-chien* reign period (454–456); some say it was the *ta-ming* reign period (457–464). Therefore I record them all.)

27. SENG-KUO
僧果

The nun Seng-kuo (Fruit of the Sangha) (b. 408) of Kuang-ling

Seng-kuo's secular surname was Chao; her given name was Fa-yu. Her family was originally from Hsiu-wu in Chi Commandery [in north China].[87]

Because she had established genuine faith during a former life, pure devotion was natural to her in her present life, and, even when she was an infant at breast, she did not transgress the monastic rule of not eating after mid-day.[88] Her father and mother both marveled at this. When Seng-kuo grew up, although she was of one mind about what she wanted to do, the karmic obstructions were mixed and multiform. Therefore she was twenty-seven years old before she was able to leave the household life, at which time she became a disciple of the nun Hui-ts'ung of Kuang-ling [on the north bank of the Yangtze River northeast of the capital]. Seng-kuo cultivated an intelligent and solid observance of the monastic regulations, and her meditative practice was so free from distractions that each time she entered into concentration she continued thus from dusk to dawn. Stretching in spirit to the pure realm of the divine, her body stayed behind looking as lifeless as dry wood, but some of her disciples of shallow understanding were doubtful of her yogic ability.[89]

In the sixth year of the *yüan-chia* reign period (429), a foreign boat captain named Nan-t'i brought some Buddhist nuns from Sri Lanka to the capital of the Sung dynasty.[90] The Sri Lankan nuns stayed at Luminous Blessings Convent.

Not long after taking up residence there, they asked Seng-kuo, "Before we came to this country, had foreign nuns ever been here?"

She replied, "No, there have not been any."

They asked again, ["If that is the case] how did the Chinese women who became nuns receive the monastic obligations from both the Assembly of Monks and the Assembly of Nuns [as they are required to do according to the rules?]"

Seng-kuo replied, "They received the obligations only from the Assembly of Monks."

"Those women who went through the ritual of entering the monastic life began the reception of the monastic obligations.[91] This reception was an expedient to cause people to have great respect for the monastic life. Our eminent model for this expedient is the Buddha's own stepmother, Mahāprajāpatī, who was deemed to have accepted the full monastic obligation by taking on herself, and therefore for all women for all time, the eight special prohibitions incumbent on women wanting to lead the monastic life. [These she accepted from the Buddha only.] The five hundred women of the Buddha's clan who also left the household life at the same time as Mahāprajāpatī considered her as their instructor."[92]

Although Seng-kuo agreed, she herself had a few doubts [about the validity of the rituals that had been observed in China regarding women leaving the household life]. Therefore she asked the central Asian missionary monk Gunavarman [who was an expert on the subject].[93] He agreed with her understanding of the situation.

She further inquired of him, "Is it possible to go through the ritual [of accepting the full monastic obligation] a second time?"

Gunavarman replied, "[The Buddhist threefold action of] morality, meditation, and wisdom progresses from the slight to the obvious. Therefore, receiving the monastic obligations a second time is of greater benefit than receiving them only once."

[Four years later] in the tenth year (433), Nan-t'i, the ship captain, brought eleven more nuns from Sri Lanka, including one named Tessara.[94] The first group of nuns, who by this time had become fluent in Chinese, requested the Indian missionary monk Sanghavarman to preside over the ritual for bestowing the monastic rules on women at the ceremonial platform in Southern Grove Monastery.[95] That day more than three hundred women accepted once again the full monastic obligation [this time from both the Assembly of Monks and the Assembly of Nuns].

One time, in the eighteenth year (441), when she was thirty-four years old, Seng-kuo sat in meditation for a whole day. [Because she had sat so long and her body was still and lifeless like dry wood] the administrator of the meditation hall tried to rouse her but could not and therefore said that she had died.[96] Alarmed, she summoned the other officers of the convent who, on examining Seng-kuo, perceived that her body was cold and stiff. Her breath was so slight as to be unnoticed, and they were on the point of carrying her away when she opened her eyes and talked and laughed like her usual self. Thereupon, those foolish ones [who had doubted her] were startled into accepting her achievements in meditation.

It is not known how or when she died.

28. CHING-CH'ENG

靜稱

The nun Ching-ch'eng (Measure of Quietude) of Bamboo Grove Convent in Tung-hsiang of Shan-yang [north of the capital on the south bank of the Huai River]

Ching-ch'eng's secular surname was Liu; her given name was Sheng. Her family was originally from Ch'iao Commandery [in the Huai River valley].[97]

Besides Ching-ch'eng's stringent practice of the monastic rules, she was also able to chant 450,000 words of scripture. The mountain grove next to the convent had no clamor or distractions, and in that fine location Ching-ch'eng's mind roamed in the silence of meditation, cutting off forever worldly corruption and trouble.

Once a man lost an ox and went searching for it. By nightfall he had come to the mountain where he saw the bright glare of firelight in the convent grove, but, when he approached it, the light disappeared.

A tiger often followed Ching-ch'eng in her comings and goings, and, when she sat in meditation, the tiger settled down nearby. If one of the nuns in the convent did not make a timely confession of an offence she had committed against the rules, the tiger would be angry, but, after she confessed, the tiger would be pleased.

Later, when Ching-ch'eng came out for a brief while from her seclusion on the mountain, on the way she encountered a woman from the north. They greeted one another without engaging in the usual formalities and were as pleased and happy as old friends. The woman's name was Ch'iu Wen-chiang, and she was originally from Po-p'ing [in northeast China, in the border region between the non-Chinese dynasty in the north and the Chinese dynasty in the south].[98] Ch'iu Wen-chiang's character was such that she particularly liked the Buddhist teaching. She had heard that in the south the Way was flourishing, and, when she was able to get across the frontier, she went as a refugee to this territory, where she became a nun.

Together with Ching-ch'eng, Ch'iu Wen-chiang led an austere life in the convent. Neither of the two women would eat millet or rice but instead ate only sesame and mountain thistles. Their reputation for strict asceticism became known in the capital of the northern barbarians who called the women sages and from afar summoned them with greetings of welcome. The two women, however, did not like the frontier region, and therefore they proceeded to besmirch their own reputation by being, as [Confucius recommended] "bold in action while conciliatory in speech" when in a country where the Way does not prevail.[99] The barbarian host had prepared for them a meal of fine delicacies, which the women immediately gobbled right down, paying no attention to manners. Because of this the ruler lost his former respect for them and detained them no longer. Ching-ch'eng and Wen-chiang returned to their convent.

Ching-ch'eng was ninety-three years old, free from any malady, when she died.

29. FA-HSIANG

法相

The nun Fa-hsiang (Mark of the Law) (ca. 375–ca. 453) of Great
Mysterious Terrace Convent of Wu Commandery [southeast of
the capital]

Fa-hsiang's secular surname was Hou. Her family was originally from Tun-huang [an outpost in far-northwest China].[100]

Fa-hsiang was outstanding in her excellence of both character and intellect. Zealous in her love of study, she would not slacken her efforts on account of scarcity; she was content in her poverty, and material prosperity did not sway her. Fa-hsiang married into the Fuh clan,[101] but the family was beset by many troubles, and, when the ruler of the Former Ch'in dynasty, Fu Chien, suffered defeat (383), all her relatives disappeared or perished in the aftermath.[102] She then left the household life and undertook the observance of the monastic rules. Her belief in and understanding of [the Buddhist religion] was profound.

Fa-hsiang often divided her clothing and food, giving the best to the nun Hui-su. The other nuns admonished Fa-hsiang saying, "The nun Hui-su is uncultivated and inarticulate. She has been totally unable to learn anything about Buddhist teaching, scriptures, or monastic rules. She wanted to study meditation, but no one would give her instruction, for she is a thorough dolt and the worst of idiots. Why is it that you do not try to harvest [greater merit for yourself by sowing the seeds of generosity] in a more spiritually worthy field instead of cultivating this very inferior one [that is unable to produce a good harvest of blessings?]"

Fa-hsiang responded [to the charge], "One would have to be a saint to know the spiritual accomplishments of the recipient of donations. I, however, because I am a very ordinary person, would rather do it this way. If I make a suitable donation, why should I be concerned with deliberately selecting [a so-called superior recipient]?"

Later, the nun Hui-su, whom the others thought to be hopeless, sponsored a seven-day meditation session. On the third night Hui-su sat down in meditation with the rest of the assembly, but she did not get up again with the others. When they observed her they saw that she was rigid like wood or stone.[103] When they tugged at her, she did not move. Some said that she had died, but three days later she got up and was her usual self. It was only then that the whole assembly recognized Hui-su's extraordinary accomplishment in meditation, and for the first time they became aware of Fa-hsiang's profound insight and ability [to recognize the spiritual capacities of others]. Things like this happened more than once.

The years went by, and Fa-hsiang in her old age was even more rigorous in her practice of austerities. She was over ninety when she died at the end of the *yüan-chia* reign period (424–453).

30. YEH-SHOU
業首

The nun Yeh-shou (First in Achievement) (373–462) of Eastern
Green Garden Convent

Yeh-shou's secular surname was Chang. She was from [the northeastern city of] P'eng-ch'eng [long a home to Buddhists].

Yeh-shou was dignified in demeanor and unsullied in observing the monastic precepts. With her profound understanding of the Buddhist teaching known as the Great Vehicle she was good at drawing out the subtle principles. Especially fond of meditation and the chanting of scriptures, she practiced both continuously without remiss.

[The first emperor of the Sung dynasty] Emperor Wu (363–420–422) greatly admired her extraordinary qualities.[104] [The third emperor] Wen (407–424–453),[105] had, when a youth, received from her the ceremony of Taking the Three Refuges.[106]

Yeh-shou lived in Eternal Peace Convent where gifts from the faithful were donated unendingly. In the second year of the *yüan-chia* reign period (425), Madame Fan, mother of Wang Ching-shen, presented to Yeh-shou the grounds of the old ancestral hall of Wang T'an-chih (330–375), where there was then built a convent called Green Garden.[107]

Yeh-shou's community of disciples was a model for the proper observance of religious life. Imperial Concubine P'an exclaimed about her, "The nun Yeh-shou's propagation of the Buddhist teaching is indeed worthy of great respect." In the fifteenth year of the *yüan-chia* reign period (438), she enlarged the convent for Yeh-shou: to the west she built a Buddha Hall; to the north she cleared the ground and built a residence hall and also donated all the necessities.

The convent flourished, and the community of two hundred nuns carried out their religious life and activities unceasingly. Through the years those who relied on Yeh-shou grew more and more numerous until she asked to retire, pleading old age, but the community would not hear of it. In the sixth year of the *ta-ming* reign period (462), she died at the age of ninety.

During that same time there were also the nuns Ching-ai, Pao-ying, and Fa-lin who were all well known in the district of the capital because of their purity of life and character. Ching-ai long cultivated meditation and chanting and carried out the duties of her office with utmost fidelity. She died in the fifth year of the *t'ai-shih* reign period (469). Pao-ying was responsible for the building of a five-story pagoda. She was diligent in the examining of principles and zealous in keeping to a vegetarian diet. She died in the sixth year of the *t'ai-shih* reign period (470). Fa-lin was widely read in both the doctrinal and monastic scriptures and in her old age did not slacken her efforts. She died in the first year of the *yüan-hui* reign period (473).

Furthermore, there was Yeh-shou's disciple, T'an-yin, who was accomplished in both meditation and the monastic discipline. Contemptuous of glory, she kept aloof from the struggle for power or wealth. She died in the sixth year [*sic*] of the *yüan-hui* reign period (478?).

31. FA-PIEN

法辯

The nun Fa-pien (Discussant of the Law) (ca. 403–463) of
Luminous Blessings Convent

Fa-pien was from Tan-yang [just to the south of the capital]. When yet a child she left the household life and became a disciple of the nun Hui-kuo (no. 14) of Luminous Blessings Convent. Respectful and modest, she lived a life of utmost simplicity, wearing worn-out clothing and eating a simple vegetarian diet, never touching strong-flavored foods.[108] Word of her eminent simplicity soon filled the capital, and the Lang-yeh prince, Yü, the governor of Yang Province, deeply admired and respected her.[109]

Later, Fa-pien sought to receive instruction in meditation from the foreign monk Kālayashas (ca. 383–ca. 442), a meditation master who was living at Grove of the Way Monastery.[110] Cultivating her meditation in accordance with the teaching, she reached the pinnacle of that spiritual practice. Whenever she joined in communal activities, she always seemed to be dozing, and, once in the refectory when the other nuns dispersed after the meal, she did not get up with them. In alarm the administrator touched her and found her body to be as inflexible as wood or stone. The administrator hurried to report the event, and everyone came to see, but a moment later Fa-pien came out of her meditative trance and spoke like her usual self. The other nuns in the community all respectfully submitted to her, redoubling their reverence for her accomplishments. Fa-pien died in the seventh year of the *ta-ming* reign period (463) when she was over sixty years old.

The day before her death, the master of the law Ch'ao-pien (420–492) of Upper Grove of Concentration Monastery dreamed of a palace that was beautifully decorated, everything down to the last trifle glowed in an aura not of this world.[111] Men and women dressed in fine array filled this palace, but no lord was to be seen. When in the dream the monk Ch'ao-pien asked why no lord was to be seen, he received the reply, "The nun Fa-pien of Luminous Blessings Convent is shortly going to be born here; she should arrive tomorrow."

On that day Fa-pien felt only that she was shivering, and she sent word to the community who, from highest to lowest, gathered around her. She said to them, "There are strangers approaching me, now visible and now faint, like shadows and clouds." Having spoken, she died as she sat there.

Afterward there were also the nuns Tao-chao and Seng-pien, who were known for their practice of the perfection of vigor [one of the six Buddhist perfections].[112] Tao-chao, whose secular surname was Yang, was from the northern province of Hsü. Keeping a vegetarian diet and chanting scriptures, she was supported with offerings from the prince of Lin-ho.

32. TAO-TSUNG
道綜

The nun Tao-tsung (Summing up the Way) (d. 463) of Three-
Story Convent in Chiang-ling

Tao-tsung, whose family origins are unknown, lived in Three-Story Convent in Chiang-ling [which was in west central China on the north bank of the Yangtze River]. As a child she had no intention of setting herself apart; as an adult she did not consider associating with others a defilement. She merely followed a course along the boundary between the wise and the foolish, and, although outwardly she seemed muddled, yet within she traversed hidden profundities.

On the full-moon night of the fifteenth day of the third month, in the seventh year of the *ta-ming* reign period (463) of the Sung dynasty, Tao-tsung, as an offering to the Buddha, purified herself in a fire fed by oil. Even though she was engulfed by flames up to her forehead, and her eyes and ears were nearly consumed, her chanting of the scriptures did not falter. Monastics and householders sighed in wonder; the demonic and upright were alike startled. When the country heard this news, everyone aspired to attain enlightenment. The appointed court scholar of Sung [*sic*], Liu Ch'iu (438–495), especially revered her and composed a Buddhist-style poetic verse to praise her.[113]

33. HUI-CHÜN
慧濬

The nun Hui-chün (Deep Wisdom) (392–464) of Bamboo
Garden Convent

Hui-chün's secular surname was Ch'en. Her family was originally
from Shan-yin [some distance southeast of the capital of Sung and very
close to Kuei-chi].

When Hui-chün was still a child, she was quite intelligent, and her
zeal in the practice of religion surpassed the multitude. In the morning
she burned incense and engaged her mind in the act of worship, thus
passing the time until noon when she ate her one meal of vegetables,
eschewing the flesh of living creatures. Although she was living in her
parents' house, she behaved as though she had already left the household life. Because her mother and father could not break her resolve,
they permitted her to enter the religious life when she was eighteen
years old.

She could recite from memory any classic text, whether Buddhist or
non-Buddhist, after having read it once. There was no deep meditation or subtle contemplation she could not enter. Hui-chün was quiet
and nonquarrelsome, agreeable, and modest; in her associations with
friends and acquaintances she never engaged in banter or joking
[behavior indeed forbidden by the monastic rules].[114]

The chief minister of the Sung state, the Chiang-hsia prince, I-kung
(413–465) [the fifth son of Emperor Wu], especially respected her and
without fail supplied clothing and medicine for her throughout the
year.[115] Hui-chün did not keep these goods for herself but used them
to build up the convent; the completion of Bamboo Garden was her
achievement.

When she grew old, Hui-chün's joy in the flavor of meditation did
not pall. In the eighth year of the *ta-ming* reign period (464) of the
Sung dynasty she died at the age of seventy-three and was buried on
Tutor Mountain.

In the same convent lived the nun Seng-hua, who was extremely
intelligent and eminently accomplished, being able to chant many doctrinal scriptures and texts of monastic rules.[116] Her renown for maintaining strict vegetarianism and ascetic practices was equal to Hui-
chün's.

34. PAO-HSIEN
寶賢

The nun Pao-hsien (Precious Virtue) (401–477) of Universal
Wisdom Convent

Pao-hsien's secular surname was Ch'en, and her family was originally
from Ch'en Commandery [in the Huai River valley, some distance to
the northwest of the Sung capital].[117]

At age 16 Pao-hsien went into mourning for her mother who had
died. For three years she did not eat any cereals but sustained herself
instead on arrowroot and taro; neither did she wear decorated silks
nor use a bed or sitting mat during the mourning period.[118]

Leaving the household life at age 19, Pao-hsien took up residence in
Establishing Peace Convent. With pure conduct and vigorous applica-
tion she thoroughly mastered both meditation and the monastic
observance.

Emperor Wen of the Sung dynasty (407–424–453) treated her with
reverend courtesy, presenting her with gifts of clothing and food.[119]
Emperor Hsiao-wu (430–454–464) also treated her with great respect, giving her ten thousand in cash every month.[120] When Emperor
Ming (439–465–472) ascended the throne he gave her the honor of
receiving her, treating her with exceeding respect.[121] In the first year of
the *t'ai-shih* reign period (465), he named her by imperial appointment
to serve as the abbess of Universal Wisdom Convent. In the second
year (466), he issued another decree making her the rector of the
assembly in the capital.[122] In this capacity she was imposing and
majestic, making decisions with divine insight. She was good at discussing the principles of things and was able to set errors aright. She
was morally upright in character; nothing could deflect her from the
proper course.

Previously, during the *sheng-p'ing* reign period (357–361) of the
Eastern Chin dynasty, the nun Ching-chien (no. 1) was the first Chinese Buddhist nun. That first reception, by women, of the monastic
obligation, was from the Assembly of Monks only. Later the nuns
Hui-kuo (no. 14), Ching-yin and others of Luminous Blessings Convent consulted [the central Asian missionary monk] Gunavarman
about the situation.[123]

He said, "China did not have both the Assembly of Monks and the

Assembly of Nuns, so the women accepted the full monastic obligation from the Assembly of Monks only."

Later, the nun Hui-kuo and the other nuns met the foreign nun Tessara and her companions when they arrived in China.[124] In the eleventh year of the *yüan-chia* reign period (434) [of the Sung dynasty], the [Chinese nuns] once again received the full monastic obligation from the Indian missionary monk Sanghavarman on the ceremonial platform at Southern Grove Monastery, and this time both the Assembly of Monks and the Assembly of Nuns [comprising the women from Sri Lanka] were present.[125] [Thus the lineage and tradition of the monastic obligation for women from the time of the Buddha's stepmother had finally been properly transmitted to China.] [Gunavarman] had not said that the first transmission to China, from the Assembly of Monks only, was invalid. He had said, rather, that the second transmission [that included the Assembly of Nuns] was augmenting the good value of the obligation that had already been received.

[After this second transmission of the monastic rules, however] those who were fond of unorthodox practices handed them on widely and repeatedly, causing the orthodox norms gradually to disappear. In the second year of the *yüan-hui* reign period (474), an expert in the study of the monastic rules, the Master of Monastic Rules Fa-ying (416–482),[126] delivered a lecture on *The Sarvāstivāda Monastic Rules in Ten Recitations* at Prospering of Chin Monastery.[127] On the day of the lecture there were ten-some nuns who, after the lecture, wished to receive again the obligation to observe the monastic rules. Pao-hsien then sent someone from the office of rector of assembly to present her orders to the lecture hall. The envoy sounded the gavel and issued the order to all the nuns that they were not at that time to receive the obligations again. If on examination it was found that any nun was not of sufficient age, the instructors had first to bring together the Assembly of Nuns, and after public confession of this fact they were to report to the office of the assembly. If the office approved, it would request someone to investigate to see whether the nuns were suitable candidates, and only then could they receive the obligation a second time. Anyone who opposed this plan would be subject to expulsion. On account of Pao-hsien's decisive action in this matter, quarrels came to an end, and the rest of her tenure in the office of rector was without untoward incident.

With great skill Pao-hsien brought matters into conformity with the spirit of the monastic life; she pacified all elements in the assembly. Detached from worldly affairs and having few desires, she was increasingly esteemed by the world. She was seventy-seven when she died in the first year of the *sheng-ming* reign period (477).

35. FA-CHING

法淨

The nun Fa-ching (Pure Law) (409–473) of Universal
Wisdom Convent

Fa-ching originally came from north of the Yangtze River. When she was twenty, her family met with civil disorder, and she accompanied her father and fled to Mo-ling [which was in the vicinity of the capital of the Sung dynasty].

The family practiced the religion of Shākyamuni Buddha. Fa-ching left the household life while still very young and dwelled in Eternal Blessings Convent. Her observance of the monastic rules was unsullied; she understood the principles of things; she immersed her thought in subtleties and deeply probed profundities. Her reputation was comparable to Pao-hsien's (no. 34).

Emperor Ming of Sung (439–465–472) considered her above the ordinary, and, in the first year of the *t'ai-shih* reign period (465), he decreed by imperial order that she live in Universal Wisdom Convent.[128] Within the royal palace she was warmly received and respected as both teacher and friend. In the second year (466) she was made, by imperial decree, the director of conventual affairs in the capital.[129] In her work she was most impartial and just; her influence spread out in waves, and those converted by her virtue were like a torrent. Of all the women of the surrounding territory of Ching and Ch'u, both nuns and other women who could claim any association through family connections, there was none who did not send letters from afar, seeking her acquaintance.

The formative power of her moral excellence was always like this, and those who consulted her as a model for the observance of the monastic rules numbered seven hundred persons.

Fa-ching died in the first year of the *yüan-hui* reign period (473) at age 65.

36. HUI-YAO
慧耀

The nun Hui-yao (Glorious Wisdom) of Eternal Quietude
Convent in Shu Commandery [in the west, far upriver from the
capital]

Hui-yao's secular surname was Chou. Her family was originally from
Hsi-p'ing [in southwest China].

Hui-yao, who left the household life while still a child, always
vowed to burn her body as a worship offering to the Three Treasures.[130] At the end of the *t'ai-shih* reign period (465–471), she spoke
about her intention to the governor, Liu Liang (d. 472), who at first
gave permission.[131] Hui-yao asked to be able to carry out her self-
immolation on the top of the tile pagoda that belonged to Madame
Wang, a concubine of a certain Chao Ch'u-ssu. Madame Wang gave
her approval, and on the full-moon night of the fifteenth day of the
first month [the day of the Lantern Festival], Hui-yao, carrying cloth
and oil, led her disciples to the pagoda.[132] They had not finished the
preparations, however, when Liu Liang sent a letter addressed to the
nuns saying, "If Hui-yao succeeds in her intention to burn herself up
as an offering, then Eternal Quietude Convent will incur a grave
offence." Hui-yao had no choice but to stop her preparations.

Madame Wang, very angry, said, "That nun, wanting fame and
profit, deceitfully indulged in unusual behavior, bribing her cronies to
do a thing like this. If that were not the case, how could someone in
the city, at midnight no less, know anything about it?"

Hui-yao [responded to the charge], "Madame, do not engage in
such confused thought. Abandoning my body is my concern. How
could others know?" Thereupon she returned to the convent, where
she gave up eating cereals, consuming instead fragrant oils [as
described in the chapter on the Medicine King bodhisattva in the
Flower of the Law], until the first year of the *sheng-ming* reign period
(477), when she offered her body by fire at the convent. Even when
the flames had reached as high as her face, she continued to chant
scriptures without ceasing.

She said to all the nuns, "Gather up the bones I leave. There should
be exactly two pints." After the fire had gone out, the result was as she
had said it would be.

A month and some days before her self-immolation, there appeared in the region a foreign monk, about twenty years old, who, although of most proper appearance, had extremely fine, soft, black hair growing on his shoulders to the length of six or seven inches. When people asked about the strange phenomenon, he answered, through an interpreter, "Because I have never covered my shoulders hair has grown there."

He said to Hui-yao, "I live in Varanasi [that is, central India] but have been here quite a few days. I heard that you intend to abandon your body. Therefore I want to give you a silver jug." Hui-yao received it with the utmost respect, but, before she could find out more about him, the foreign monk departed in a great hurry. She sent people to follow and bring him back, but he had already gone out the city gate and disappeared. The silver jug was used to hold the *sharīra* [the pearl-like relics of sanctity], recovered from Hui-yao's bones. The relics came to not quite a fifth of a pint.[133]

3. The Ch'i Dynasty
(479–502)

37. FA-YÜAN
法緣

The nun Fa-yüan (Affinity with the Law) (424/426–479/482) of
Tseng-ch'eng in Tung-kuan [in south China]

Fa-yüan's secular surname was Lun. She was from Tseng-ch'eng [in
Tung-kuan in south China].[1]

In the ninth year of the *yüan-chia* reign period (432) of the Sung
dynasty, Fa-yüan was ten years old, and her sister Fa-ts'ai was nine. At
that time they knew nothing of the teachings or scriptures of Buddhism. In that year, the eighth day of the second month [the day com-
memorating the Buddha's final nirvana], both sisters disappeared.
Three days later they reappeared saying that they had reached the
heavenly palace of the Pure Land and had seen the Buddha, who had
converted them.

On the fifteenth day of the ninth month [the full-moon day], they
disappeared again for ten days before returning.[2] After that sojourn
they were able to speak and write a foreign language as well as chant
Buddhist scriptures. When they chanced to see anyone from the foreign lands to the west of China, they bantered with them, communi-
cating with them fluently.

In the tenth year (433), on the fifteenth day of the first month [the
day of the Lantern Festival], they vanished once again.[3] People working in the fields saw the two girls blown whirling by a wind up to the
sky. Their parents, worried and afraid, petitioned the spirits with sacrifice for the happy fortune of the sisters' return, but it was a month
before they came back.

When the two sisters returned, they had already embraced the monastic life, signified by their wearing monastic robes and carrying their cut-off hair. They reported that they had seen the Buddha and also a nun who had said, "Because of affinities established between us in a previous life, you should become my disciples." She rubbed their heads with her hands, and their hair fell out of its own accord. The nun bestowed religious names on them, calling the elder sister Fa-yüan and the younger Fa-ts'ai. On the point of sending them back, the nun said, "You should build a monastic dwelling, and I shall give you scriptures."

When Fa-yüan and her sister returned home, they demolished the altar to the spirits and in its place built a monastic dwelling where they discussed and chanted scriptures day and night. Every evening multicolored lights, as though from lanterns or candles, played over the mountain peaks. From this time forward the sisters' demeanor was elegant and their speech correct and clear. The chanting in the capital itself could not surpass theirs.

The provincial governors Wei Lang and K'ung Mo both humbly made offerings, and, when they heard the two sisters' speech, they even more deeply honored the nuns' unusual quality. Because of this all the people in the region served the True Law of the Buddha.

Fa-yüan died at the age of fifty-six in the *chien-yüan* reign period (479–482).

38. T'AN-CH'E

曇徹

The nun T'an-ch'e (Discerning the Dharma) (422–484) of
Southern Eternal Peace Convent

T'an-ch'e's origins are unknown. When still a child she became a disciple of the nun P'u-yao and lived together with her in Southern Eternal Peace Convent. P'u-yao, whose practice of religion was pure and learning excellent, was well known to her contemporaries.

T'an-ch'e maintained her principles without pride and practiced her vocation without neglect. She determined to grasp fully the profound meaning of the Buddhist teaching, and, before she became a full-fledged nun, she had become learned in the scriptures and their commentaries. After accepting the complete obligation of the monastic life she became thoroughly versed in the precepts of the monastic texts.

T'an-ch'e had the talent to handle important affairs, and she was particularly capable in exposition. She distinguished fine points and resolved impasses, probing deeply into the abstruse and hidden. All the other nuns, irrespective of rank, requested to be her subordinates. Taking advantage of the opportunity, a multitude of students flocked to her. From women of noble rank on down there was no one who did not revere her.

In the second year of the *yung-ming* reign period (484) of the Ch'i dynasty T'an-ch'e died at the age of sixty-three.

39. SENG-CHING

僧敬

The nun Seng-ching (Respect in the Sangha) (402–486) of
Exalted Sanctity Convent

Seng-ching's secular surname was Li. Her family was originally from Kuei-chi [some distance to the southeast of the capital].[4] They resided, however [in the immediate vicinity of the capital] at Mo-ling.

When Seng-ching was still in her mother's womb, the family arranged a meeting, requesting the monk Seng-chao from Pottery Office Monastery and the nun T'an-chih from Western Convent each to point at the mother's belly and address the unborn baby as a disciple. The mother, on behalf of her unborn child, addressed the two monastics as teacher, thereby agreeing that the child, whether boy or girl, would be committed to the religious life.

On the day when she was about the give birth, the mother dreamed of a supernatural being who said to her, "You may sponsor a ceremony of taking the eight precepts of the householder."[5] She forthwith gave orders to begin the preparations, but, before the monks and the statues had been gathered together, Seng-ching was born. A voice out of nowhere said, "You may give her as a disciple to the nun Pai of Establishing Peace Convent." The mother complied.

Seng-ching, by the age of five or six, was able to repeat from memory scriptures that she had heard others chant. She read several hundred scrolls of scripture, and her marvellous understanding of them increased daily. Practicing sacrificial vegetarianism her pure manner became more and more manifest.

In the *yüan-chia* reign period (424–453) [of the Sung dynasty], when K'ung Mo went out as an officer to keep order in Kuang Province [in south China], he took Seng-ching along in his retinue. Seng-ching happened to meet the foreign nun Tessara and the others who were on their way to the Sung capital. They were all of highly exceptional conduct and appearance, and [Seng-ching, in order to accord fully with the monastic regulations and tradition that required that she receive the monastic obligation from both the Assembly of Monks and Assembly of Nuns] went through a second ceremony [of receiving the complete monastic obligation, accepting the rules from the foreign nuns as well as from the monks].

Seng-ching, deeply awakened to the truth of impermanence, wanted to embark on a pilgrimage across the ocean to seek out the holy traces of the Buddha's life on earth. The monastics and householders prevented her, however, and she remained in the Ling-nan region in south China for more than thirty years.[6] Her manner gradually changed the hearts of the barbarian peoples of the south among whom she lived. A total of thirteen families donated land and went together to build a convent for her at Ch'ao-t'ing, calling it Built by the Multitude.[7]

Emperor Ming (439–465–472) of the Sung dynasty heard about Seng-ching and issued an invitation all that distance to her, to welcome her to his presence.[8] The monastics and householders of P'an-yü [the region in south China where she lived] grieved at the thought of losing her.

When Seng-ching returned to the capital, she lived by imperial decree in Exalted Sanctity Convent, where monastics and householders alike submitted to her instruction. A certain Yüeh Tsun of Tan-yang donated land and built a convent for her to which she later moved.[9]

The Ch'i heir apparent, Wen-hui (458–493) [who was the first son of Emperor Wu], and the prince of Ching-ling, Wen-hsüan (460–494) [who was the second son of Emperor Wu], both admiring her virtuous practice, personally made donations without fail.[10]

Seng-ching died on the third day of the second month of the fourth year of the *yung-ming* reign period (486) at the age of eighty-four and was buried on the south side of Bell Mountain.[11] Her disciples erected a memorial stone for which the vice president of the department of the imperial grand secretariat, Shen Yüeh of Wu-hsing County,[12] wrote the inscription.[13]

40. SENG-MENG
僧猛

The nun Seng-meng (Courageous in the Sangha) (418–489) of
Brightness of Ch'i Convent of Yen-kuan County

Seng-meng's secular surname was Ts'en. Her family was originally
from Nan-yang [near the old northern capital of Lo-yang],[14] but they
had removed to Yen-kuan County [on the seacoast some distance
southeast of the Ch'i dynastic capital of Chien-k'ang] and, by the time
Seng-meng was born, had lived there for five generations.[15] Her great-
grandfather Ts'en Shuai, in the Eastern Chin dynasty (317–420), was
the secretary to the head of the subprefectural personnel and magistrate of Yü-hang [which lay to the west of Yen-kuan].[16]

For generations the family had followed the Taoist religion of the
Yellow Emperor and Lao-tzu and had also believed in and worshipped
demonic spirits. Nevertheless, Seng-meng, even as a child, resolutely
determined to uproot these vulgar practices.

When she was twelve, her father died. Weeping bitterly until she
vomited blood, she died and then revived.[17] After the three-year
mourning period was completed, she demonstrated her unquenchable
spirit by taking leave of her mother and going forth into the homeless
life.[18]

Seng-meng's conduct was already pure, and she respectfully served
her teacher. Her food of plain vegetables and coarse rice was sufficient
just to preserve life and limb. In practicing the ritual of confession she
was never weary nor remiss, and, when she was repenting her former
sins, her tears flowed in utmost sincerity. She was able to do what others could not do.

When the governor of I Province, Chang Tai (413–483) of Wu
Commandery, heard of her good reputation, he highly honored her
and requested her to become his family teacher.[19]

In the first year of the *yüan-hui* reign period (473) of the Sung
dynasty the nun Ching-tu entered the region of Wu and took Seng-
meng to the capital city of Chien-k'ang to live in Establishing Blessings
Convent. Seng-meng read through many scriptures day and night;
when she followed lectures her mind was never weary; she learned
much and remembered well, always able to recall whatever she had
heard. Thus she studied and comprehended all the scriptures and

books of monastic discipline, and with pure desires she sat quietly in meditation, immeasurably tranquil.

In the fourth year of the *chien-yüan* reign period (482) of the Ch'i dynasty when her mother became ill, Seng-meng returned east to her home in Yen-kuan County and made the house there into a convent that she called Brightness of Ch'i. She built shrine rooms and halls and planted rows of bamboo. Tranquil both within and without, it looked like the dwelling place of the immortals.[20] She gave her food to the hungry and her clothes to those suffering from the cold.

Once a hunter approached the convent from the south. The flying birds and running beasts rushed to Seng-meng for refuge with the pursuing falcons and dogs very close behind.[21] Seng-meng blocked them with her body and arms, and, although she was pecked and bitten, the creatures who had fled to her escaped from harm.

Several dozen persons lived together with her for more than thirty years without once seeing her angry. She was seventy-two years old when she died in the seventh year of the *yung-ming* reign period (489) of the Ch'i dynasty.

At that time there was also the nun Seng-yüan who was the daughter of Seng-meng's cousin on her father's side. Seng-yüan was also known for her filial behavior. Her conduct was exalted and her wisdom deep.

41. MIAO-CHIH
妙智

The nun Miao-chih (Marvellous Sagacity) (432–495) of Flower
Garland Convent

Miao-chih's secular surname was Ts'ao, and her family was originally from Ho-nei [north of the Yellow River and the old northern capital of Lo-yang].

Of gentle and intelligent disposition, she formed her mind in accordance with the Great Conversion of Buddhism.[22] She kept the monastic rules as carefully as though she were guarding bright pearls. Untiring in patience, she displayed no irritability with regard to worldly matters. Although faced with vexations, she never had other than a pleasant countenance. Withdrawn from the world for a lifetime of study, she was nevertheless happy the whole day. She thoroughly penetrated the Buddhist teaching about the characteristics of existence, and the world honored her.[23]

When the meditation hall was first built, Emperor Wu (440–483–493)[24] of the Ch'i dynasty by imperial order requested Miao-chih to lecture on the *Shrīmālā*[25] and the *Vimalakīrti*.[26] As she began and carried out the lectures, several times the emperor personally attended, asking questions without limit. Miao-chih made connections and distinctions, from the first neither losing a point nor being stumped. The emperor praised her again and again, and the four groups [monks, nuns, laymen, and laywomen] very respectfully acknowledged her learning.

Wen-hsüan (460–494), the Ch'i prince of Ching-ling [and second son of Emperor Wu], marked off some land on Bell Mountain as a cemetery in which to bury those of renowned virtue.[27]

Miao-chih died at the age of sixty-four in the second year of the *chien-wu* reign period (495) and was buried on the south side of Grove of Concentration Monastery on Bell Mountain. Madame Chiang, wife of Palace Attendant Wang Lun (d. 494–498) of Lang-yeh, composed the eulogy that was inscribed on the stone tablet set up on the left side of the grave mound.[28]

42. CHIH-SHENG

智勝

The nun Chih-sheng (Victorious Sagacity) (427–492) of
Establishing Blessings Convent

Chih-sheng's secular surname was Hsü. Her family was originally from [the northern city of] Ch'ang-an, but had lived [in the south] in Kuei-chi, for three generations.

When she was six, Chih-sheng went along with her grandmother to the capital to visit Pottery Office Monastery. When she saw the magnificence of the monastery, the precious decorations, and adornment, she wept copiously and begged leave from her grandmother to cut off her hair and cast aside secular garments to become a nun. Her grandmother questioned her in detail, and Chih-sheng fully explained her intention, but her grandmother said she was too young and did not permit it.

During the Sung dynasty many hardships caused people in all

classes of society to lose their livelihood.[29] The times were very confused, and the years went by, so that Chih-sheng was close to twenty before she was able to leave the secular life and take up residence in Establishing Blessings Convent.

Walking alone without peer, her practice of the Buddhist monastic life was inimitable. She listened to a recitation of the *Great Final Nirvāna Scripture,* and, hearing it once, was able to hold it in mind.[30] Later, when she was studying the books of monastic discipline, she mastered them thoroughly without having to be taught twice. The fame of her memory in all respects increased. She herself wrote several tens of scrolls of commentaries in which the phrasing was concise and the meaning far-reaching; her interpretations were recondite and her reasoning subtle.[31]

Encountering filth she was not soiled; meeting with adversities she was not worn down. In the *ta-ming* reign period (457–464) there was a fellow who used deceit to meet with her, to try to embrace her in a lascivious way, hoping she would not keep to her rules. But Chih-sheng with deep-seated purpose upheld her purity and stood firm as a wall. With grave countenance she reported everything to the Assembly of Nuns, who recorded what had happened and reported it to the civil authorities. Chih-sheng maintained the pure precepts of the monastic life as though she were guarding bright pearls.

At one time the monks Seng-tsung (438–496) and Hsüan-ch'ü, disciples of the master of the law T'an-pin of Splendidly Adorned Monastery, together were on duty in the Buddha Hall, but, because they were careless in storing things, they invited a theft in which the bodhisattva necklace and the seven-jeweled water bowl were stolen.[32] T'an-pin's own room, except for his robe and begging bowl, was as bare as a hanging gong, and therefore he had nothing with which to replace what had been taken. Distressed and sad, he suspended his lectures and remained in his own quarters for three days. When Chih-sheng made this known to the four groups of monks, nuns, laymen, and laywomen, everything was provided within ten days. The response to her virtue and influence was always like this.

The Ch'i heir apparent, Wen-hui (458–493) [the eldest son of Emperor Wu], hearing of her reputation, often summoned her to his presence.[33] Whenever she was invited to the imperial palace to give lectures on the various Buddhist scriptures, the minister of education, the prince of Ching-ling, Wen-hsüan (460–494) [the second son of Emperor Wu,] respected her even more.[34]

Chih-sheng's sense of purpose was as durable as southern gold, and her heart as pristine as northern snow. Because she was indeed highly respected for the discerning moral advice she gave her Assembly of Nuns, the empress dowager ordered that she serve as abbess of the convent. The whole community loved and respected her as though they were serving their elders.

Chih-sheng made the vows of one aspiring to be a bodhisattva[35] from Master of the Law Seng-yüan (ca. 430–ca. 490) of [Upper] Grove of Concentration Monastery on Bell Mountain.[36] A censer was always placed beside the seat, and Chih-sheng picked up some incense to put in it, but Seng-yüan tried to stop her, saying, "The censer has not been lit for the past three days." But when clouds of smoke arose from the incense that she had dropped into the censer, everyone marveled at her awesome devotion that brought forth such a response.[37]

During the *yung-ming* reign period (483–493), while she was holding a vegetarian religious feast in honor of the Holy Monk [Pindola], she concentrated her mind in earnest supplication.[38] When she unexpectedly heard fingers snapping in the air, she brought her palms together in a gesture of reverence and bowed her head to listen.

Because Chih-sheng lived in the convent for thirty years without attending the vegetarian meals given outside the convent and without roaming about visiting either nobles or commoners, and because she dwelt in quiet seclusion and remained in contemplation, the fragrance of her reputation was not widespread.

The heir apparent, Wen-hui, especially made offerings to her, and as time went by they were so abundant that she built more buildings and that the entire convent was splendidly beautiful.

Chih-sheng sacrificed her own religious robes and begging bowl, selling them to raise money to make stone images at Sheh Mountain Monastery for the sake of seven emperors of the Sung and Ch'i dynasties.

In the tenth year of the *yung-ming* reign period (492), when she was confined to bed with an illness, she unexpectedly saw golden chariots with jade canopies all coming to welcome her. On the fifth day of the fourth month she told all her disciples, "I am now going to leave." The disciples wept. She then pulled aside her robe to expose her chest on which there appeared, written in the highly cursive style, the character *Fo* (Buddha), clear and white in form and color.[39] At noon on the eighth day [the day of the Buddha's birthday], she died at the age of sixty-six. She was buried on Bell Mountain. The heir apparent, Wen-hui, had supplied her medicines, and imperial officials provided everything needed for the funeral.

43. SENG-KAI

僧蓋

The nun Seng-kai (Canopy of the Sangha) (430–493) of
Foundation for Meditation Convent

Seng-kai's secular surname was T'ien, and her family was originally from Chün-jen in the Chao region [north of the Yellow River]. Her father, T'ien Hung-liang, was administrator of T'ien-shui in [northwest China].

Seng-kai was still a child when she left secular life to become a disciple of the nun Seng-chih in Flower Grove Convent [of the northeastern city] of P'eng-ch'eng, where she forgot about gaining personal advantage and ignored slander or praise.

In the first year of the *yüan-hui* reign period (473), when the northern barbarians invaded the province, she, together with her fellow student Fa-chin, went south to the capital [Chien-k'ang], and took up residence in Wonderful Appearance Convent.[40] Seng-kai listened extensively to the scriptures and to the texts of monastic discipline, inquiring deeply into their meanings. She especially cultivated the practice of meditation and [as the *Classic of History* says], "A single day was not enough."[41] In cold weather or hot she did not change the amount of clothing she wore, and throughout the four seasons she did not vary her food or drink but sustained herself with only one dish of vegetables at the noon meal.

[Seng-kai received] instruction from the two masters of meditation Fa-yin and Seng-shen (416–490), both of whom marveled at her easy awakening.[42] During the *yung-ming* reign period (483–493) of the Ch'i dynasty she moved to Foundation for Meditation Convent, where she wanted to propagate the way of contemplation, but monastics and laity alike came to consult her, greatly increasing the hubbub. Thereupon, on the left side of the convent she built a separate meditation

the tenth year of the *yung-ming* reign period (492), she died at the age of seventy-two.

At that time in the convent were the nuns Seng-yao and Kuang-ching, who were also known for their study and practice of Buddhism.

46. T'AN-CHIEN
曇簡

The nun T'an-chien (Simplicity of the Dharma) of Voice of the Teaching Convent

T'an-chien's secular surname was Chang, and her family originally was from Ch'ing-ho [in northern China].[50] She was a disciple of the nun Fa-ching.[51] She traveled throughout the valley of the Huai River [north of the Yangtze River], to study with various teachers, so that she might widely proclaim the True Law of the Buddha.[52] Putting others first and herself last, her ambition was to help all living beings.

In the fourth year of the *chien-yüan* reign period (482) of Ch'i, she built Voice of the Teaching Convent, where she practiced the quiet of meditation and achieved [the highest concentrative state known as] *samādhi*. She was widely known for her virtue, and her meritorious influence spread daily. Both religious and laity respected her and made plentiful offerings.

At that time there was a master of the law Hui-ming who deeply appreciated silence and quietude.[53] Originally he lived in Grove of the Way Monastery, which had been refurbished and adorned by the heir apparent, Wen-hui (458–493) [eldest son of the emperor], and the prince of Ching-ling, Wen-hsüan (460–494) [second son of the emperor], during the *yung-ming* reign period (483–493) of Ch'i.[54] Many of the monks there were students of doctrine and were constantly debating topics in the scriptures and explanatory treatises. Because of the hustle and bustle of all the coming and going, Hui-ming wanted to get away. T'an-chien made a gift to him of her convent, and she herself moved to White Mountain, where she built a grass shelter to protect her from wind and rain.[55] At the appropriate times she went out begging and was sustained by the alms she received.

She often gathered firewood, saying that she was going to carry out a meritorious act, and [on the day celebrating the Buddha's final nirvana], the eighth night of the second month in the first year of the *chien-wu* reign period (494), she mounted this pile of firewood and kindled a fire, immolating herself, thereby abandoning her body of birth and death as an offering to the Three Treasures.[56] When the people in the neighboring village saw the fire, they raced to rescue her, but, when they arrived, T'an-chien had already died. Religious and laity alike lamented, their cries reverberating through the mountains and valleys. They then built a tomb to bury her remains, which they had gathered up.

47. CHING-KUEI
淨珪

The nun Ching-kuei (Pure Symbol) (d. 494) of Voice of the Teaching Convent

Ching-kuei's secular surname was Chou. Her family was originally from Chin-ling [to the southeast of the capital, Chien-k'ang], but they had lived in the Chien-k'ang district for three generations by the time she was born.[57]

As a child Ching-kuei was very intelligent and often needed to hear something only once to understand it. By natural inclination she did not associate with worldly people and very early on wished to leave the household life. Her parents, sympathizing with her, did not oppose her resolve, and she took up residence in Voice of the Teaching Convent as a disciple of the nun Fa-ching.

She was pure in conduct, broadly versed in both the scriptures and the monastic rules, and well accomplished in all the meditative secrets of the three types of Buddhist paths.[58] In short, Ching-kuei's spiritual capacity was so vast that no one could fathom it; on the other hand she neglected her body and forgot the taste of food to the point that she was always emaciated. Her vigor and memory were models for the world, and her teaching and guidance greatly benefited everyone of that time who turned to her.

Ching-kuei lived together with the nun T'an-chien in Voice of the Teaching Convent, and she [too] eventually moved to White Mountain, where she dwelt beneath the trees, her meritorious influence spreading far.

In the first year of the *chien-wu* reign period (494), on the night of the eighth day of the second month [traditionally thought to be the day of the Buddha's complete and final entry into nirvana], Ching-kuei burned her body at the same time as the nun T'an-chien (no. 46). Religious and laity, all grieving and weeping, collected her relics and buried them in a tomb.

48. HUI-HSÜ

慧緒

The nun Hui-hsü (Wisdom's Thread) (431–499) of Collected
Goodness Convent

Hui-hsü's secular surname was Chou. Her family was originally from the city of Kao-p'ing in the Lü-ch'iu district [quite far north of the Ch'i capital].⁵⁹

High-minded and distant in character, in physical appearance she looked like a man rather than a woman. Her statements and opinions were extremely straightforward without the slightest circumlocution.

By the time she was seven years old, Hui-hsü ate vegetarian food, observed the fasts, and was resolute in her determination to maintain her chastity. At the age of eighteen she left the secular household life to take up residence in Three-Story Convent of Ching Province [along the Yangtze River, an important center of Buddhism, far to the west of the capital].⁶⁰ Religious and laity alike admired her complete practice of the monastic rules.

At that time in Chiang-ling [the provincial capital of Ching Province], there was an eremitic nun who had a reputation for virtue in those western regions.⁶¹ When she saw Hui-hsü, she regarded her as extraordinary, and therefore, forgetting any difference in age, they together followed the Way of Buddhism. Once they lived together for a summer to practice [the meditation of visualizing the Buddha in one's presence], during which time they carried out austerities of mind and body both day and night without rest.⁶²

When Shen Yu-chih (d. 478) was governor of the province he sifted and weeded the monastic communities, at which time Hui-hsü, to avoid the difficulty, fled to the capital.⁶³ She returned to the west only after the defeat of Shen [during the struggles between the Sung and the eventually victorious Ch'i]. The Ch'i grand general of the army and grand marshal, the prince of Yü-chang, Hsiao I (444–492) [second son of Emperor Kao, first emperor of Ch'i], at the end of the *sheng-*

ming reign period (477–479) of the Sung dynasty,[64] went out as a commander of the garrison for the provinces of Ching and Shan.[65] Knowing of her religious practice, he requested her presence at his residence where he provided her with the four essentials of a monastic.[66]

At that time the master of meditation Hsüan-ch'ang came to Ching from the [far western] province of Shu.[67] He taught methods of meditation to Hui-hsü, who investigated to the utmost their subtle mysteries, causing Hsüan-ch'ang often to praise her depth of mind inherited from experience gained in previous lives. Hui-hsü thus became proficient in meditation as well as continued to maintain her vegetarianism and strict observance of the moral precepts.

The wife of the prince of Yü-chang and other ladies of the royal family were greatly devoted to her and from her received instruction in meditation. Whenever she received donations, she dispersed them to others, never having any intention of keeping them for herself. Hui-hsü, far above such matters, had no concern for her material livelihood.

The prince requested her to return with him to the capital, where, east of the eastern fields of his family's estate, he built for her Field of Blessings Convent. She was frequently invited to the prince's residence to carry out various religious practices.

In the ninth year of the *yung-ming* reign period (491), Hui-hsü announced that she had suddenly taken very ill, but it was not a genuine disease; it was only that she was no longer willing to eat. When she had become quite haggard and emaciated, she earnestly begged to be able to return to her convent, and as soon as she returned she immediately improved. Ten days later, however, she was again summoned to the prince's residence, and, having once arrived, her illness reappeared as before. No one knew the reason why, but suddenly the prince died (492), and one calamity after another befell his family. Because the eastern estate was in a distant suburb, Emperor Wu (440–483–493) [the prince's elder brother and second emperor of Ch'i], built Collected Goodness Convent and moved all the nuns to this new convent while using Field of Blessings Convent to house the foreign monk Ārya.[68] The monk, who received support from the royal family, was good at chanting Buddhist magical spells.[69]

After Hui-hsü herself had moved to Collected Goodness Convent, she did not again set foot in the palace for several years. During that time everyone, both within and without the palace, greatly respected the nun and often urged her to return for short visits to the women's apartments of the palace. Lady Chu wished to hold a religious vegetarian feast and sent a message to invite Hui-hsü to consult with her ahead of time about the affair.

The nun said, "This is very good. Because I am now old, I truly want at this time to visit the palace once more to bid farewell to all the ladies." Thus she attended the vegetarian feast and, when it was over, she asked for paper and brush and wrote a poem:

> *Worldly people who know me not*
> *Call me by my worldly name of Old Chou.*
> *You invite me to a week-long feast of food,*
> *but the feast of meditation has no end.*

(I, Pao-ch'ang, the compiler, note here that there were ten more words in this poem of farewell, but they have been lost.) After she finished the poem, she talked and laughed with the people there and comported herself in no way different from her usual dignity.

She then took her leave, saying, "This time when I go out to the convent, it will be farewell forever. Because I am old, I shall not again be able to enter the palace." She was healthy at that time, but a little over a month after she had gone back to the convent she said she was sick, and, even though she seemed no different from before, she died a few days later on the twentieth day of the eleventh month of the first year of the *yung-yüan* reign period (499). She was sixty-nine years old. The scholar Chou Sheh (469–524) wrote a statement in praise of her.[70]

The nun Te-sheng was a companion in the Way [of Buddhism], the same in virtue and will, and received Hui-hsü's instruction in religious practice and contemplation.

49. Ch'ao-ming

超明

The nun Ch'ao-ming (Superior Clarity) (ca. 438–498) of
Brightness of Ch'i Convent in Ch'ien-t'ang

Ch'ao-ming's secular surname was Fan. Her family was from Ch'ien-t'ang [southeast of the capital], and her father, Fan Hsien, as a young man had been a student at the imperial academy.[71] The family had been Buddhist for a long time.

When a young girl, Ch'ao-ming had been very intelligent and had exalted ambitions. She studied the five Confucian classics and was well versed in literature.[72] Her polite and proper deportment drew the respect of everyone both within and without her family.

When she was twenty-one, her husband died, leaving her a widow. A neighbor sought to marry her, but she vowed not to allow it. Therefore she left the secular life and took up residence in Venerating Seclusion Convent. Of brilliant intellect, she well apprehended the body of [Buddhist] knowledge, and, when she heard that Master of the Law T'an-cheng of North Chang Monastery in Wu County [northeast of Ch'ien-t'ang], was vigorously ascetic in his practice, she received from him the full obligation to observe the monastic rules. Afterward she went to Mud Mountain [a short distance southeast of Ch'ien-t'ang][73] to receive instruction from the well-known master of the law Hui-chi (412–496).[74] When he lectured on the various scriptures she comprehended the meaning, and whatever she heard once she always remembered. Everyone in the surrounding region, whether religious or lay, held her in great esteem.

Ch'ao-ming subsequently returned to Ch'ien-t'ang to Brightness of Ch'i Convent where she died in the fifth year of the *chien-wu* reign period (498) at the age of sixty-some years.

There was also at that time the nun Fa-tsang, who was [like Ch'ao-ming] well known for her learning and practice.

50. T'AN-YUNG

曇勇

The nun T'an-yung (Courageous in the Dharma) (d. 501) of
Voice of the Teaching Convent

T'an-yung was the elder sister of the nun T'an-chien (no. 46). By nature she was firm in her principles, unswayed by any outside circumstance. Always considering the practice of meditation and the strict observance of the monastic rules as her duty, she never thought of food and clothing as matters for her concern. She lived in Voice of the Teaching Convent, where she deeply comprehended the Buddhist teaching of impermanence and highly venerated the joy of cessation in nirvana.

In the first year of the *chien-wu* reign period (494), she moved to White Mountain together with T'an-chien, and, on the night of the fifteenth day of the second month of the third year of the *yung-yüan* reign period (501), she piled up firewood and burned up her body as an offering to the Buddha.[75] Those who saw and heard her at that time all aspired to attain Buddhist enlightenment, and together they built a tomb to bury her remains that they had gathered up.

51. Teh-leh
德樂

The nun Teh-leh (Joy in Virtue) (421–501) of Brightness of Ch'i Convent

Teh-leh's secular surname was Sun. Her family was from P'i-ling [to the southeast of the capital].[76] Her great-great-grandfather, Sun Yü,[77] during the Chin dynasty, was the governor of Yü Province [which lay west of the capital on the north bank of the Yangtze River].[78]

Teh-leh was born with two teeth in her mouth and, as she grew up, was often able to see clearly in a dark room without using either lamp or candle. She wished to leave the secular life, and her parents, who loved and cherished her, did nothing to stand in her way. When she reached the age of eight they gave permission for Teh-leh and her sister to enter the religious life together and become the disciples of the nun Kuang of Chin-ling.[79]

After they had received the obligation to observe all the precepts of the monastic life, they both went to the capital [to pursue their study of Buddhism] and lived in Southern Eternal Peace Convent. Teh-leh, of steadfast determination, diligently labored at her studies day and night, thoroughly investigating both the scriptures and monastic rules, conversing about them in an elegant and refined way that gained the approval of Emperor Wen (407–424–453) of the Sung dynasty.[80]

In the seventh year of the *yüan-chia* reign period (430), the foreign monk Gunavarman arrived in the capital.[81] The grand general of the Sung [I-k'ang, prince of P'eng-ch'eng] (409–451),[82] built Kingdom Convent (I, Pao-ch'ang, the compiler, note that it was located north of

Hedge Garden Monastery) and invited Teh-leh and other nuns to live there.[83] In the eleventh year (434), more than ten nuns from Sri Lanka arrived and thus the Chinese nuns were able to receive from the foreign monk Sanghavarman the obligation to keep all the monastic precepts [in the proper form].[84]

In the twenty-first year (444), the nuns Fa-ching and T'an-lan of that same convent,[85] because of their involvement in K'ung Hsi-hsien's (d. 445) plots and intrigue against the government, brought about great harm to the Way [of Buddhism] and the destruction of their own convent, forcing all the nuns there to disperse.[86] Teh-leh moved to Eastern Green Garden Convent, where she delved deeply into the practice of meditation, thoroughly investigating that marvellous realm.

After Emperor Wen died (453), she left the capital and traveled east toward Kuei-chi and took up residence in Reflecting Brightness Convent on White Mountain in the Yen region [to the southeast of Kuei-chi].[87] She taught easily and without fuss the students who gathered around her like clouds, causing [the Buddhist] religion to flourish in the southeast.

In the fifth year of the *yung-ming* reign period (487) of Ch'i, the devout [Buddhist] layman Yüan Chien, originally from Ch'en-liu [west of the capital],[88] donated his own residence to set up Brightness of Ch'i Convent.[89] The nuns, young and old alike, happily submitted to Teh-leh's leadership while those near and far, admiring her character, all wished to rely on her as their teacher, with the result that her disciples numbered over two hundred persons. She did not keep the donations made to her but rather, making no distinctions, distributed them equally to both monks and nuns who came to participate in the great gathering for lectures and preaching that she convened every year.

Teh-leh died in the third year of the *yung-yüan* reign period (501) at the age of eighty-one.

In the region of Yen there was also the nun Seng-mao, whose secular surname was Wang and whose family was originally from P'eng-ch'eng [in northeast China]. She kept a strict vegetarian diet and vigorously cultivated asceticism. Whatever was given to her she bequeathed to Bamboo Garden Convent.

4. The Liang Dynasty

(502–557)

52. Ching-hsiu

淨秀

The nun Ching-hsiu (Pure Refinement) (418–506) of Meditation
Grove Convent

Ching-hsiu's secular surname was Liang,[1] and her family was originally from Wu-shih in An-ting [northwest of the old northern capital
of Ch'ang-an].[2] Her grandfather, Liang Ch'ou, was a military commander of the title marshal in charge of subjugating barbarians; her
father, Liang Ts'an-chih, was the marquis of Tu-hsiang in Lung-
ch'uan County [in the far south of the country].[3]

Ching-hsiu, when still very young, besides being intelligent, liked
performing compassionate deeds. At the age of seven she took up the
observance of the Buddhist vegetarian regulations on her own. The
family had requested monks to come to recite the *Nirvāṇa Scripture,*
and, when Ching-hsiu heard the section that talks about giving up fish
and flesh, she thereupon became a vegetarian, but she did not dare to
let her parents know.[4] If she was served any flesh food, she would
secretly throw it away. After receiving the obligation for the five fundamental precepts of Buddhism from the foreign monk P'u-lien, she
kept them scrupulously without once transgressing.[5] Day and night
she ceaselessly offered worship and recited and chanted the scriptures.
When she was twelve, she sought to leave the secular life, but her parents forbade it. After she had learned to write, she often copied out
scriptures. Whatever valuables she had she used entirely for meritorious deeds, neither enjoying secular pleasures nor wearing silks and
brocades nor applying any cosmetics. In this way she lived until she
was twenty-nine years old, at which time she finally received permission to become a nun.[6]

Ching-hsiu became a disciple of the nun Yeh-shou (no. 30) of Green Garden Convent, whom she served in absolute sincerity, all the while fearing that she was not coming up to the mark. Day and night, without remiss, she cultivated the threefold Buddhist work [of morality, meditation, and wisdom]. In every communal effort she took the lead, laboring without stint and taking on the most difficult matters. Benevolent deities were always nearby respectfully protecting her. At that time a certain Mr. Ma, whom the world considered divinely sagacious, saw Ching-hsiu and predicted, "This nun will be born in the Tushita Heaven."

One night three nuns were sitting in meditation in the Buddha Hall when they suddenly heard a voice in the air like the bellowing of a bull, which frightened two of them. Ching-hsiu alone retained her composure and went to her room to fetch a candle. After her return to the hall, as soon as she began to go up the steps they again heard a voice saying, "Nuns, make way, Master of Meditation Ching-hsiu is returning."

On another occasion she was sitting in meditation with several other nuns in the meditation hall. One of the nuns who had dozed off was snoring. In her sleep she saw a person supporting the hall with his head who said, "Do not startle the nun Ching-hsiu with your snoring." Another time after that when she was sitting in meditation together with all the other nuns, one of them briefly stood up to return to her room, but she saw an apparition of a person who clapped his hands to stop her, saying, "Do not disturb the nun Ching-hsiu."

In her behavior toward everyone Ching-hsiu followed all the monastic regulations and standards.

She wanted to request the master of the law Yao[7] to lecture on the text *The Sarvāstivāda Monastic Rules in Ten Recitations,*[8] but she had only one thousand in cash and was distressed that the money might not be enough to complete the arrangements. That night in a dream she saw a flock of ravens, magpies, mynahs, and sparrows, each riding in a carriage appropriate to its size and singing together, "We are going to help the nun Ching-hsiu arrange the lecture," and, when she began to plan for it, seventy donors vied to give her fine offerings.

Later, she also invited the master of monastic rules Fa-ying (416–482) to give a lecture again on *The Sarvāstivāda Monastic Rules in Ten Recitations.*[9] On the first day of the lectures the water in the water jar became fragrant spontaneously. On that day, because she was the only one sitting in attendance for the lecture and she feared that she might be transgressing the rule [forbidding a nun from sitting alone with a monk], Ching-hsiu consulted the master of monastic rules who replied, "You are not transgressing the rule."

Ching-hsiu, observing that the rest of the nuns were not living in complete accordance with all the requirements of the religious life, lamented, "[The Buddha] the great fountain himself, is not yet so far in the past; but the springs of his teaching are slowing to a trickle.[10] If I do not rectify myself, how can I guide others?" Therefore she carried out the *mānatta* ceremony for the confession of offenses against the monastic rule, she herself confessing her own faults.[11] When the Assembly of Nuns saw what she was doing, they, too, followed suit and, reflecting on their behavior and desiring to make amends, confessed their faults in a spirit of contrition.

In the seventh year of the *yüan-chia* reign period (430) of Sung, the foreign monk Gunavarman (ca. 367–ca. 431) arrived at the capital.[12] His knowledge and practice of the monastic rules and regulations were of the highest caliber, and from him Ching-hsiu received once again the full obligation to observe the monastic precepts. Nevertheless, because the rest of the nuns at Green Garden Convent had a different understanding, she wished to live elsewhere so that, exteriorly—observing strictly the monastic rules—and interiorly—resting peacefully in the silence of meditation—she might come near to satisfying her religious intentions.

In the seventh year and eighth month of the *ta-ming* reign period (463), the princess of Nan-ch'ang of Sung and Huang Hsiu-i together donated a suitable piece of land to build a convent. In the construction work Ching-hsiu, wearing hempen clothing and eating coarse vegetables, personally carried mud and tile, laboring strenuously from morning until night. In the building of the shrines and the making of the statues, there was nothing that was not provided to complete the project. The more-than-ten nuns who lived together with Ching-hsiu in the new convent all practiced meditation as their work, and, in the third year of the *t'ai-shih* reign period (467), Emperor Ming (439–465–472) decreed that the convent should be named Meditation Grove Convent to identify the work of those who had gathered there.[13]

Ching-hsiu copied many scriptures in her own hand and placed them on a specially built scripture platform housed in the convent.

Throughout the day the two Sāgara Dragon King brothers, to show their protection and support, left footprints that were seen by everyone who came to the convent.[14] Each time she made offerings to the Holy Monk [Pindola] strange tracks appeared on the fruit and food.[15]

As another example of her sanctity, once she held a seven-day offering ceremony for the holy arhats, solitary Buddhas, and bodhisattvas.[16] From the beginning to the end of the ritual she concentrated her mind and fixed her thoughts, whereupon she saw two foreign monks gesticulating and talking. One was called Mikhala and the other Bhikhala. Because the color of the robes that they wore was like ripe mulberry fruit, Ching-hsiu then dyed her clothing with mud to match the color she had seen.[17] On another day she held a ceremony for the five hundred arhats of the Himalayan Lake Anavatapta and for the five hundred arhats of Kashmir.[18] Finally, she invited the monks in the capital to attend a two-day assembly.[19] On the second day a foreign monk appeared, and everyone there thought it suspicious. When they made an inquiry, he said that he had come from Kashmir a year ago. They asked the gatekeeper to keep watch on him. Many people saw him go out through the Sung-lin Gate, walk ten-some steps farther and then suddenly disappear.

On another occasion when she held a ceremony of inviting the Holy Monk Pindola to bathe, all was quiet both within and without the hall, except for the sound of the dipper ladling water, indicating that Pindola was truly present.[20] Ching-hsiu's auspicious omens and unusual spiritual experiences were all of this type.

The Ch'i heir apparent, Wen-hui (458–493), and the prince of Ching-ling, Wen-hsüan (460–494), treated her with great honor, making donations to her all the time.[21] Ching-hsiu grew old and feeble and was unable to walk. In the third year of the *t'ien-chien* reign period (504) of the Liang dynasty she received imperial permission to ride in a sedan chair to the imperial palace. On the seventeenth day of the sixth month of the fifth year (506), she became severely ill and depressed, unable to eat or drink. On the nineteenth day of the sixth month the master of the law Hui-ling of P'eng-ch'eng Monastery dreamed of an extraordinarily beautiful pavilion that he was told was the palace in Tushita Heaven.

When he saw Ching-hsiu within it, Hui-ling requested of her, "When you attain birth in that excellent place, do not forget to receive me there."

Ching-hsiu replied, "Because you, Master of the Law, are a great man widely conversant in the scriptures and religion of Buddhism, you shall surely live in this superlative land."

When Hui-ling heard that Ching-hsiu was sick, he went to see her and to tell her about his dream.

On the thirteenth day of the seventh month, she improved slightly, and in a dream she saw people on the west side of the Buddha Hall welcoming her with banners, parasols, and musical instruments; on the twenty-second day she invited all the religious whom she knew to gather together so that she might bid them farewell; on the twenty-seventh day she told her disciples, "I am ascending to the palace in the Tushita Heaven."[22] As soon as she finished speaking, she died. Ching-hsiu was eighty-nine years old.

53. SENG-NIEN

僧念

The nun Seng-nien (Remembrance of the Sangha) (415–504) of
Meditation Grove Convent

Seng-nien's secular surname was Yang, and her family was from Nan-ch'ang in T'ai-shan Commandery [in northeast China].[23] Her father, Yang Mi, was an assistant to the provincial governor. Seng-nien was the aunt of Master of the Law T'an-jui of Chaturdesha Monastery.

From early on Seng-nien's noble character was remarkable; her understanding was clear. She was established in virtue while still very young. At age 10 she left the secular life to become a disciple of the nun Fa-hui and live with her in Empress Dowager Convent. Living a strict and ascetic life, Seng-nien's practice of meditation was very profound. She read widely and comprehended much; her literary compositions were admired both for their form and for their meaning. As she grew older, she was even more intensely devoted to her vegetarianism and religious practices. For example, she would chant the *Flower of the Law Scripture* seven times through in a day and a night.[24]

The Sung dynasty emperors Wen (407–424–453) and Hsiao-wu (430–454–464) often provided for her material needs.[25]

During the *yung-ming* reign period (483–493) of the Ch'i dynasty she moved to Meditation Grove Convent, where her standard for the practice of meditation flourished and where those who sought instruction from her were many. The minister of education, the prince of Ching-ling [Wen-hsüan (460–494), second son of Emperor Wu of Ch'i], provided for her the four requisites of clothing, food, bedding, and medicine.[26]

In the third year of the *t'ien-chien* reign period (504) of the Liang dynasty she died at the age of ninety and was buried in Chung-hsing Village in Mo-ling County [very close to the southwest outskirts of the capital].

54. T'AN-HUI
曇暉

The nun T'an-hui (Radiance of the Dharma) (422–504) of
Enduring Joy Convent in Ch'eng-tu

T'an-hui's secular surname was Ch'ing-yang and her given name Pai-yü. She was from Ch'eng-tu [a city in the far-western region of Shu].[27]

When she was a child T'an-hui delighted in the thought of practicing the [Buddhist] religion, but her parents would not permit it. Nevertheless, in the ninth year of the *yüan-chia* reign period (432), when the foreign master of meditation Kālayashas entered the region of Shu to propagate the practice of meditation and contemplation, T'an-hui, eleven years old at the time, asked her mother to invite the master of meditation to visit them, for she wished to consult him about methods of meditation.[28] Her mother agreed to do so. The moment Kālayashas saw T'an-hui he marveled at her natural propensity and ordered her to cultivate the practice of meditation and also requested the nun Fa-yü to keep her under supervision. T'an-hui's mother, however, had already arranged her betrothal to the son of T'an-hui's paternal aunt. Because the day for the marriage had been set and was not to be changed, the nun Fa-yü took her in secret to the convent.

T'an-hui made a solemn vow, saying, "If I cannot carry out my intentions to lead the religious life but instead am compelled to marry, then I shall burn myself to death."

When the governor [of I Province],[29] Chen Fa-ch'ung, heard about this he sent an envoy to summon T'an-hui.[30] He gathered together greater and lesser officials, as well as other prominent individuals, and then requested all the monks and nuns to investigate the difficult problem thoroughly.

Chen Fa-ch'ung asked, "Are you truly able to lead the life of a Buddhist nun or not?"

T'an-hui replied, "It has been my humble wish for a long time, and I especially beg your help in my distress."

Chen Fa-ch'ung said, "I approve," and he sent an envoy to consult with her aunt, who then obeyed his instructions and released T'an-hui from her betrothal.

T'an-hui had just turned thirteen when she entered the religious life as a disciple of the nun Fa-yü, under whom she learned the practice of contemplation. When she had first received instruction, one time near the end of a meditation period she entered into a state of *samādhi,* or deep mental concentration, in which she saw two rays of light in the east, one bright like the sun and the other darker like the moon. While still in that state of concentration she had the thought, "The bright light must symbolize the way of the bodhisattva and the darker one the way of the hearer. If this is truly so, then the darker ray should fade away and the white one should blaze forth even brighter."[31] Then in response to her thought the darker ray vanished and the bright ray shone in full splendor. When she arose from her concentration, she told the nun Fa-yü what had happened. Fa-yü, skilled in the way of contemplation, was very happy when she heard about this and praised her accomplishment. At that time the nuns who had been sitting together with her, more than forty in number, all marveled at this rarity.

Later, when T'an-hui was sixteen years old, her fiancé, suspecting that he had been deceived, took some other fellows with him to seize her and take her back with him, but T'an-hui, because her maidservant helped to protect her, did not suffer violation, and there was nothing the fiancé could do. The case was again reported at the provincial level.

The governor, appreciating the unusual nature of the case, conferred with the monk Kālayashas who said, "This woman is very intelligent, so be careful not to oppose her. If there is insufficient money for her fiancé's family to break the engagement, I have an old servant who can go from place to place, collecting money for that purpose."

Later in meditation she herself came to understand the immutability of the Buddha nature and other doctrines of the Mahāyāna, or Great Vehicle, of Buddhism, none of which she had learned from her teacher.[32] At that time famous Buddhist masters exerted themselves to the utmost in posing difficult questions for her to answer, but none of them could stump her. Thus her reputation spread far and wide, and everyone looked up to her.

In the nineteenth year of the *yüan-chia* reign period (442) of the Sung dynasty, when the prince of Lin-ch'uan (403–444) went to his administrative post in the province of Nan Yen,[33] he invited T'an-hui to come to the town where he had his headquarters [a short distance to the northeast of the capital].[34] She was then twenty-one years old. When the general of the cavalry governing the region of Shan[35] invited her to accompany him to the district of southern Ch'u,[36] twelve hundred persons, male and female, religious and lay, welcomed her as their spiritual sovereign. Nevertheless, as the months and years slipped by, she thought of her mother more and more and finally insisted that she be allowed to return to her native place.

Because of her virtuous conduct, T'an-hui's disciples increased daily in number. Northwest of the town bridge she built a pagoda and a temple in which the halls, rooms, side rooms, and porches were completed most quickly.[37] She also built three convents wonderfully fast, and everyone marveled in admiration, saying that she had the power of the divine.

T'an-hui died in the third year of the *t'ien-chien* reign period (504) at the age of eighty-three.

Earlier when Chang Chün was with his father in I Province,[38] he once went unexpectedly with more than thirty other persons to visit T'an-hui without giving advance notice.[39] Nevertheless, they had no sooner sat down when they were served with fruit, dumplings, and other seasonal delicacies. The provincial governor, Liu Chün (ca. 439–499), also went to visit T'an-hui, and the same thing happened.[40]

The prince of Hsüan-wu (d. 500)[41] of the Liang dynasty once sent supplies to T'an-hui for her to prepare a feast for one hundred monks and originally said he would not go.[42] When the time came, however, he himself went. When he arrived, in addition to three hundred monks, there were also various government officials bringing the number close to four hundred persons. Just as the religious ceremony was about to begin, he sent a maidservant to ask for the assistants to help serve the food, but, when T'an-hui sent them in, everyone saw that there were only two disciples and two serving maids setting out and offering the food entirely without additional help. The prince again admired her immeasurable capacity.

Someone once asked T'an-hui, "Because your disciples seem to have only an average amount of material goods, and yet what you have built has been said to be like a divine transformation, how is this possible?"

She replied, "Often I have nothing saved up, and, if I must pay any expenses, I use a few coins and that is all. Immediately I have more available, but I do not know how this happens."

The one who had talked to her about this therefore thought that she had a miraculous inexhaustible treasury.[43]

At that time there was also the nun Hua-kuang, whose secular surname was Hsien-yü. She deeply comprehended abstruse elements of profound meditation and subtle contemplation. She was thoroughly versed in all the Buddhist scriptures as well as in the teachings of the non-Buddhist philosophers of the Hundred Schools. Especially skilled in literary composition, she wrote an encomium for T'an-hui that was both appropriate in content and elegant in form.

55. Nun Feng

馮尼

Nun Feng (409–504) of Capital Office Convent in the illegitimate kingdom of Kao-ch'ang[44]

Nun Feng[45] was a native of Kao-ch'ang [in the far northwest].[46] Because the people there respected her very much, they called her by her original surname of Feng. When she was thirty years old she became a nun in Capital Office Convent in Kao-ch'ang. She ate vegetables for her one meal a day, and her observance of the monastic rules was very strict. As an offering to the Buddha she burned six fingers down to the palms of her hands.[47] She was able to chant through the entire *Great Final Nirvāna Scripture* in only three days.[48]

At that time there was a master of the law Fa-hui (d. ca. 500), whose vigor in the practice of religion surpassed all others.[49] He was the chaplain for all the nuns in the kingdom of Kao-ch'ang.

Later, for she was the chaplain's spiritual friend of good discernment and influence, Nun Feng suddenly said to Fa-hui, "You, Āchārya, are not yet perfect.[50] You may go to the kingdom of Kucha in central Asia to Gold Flower Monastery, where you should listen to the monk Chih-yüeh, and then you will surely attain the superlative teaching."[51]

Fa-hui heeded her advice and went to that monastery to see Chih-yüeh, who, delighted by his arrival, gave him a pint of grape wine and bid him to drink.

Fa-hui, startled, said, "I have come to seek the superlative teaching, but instead you have offered me that which is unlawful and that which I am therefore not willing to drink."

Chih-yüeh pushed him around and quickly ordered him to leave. Fa-hui thought to himself, "Because I have come a long way but have not yet come so far as to understand the purpose of this, perhaps I should not disobey," and gulped it down. Drunk, he vomited and, dazed and confused, passed out, while Chih-yüeh betook himself elsewhere. When Fa-hui regained consciousness, realizing that he had violated the monastic rule against drinking wine, in his great shame he struck himself and, in penance for what he had done, wished to take his own life. As a consequence of this reflection he attained the third fruit [of Buddhist practice].[52]

Chih-yüeh returned and asked him, "Have you got it now?"[53]

Fa-hui replied, "Yes," whereupon he returned to Kao-ch'ang.

Fa-hui was still over two hundred Chinese miles away when, without advance verbal or written news of his impending arrival, Nun Feng summoned the Assembly of Nuns to go out to wait for him. Examples of her foreknowledge were all like this.

All the nuns of Kao-ch'ang revered Nun Feng as a teacher. When she was ninety-six years old, she died in the third year of the *t'ien-chien* reign period (504) of the Liang dynasty.

56. HUI-SHENG

慧勝

The nun Hui-sheng (Victorious Wisdom) (425–505) of Solitude
Convent of Liang

Hui-sheng's secular surname was T'ang. Her family was originally from the city of P'eng-ch'eng [in northeast China], but her father, T'ang Seng-chih, took up residence in Chien-k'ang [the capital of the Liang dynasty].

When still a child Hui-sheng wanted to leave the household life to become a nun. She was upright in character and restrained in speech; her deeds matched her words. Lacking any tendency to frivolity, she would remain indoors for as long as ten days. All who saw her respected her extraordinary qualities.

In the twenty-first year of the *yüan-chia* reign period (444) of the Sung dynasty, when Hui-sheng was eighteen years old, she left the secular life and lived at Meditation Grove Convent as a disciple of the nun Ching-hsiu (no. 52). After her reception of the obligation to observe all the monastic precepts, she lectured on the *Flower of the Law Scripture*. Under the tutelage of the nun Hui-hsü (no. 48) of Collected Goodness Convent she studied the five ways of meditation.[54]

Later, under Hui-yin of Grass Hall Monastery and Fa-ying of Spiritual Root Monastery, Hui-sheng cultivated the practice of contemplation in which she grasped to an exceptional degree the marvellous realization of the [Buddhist Way].[55] Whenever others perceived this and asked her about it, she always replied, "Sins, whether serious or slight, should be disclosed at once. Confess them diligently day and night."

Exalted and humble alike respected her, giving her offerings without cease.

In the fourth year of the *t'ien-chien* reign period (505) of Liang she died at the age of eighty-one and was interred on Bare Plank Mountain.

57. CHING-HSIEN

淨賢

The nun Ching-hsien (Pure Virtue) (431–505) of Eastern Green
Garden Convent

Ching-hsien, whose secular surname was Hung, was originally from Yung-shih [to the southeast of the capital].[56] She lived in the capital in Eastern Green Garden Convent. Capable and talented, she liked to practice meditation; well read in both the scriptures and the books of monastic precepts, her words were certainly elegant and seemly. Although she did not give lectures on these texts, she had thoroughly examined their essential teachings.

Emperor Wen (407–424–453) of the Sung dynasty held her in esteem.[57] When the prince of Hsiang-tung [eleventh son of Emperor Wen] was a young child, he often had nightmares.[58] After the emperor ordered him to take the Three Refuges [in the Buddha, in his teaching, and in the monastic assemblies] from the nun Ching-hsien, the prince's disturbed sleep was cured. The emperor thus esteemed her all the more and generously honored her with gifts, and everyone both within and without the palace personally rewarded her.

When the prince ascended the throne as Emperor Ming (439–465–472), he treated her with even greater courtesy and presented gifts in even greater abundance. Religious feasts and meetings for talks on the scriptures were held one after another, and all the famous scholars of that time honored and respected her.

Later she was in charge of the convent for more than ten years. She died in the fourth year of the *t'ien-chien* reign period (505) of Liang at the age of seventy-five.

There were also the nuns Hui-kao and Pao-yung, who were both famous. Hui-kao practiced meditation and chanted the scriptures in addition to diligently managing the affairs of the Assembly of Nuns. Pao-yung expounded on the *Flower of the Law Scripture* and was adept in the practice of contemplation.[59]

58. CHING-YÜAN

淨淵

The nun Ching-yüan (Pure Profundity) (436–506) of Bamboo
Garden Convent

Ching-yüan's secular surname was Shih, and her family originally was from the Chü-lu region [in far north China].[60] When she was a child, she had the wisdom of an adult, and at the age of five or six she used to pile up sand to make little pagodas and carve wood to make little images.[61] Burning incense and offering worship, the whole day was not long enough for her. Whenever she heard people discussing anything, she would relentlessly pursue the topic to grasp the essential principles.

When she was twenty, Ching-yüan left secular life to become a nun. Out of devotion to her parents she did not eat or sleep and drank only water to keep her fast.[62] She went on like this, not acquiescing to remonstrances, until seven days were over, after which she always kept a vegetarian diet. Ching-yüan observed all the monastic precepts most diligently, needing no exhortation or encouragement from others. Her teachers and friends respected her; those far and near commended her. The Ch'i heir apparent Wen-hui (458–493) honored her greatly,[63] giving her the four necessities of a monastic life, while messages and envoys came thick and fast.[64]

Ching-yüan died in the fifth year of the *t'ien-chien* reign period (506) at the age of seventy-one.

59. CHING-HSING
淨行

The nun Ching-hsing (Pure Conduct) (444–509) of Bamboo
Garden Convent

Ching-hsing was the nun Ching-yüan's (no. 58) fifth younger sister.
While yet a child she had remarkable intelligence and great foresight;
ardent in determination and elegant in behavior, in every way she
stood far above the crowd.

When Ching-hsing was young she was acquainted with Madame
Tsang, the wife of Kuo Hsia, who was the district magistrate of Ta-
mo. Kuo Hsia wanted to murder his wife, and, when word of his
intention leaked out, Ching-hsing requested her elder brother to
remonstrate with him, but Kuo Hsia refused to listen. Ching-hsing
secretly spoke to his wife, but she did not believe her. Holding
Madame Tsang's hands, Ching-hsing wept sorrowfully and then
departed. A day or two later Kuo Hsia indeed killed his wife.

When Ching-hsing was seventeen years old, she left secular life,
becoming a nun under the direction of the nun Fa-shih and living in
Bamboo Garden Convent, where she studied the *Discourse on the
Completion of Reality,* the *Discourse on the Abhidharma,* the *Nirvāna,* and the *Flower Garland.* Whenever she first encountered a
topic, she immediately grasped the essential meaning and tirelessly
searched out its nuances and profundities.[65]

Hsiao Tzu-liang, the Ch'i prince of Ching-ling, Wen-hsüan (460–
494) [second son of Emperor Wu], abundantly provided her with
material goods.[66] The two masters of the law Seng-tsung (438–496)
and Pao-liang (444–509) regarded her highly.[67] Whenever she was
asked to give lectures on the Buddhist scriptures and teachings, the
audiences numbered several hundred persons. In official residences
and in convents religious activities were carried out continuously. No
scholars were able to confound her. The prince of Ching-ling, when
later ranking the Assembly of Nuns with the intention of composing
records about them,[68] found that none could equal Ching-hsing.

Later there was a very intelligent and accomplished nun who was
extraordinarily competent in disputation. Ching-hsing was especially
intimate with her, and the whole community considered her to be a
talented and bright woman of the younger generation who could be
favorably compared to Ching-hsing.

In her old age Ching-hsing especially liked to practice meditation, and she rigorously maintained her vegetarian diet. When the emperor heard of her, he praised her highly.[69] In the eighth year of the *t'ien-chien* reign period (509), she died at the age of sixty-six and was buried on Bell Mountain [located immediately to the northeast of the capital].

60. SHIH LING-YÜ

釋令玉

The nun Shih Ling-yü (Esteemed Jade) (in the lineage of
Shākyamuni) (434–509) of Southern Chin-ling Convent

Ling-yü's secular surname was Ts'ai, and she was from [the capital city of] Chien-k'ang. While still very young she left secular life and went to live in the meditation hall of Empress Ho Convent as a disciple of the nun Ching-yao, whose adherence to the monastic precepts was perfect and whose intellect was superior to others.

Ling-yü as a young girl served her instructor with great respect and diligence, and, when she first received the ten initial precepts of a novice, one could already behold her great dignity of behavior. After she received the obligation to keep all of the monastic precepts, her observation of the prohibitions was as pure as snow.

She widely perused the texts of the five sectarian divisions of Buddhist monastic rules, admirably delving into the deep teachings with an excellent capacity for transmitting them to others.[70]

The prince of Shao-ling (?470–479) of the Sung dynasty [seventh son of Emperor Ming (439–465–472)], very much respected her and requested her to serve as abbess of Southern Chin-ling Convent, but she firmly declined to accept the position.[71] Because the prince was unable to make her submit to his request, he reported it [to his elder brother who was the emperor] during the *yüan-hui* reign period (473–477).[72] [When the emperor] during the *yüan-hui* reign period issued an imperial decree repeating the request she was unable to avoid accepting the position that she then held for many years. During that time she maintained a dignified but not overbearing manner and was serious without being severe.

In the eighth year of the *t'ien-chien* reign period (509), Ling-yü died at the age of seventy-six.

In the same convent there were also the nuns Ling-hui, Chieh-jen, and Hui-li, all of whom had illustrious reputations. Ling-hui chanted the *Lotus Flower of the Wonderful Law,*[73] the *Vimalakīrti,* the *Shrī-mālā,*[74] and other scriptures, kept a rigorous vegetarian diet, and was an eminent example for the Assembly of Nuns. Chieh-jen was very bright and excelled in studies; whatever she read she did not forget. Hui-li was spiritually accomplished and not given to contention.

61. SENG-SHU

僧述

The nun Seng-shu (Transmitter for the Sangha) (430–513) of
Solitude Convent

Seng-shu's secular surname was Huai. Her family was originally from [the northeastern city of] P'eng-ch'eng, but her father Huai Seng-chen had moved to [the capital city of] Chien-k'ang.

When Seng-shu was a child, she set her mind on the practice of religion and at age 8 undertook a vegetarian diet. When she was nineteen, in the twenty-fourth year of the *yüan-chia* reign period (447) of Sung, she left the secular life under the direction of the nun Ching-hsiu (no. 52) of Meditation Grove Convent. She was extremely rigorous in her practice of morality, keeping all the regulations without fail. She widely read both the scriptures and the texts of monastic precepts, carefully perusing them all, and later made a particular study of the *Sarvāstivāda Monastic Rules in Ten Recitations,* whose meaning she thoroughly comprehended.[75] Further, under the direction of the two masters of meditation, Fa-yin and Seng-shen (416–490), she received instruction in all the many abstruse methods of meditation.[76]

Seng-shu then took up residence in Meditation Grove Convent as the head of meditation studies, but, because the hubbub of all the people coming, going, and gathering together became too great, she resolved to live in seclusion. When Lady Chang, mother of the prince of Lin-ch'uan, heard about this she gave up her own residence, intending to convert it into a convent for Seng-shu, but at that time regulations forbid her to do this.[77] It was not until the first day of the ninth month of the second year of the *yüan-hui* reign period (474), when Wu Ch'ung-hua, the mother of the prince of Ju-nan, requested an imperial decree, that the convent was allowed to be built. There were altogether over fifty units of halls, shrines, and cells. Seng-shu, together with her companions, twenty women in all, delighting in the quiet of meditation, named their new convent Solitude.

In all circumstances Seng-shu held fast to her own sense of propriety and did not encourage any outward ostentation. At the close of both the Sung and Ch'i dynasties the world was in turmoil, but Seng-shu, sitting in the quietude of meditation, was not at all vexed by the clamor of worldly affairs.

The Ch'i heir apparent, Wen-hui (458–493), and the prince of Ching-ling, Wen-hsüan (460–494), treated her with great courtesy and respect.[78] They refurbished and adorned the entire convent, giving everything remarkable splendor. They provided for her necessities throughout the four seasons without cease.

When the great Liang dynasty came to power,[79] and the empire once again was established in order and good principles, both religious and laity paid her great respect, gathering like clouds from the four directions, but Seng-shu did not store up any of the material goods offered to her. Rather, she distributed them as soon as she received them. Sometimes she used the wealth she received to help the Buddhists of the four groups—the monks, nuns, laymen, and lay-women. Sometimes she used it to buy freedom for captured animals. She begged for donations to commission five golden images, all of which were of magnificent beauty. She also commissioned the copying of more than a thousand scrolls of Buddhist scriptures and texts of monastic precepts, the cases and rollers of which were adorned with precious ornaments.

Seng-shu died in the twelfth year of the *t'ien-chien* reign period (513) at the age of eighty-four and was buried on the south side of Bell Mountain [close to the northeast outskirts of the capital].

62. MIAO-WEI

妙禕

The nun Miao-wei (Wonderful Beauty) (444–513) of Western
Green Garden Convent

Miao-wei's secular surname was Liu, and her family was from [the capital] Chien-k'ang. When she was a very small child, her extraordinary capacities were abundantly evident, and while still a young girl she left secular life to take up residence at Western Green Garden Convent. Her spotless practice of the monastic precepts, her highly awakened spiritual sensibilities, and her sincere faith that spread kindness led everyone to cherish her.

Miao-wei liked conversation and was particularly good at witticisms. She lectured on the *Great Nirvāna Scripture,* the *Flower of the Law,* and the *Ten Stages,* altogether over thirty times.[80] She promoted the *Mother of Monasticism Scripture*[81] of the Sarvāstivāda sect of Buddhism. In all circumstances she benefited a great number of people with her skillful guidance.

In the twelfth year of the *t'ien-chien* reign period (513), she died at the age of seventy.

63. SHIH HUI-HUI

釋惠暉

The nun Shih Hui-hui (Radiance of Wisdom) (in the lineage of
Shākyamuni) (442–514) of Joyful Peace Convent

Hui-hui's secular surname was Lo, and her family was from Ch'ing Province [some distance northeast of the capital].[82] When she was six years old, she wanted very much to delight in the religious life, but her parents would not hear of it. At age 11 [to conform to the monastic precepts], she stopped eating all strong-flavored vegetables such as garlic and onions.[83] Clear and placid in mind and elegant in manner she recited the *Great Nirvāna Scripture* and chanted the *Flower of the Law Scripture.*[84] When she was seventeen, she went with her father to the capital, where, resolute in her vigor, she accomplished in her practice of religion what others could not achieve. Her parents, filled with affection on account of her efforts, permitted her to fulfill her aspirations, and, when she was eighteen, she left secular life to take up residence in Joyful Peace Convent.

Hui-hui received instruction in the *Discourse on the Completion of Reality,* the *Nirvāna,*[85] and other scriptures from the four masters of the law T'an-pin (407/411–473/477),[86] T'an-chi, Seng-jou (431–494), and Hui-tz'u (434–490),[87] and in ten-some years her learning became as well established as a veritable forest, and all the nuns in the capital turned to her as their instructor. Thus religious activities were set up one after another, drawing together people from all directions like clouds. Hui-hui continuously carried on her lectures as well as her meditation and chanting of scriptures. Her mind a standard of upright thought, she went day and night forgetting to sleep. Royalty, nobility, and commoners all greatly respected her, coming from everywhere to bestow gifts in great number throughout the year. The wealth that she received she used for copying scriptures, making images, and distributing as alms wherever appropriate. At that time someone, whose name has not come to light, renovated Joyful Peace Convent, refurbishing everything so that it looked new.

Hui-hui died in the thirteenth year of the *t'ien-chien* reign period (514) at the age of seventy-three and was buried at Stone Top Hill [in the southwestern part of the capital].

At that time there was also the nun Hui-yin, whose particular vocation was engaging in the ritual of offering worship [to the Buddha] and in the chanting [of scriptures].

64. SHIH TAO-KUEI

釋道貴

The nun Shih Tao-kuei (Honor of the Dharma) (in the lineage of
Shākyamuni) (431–516) of Ti Mountain Convent

Tao-kuei's secular surname was Shou, and her family originally was from Ch'ang-an [the old capital in the north]. As a child she was pure and serene and fond of searching out the principles of things. Energetic in her determination, her efforts surpassed others. Vowing to spread the Buddhist religion she did not eat flesh or strong-flavored vegetables, and, devoting herself to the salvation of all living beings, she was content to wear ragged clothing. Tao-kuei chanted the *Shrīmālā*[88] and *Infinite Life Scriptures,*[89] keeping to the task day and night. With loving thoughts her parents allowed her to take up the practice of religion, and, when she was seventeen, she left the secular life to become a nun.

Tao-kuei read widely in the scriptures and monastic texts, fully investigating their content. Coveting neither name nor fame, she took the practice of religion as her calling, and in the realm of contemplation she entered into meditative trance that did not cease regardless of her activity. When confessing her faults or making her vows, her words of sincere entreaty greatly moved those who heard them.

Hsiao Tzu-liang (460–494), the prince of Ching-ling, Wen-hsüan,[90] of the Ch'i dynasty, regarded her with great respect and built Peak Mountain Convent for her to have a place to bring together a community of nuns devoted to the practice of meditation.[91] When he asked her to serve as the manager of affairs of the new convent she firmly refused, but, when he asked her to serve as the model for the practice of meditation, she agreed.

Thus Tao-kuei lived for the rest of her life in the convent in Cassia Park.[92] Although repeatedly the gathered clouds might obscure every view or deep snow might bury the whole mountain, she circumspectly cultivated her practice of sitting in meditation, never becoming weary in spirit. With whatever donations she received from the faithful she widely promoted good works, keeping not a penny to benefit herself.

Tao-kuei died in the fifteenth year of the *t'ien-chien* reign period (516) at the age of eighty-six and was buried on the south face of Bell Mountain.

65. SHIH FA-HSÜAN

釋法宣

The nun Shih Fa-hsüan (Comprehensive Law) (in the lineage
of Shākyamuni) (434–516) of Beckoning Clarity Convent in
Shan-yin

Fa-hsüan's secular surname was Wang, and her family came from Yen [near Kuei-chi, southeast of the capital].[93] Her father, Wang Tao-chi, continued his family's profession of the True Law [of Buddhism]. Already as a child Fa-hsüan had determined to leave the secular life and become a nun, and beginning at age 7 she undertook a vegetarian diet and other austerities. At age 18 she chanted the *Flower of the Law Scripture* and fully studied and understood its purport from beginning to end.[94] Whether sitting or lying down for sleep, Fa-hsüan always had a vision of a canopy hovering over her.[95]

Unexpectedly a matchmaker appeared to arrange a betrothal, but Fa-hsüan made a vow that she would not be married. When she was twenty years old,[96] her parents took her to the nun Teh-leh (no. 51) of Brightness of Ch'i Convent in Yen where she donned the garb of a nun and undertook to follow all the precepts of the monastic life. From that day forward the vision of the canopy vanished.

Fa-hsüan read widely in the scriptures, fully savoring the flavor of their doctrines. After she received the full obligation of a monastic life, her contemporaries in the region all looked up to her, acknowledging her excellent practice [of Buddhism].

At the time of the end of the Sung dynasty (420–479) the master of the law Seng-jou (431–494) traveled around eastern China preaching and explaining the scriptures and commentaries, going from T'u and Sheng mountains in Yen [north] to Yü Cave on Kuei-chi Mountain, or [going on farther west] to ascend Ling-yin Mountain, or [going on farther north to Ku-su Mountain, way up in Wu Commandery].[97] Fa-hsüan took pleasure in the subtleties of Seng-jou's explication of the trends of thought in the commentaries to the scriptures, and she looked deeply into the profundities of the essentials in the scriptures themselves as explained by Hui-chi (412–496), another master of the law who had also been traveling in the region.[98] During the *yung-ming* reign period (483–493), she received instruction in the *Sarvāstivāda Monastic Rules in Ten Recitations*[99] from the master of the law Hui-hsi.[100] Thus, day by day her knowledge increased in both breadth and depth.

Fa-hsüan then moved to Beckoning Clarity Convent in Shan-yin County, where she repeatedly lectured on the scriptures and the books of monastic rules until her fame spread beyond the immediate region [which included what was, in olden times] the kingdom of Yüeh.[101] Rather than build up a private fortune for herself she used the donations given her to renovate the convent buildings, whose reconstruction was so splendid that it seemed to be of divine workmanship. She had scriptures copied and images made, and there was nothing that was not completed to perfection.

Chang Yüan of Wu Commandery, Yü Yung of Ying-ch'uan[102] and Chou Ying[103] of Ju-nan,[104] famous literary men of the time, all went personally to Fa-hsüan to pay their respects. When Hsiao Chao-chou, the Ch'i dynasty prince of Pa-ling, was serving as the administrator of Kuei-chi, he treated her most generously.[105] [Hsiao] Yüan-chien (d. 519), prince of Heng-yang of the Liang dynasty, asked her to serve as his mother's religious instructor when he came to the commandery.[106]

Fa-hsüan died in the fifteenth year of the *t'ien-chien* reign period (516) of the Liang dynasty at the age of eighty-three.

APPENDIX A: THE TEXT

The biographical collection, the *Lives of the Nuns*,[1] one of a number of Chinese Buddhist biographical writings, is unique not only because it is devoted to women but also because it covers the time of the founding of the Buddhist assembly for women. Several other collections survive from the same period, but these are all devoted to the lives of monks.

The most important complete biographic documents in addition to the *Lives* is Shih Hui-chiao's *Kao seng chuan* (Lives of eminent monks) consisting of 257 major biographies and a number of subbiographies completed "around A.D. 530."[2] Another collection, much smaller, is found in the last three *chüan* of Shih Seng-yu's[3] *Ch'u san-tsang chi chi* (Collected notes on the translation of the Buddhist scriptures into Chinese).[4]

A third collection, by Shih Pao-ch'ang, the compiler of the *Lives of the Nuns*, was a collection of monks' biographies titled the *Ming seng chuan* (Lives of famous monks) (hereafter *MSC*).[5] This work is now lost, except for the table of contents and a few extracts made by the Japanese monk Shūshō in the year 1235.[6] Coincidentally, one extract is also found nearly word for word in the *Lives* in the biography of the Nun Feng (no. 55). This strengthens the assumption that Pao-ch'ang is truly the compiler of the *Lives* because his name is not associated with the *Lives* in any extant Chinese bibliographic catalogue,[7] Buddhist or non-Buddhist, until the T'ang dynasty (618–907) catalogue *K'ai-yüan shih chiao lu* (The T'ang *k'ai-yüan* reign period collection of Buddhist writings),[8] and the *K'ai-yüan shih chiao lu lüeh ch'u* (The condensed T'ang *k'ai-yüan* reign period catalogue of Buddhist writings).[9] Although the attribution of the *Lives* to Pao-ch'ang first appears in a T'ang-dynasty catalogue, we need not suspect that the *Lives* is an orphan text to which a name has been arbitrarily assigned.

Nevertheless, in the T'ang-dynasty encyclopedia, *Fa yüan chu lin* (The forest of pearls in the garden of the law) (hereafter *FYCL*),[10] the *Lives* is not to be found in the *FYCL* list of nine titles attributed to Pao-ch'ang.[11] The *FYCL* does not quote from the *Lives*, nor does it quote from Pao-ch'ang's *MSC*. The *Li tai san pao chi (LTSPC)* lists only the first eight of the nine titles given in the *FYCL*.[12] Of the eight, only the *MSC* is undated. Elsewhere in the *LTSPC*, however, a date of 519 is given to the *MSC*.[13] Therefore, the *Lives* was most likely compiled between 516 and 519, despite the late attribution of the date.[14]

It is a curious detail that the *Lives* is not quoted in the major encyclopedic collections, whether Buddhist or not, from which are taken the surviving fragments of lost works such as the *Ming hsiang chi* (Records of mysterious omens) (hereafter *MHC*). The collections thus do not quote from the *Lives,* although they quote the sources of many of the *Lives.* These major collections were compiled in the north, and probably the *Lives* circulated only in the limited area of the south where it was originally compiled. The T'ang dynasty, consolidating the rulership of the entire country, which had been unified under the Sui dynasty (581–618), brought easier travel and concourse than was possible during the chaotic and warring disunion of the Northern and Southern dynasties. Only then could the *Lives* became more widespread and thus finally appear in the T'ang catalogues of scriptures with their attribution to Pao-ch'ang.[15]

The text of the *Lives* as it now stands is part of the Chinese Buddhist canon, the *Ta tsang ching* (Great storehouse of scriptures), in the *Taishō* edition *(T.)* (vol. 50, no. 2063), which is the basic text for our translation. The *Lives,* with the exeption of one biography, also appears in the *Ku chin t'u shu chi ch'eng* (Complete collection of books and records ancient and modern) (hereafter *KCTSCC*), vol. 506, a Ch'ing-dynasty (1636–1911) encyclopedia. The text of the *Lives* in *KCTSCC* corresponds to the Ming-dynasty (1368–1644) edition of the Buddhist canon as given in the *Taishō* edition.

One other of Pao-ch'ang's works to survive, the *Ching lü yi hsiang* (Different manifestations of the scriptures and the law) (*T.* 53, no. 2121), is the first title of the nine mentioned above in the *FYCL*.

Sources of the Text

In his preface Pao-ch'ang declares, "I have been examining epitaphs and eulogies, and searching in collections of writings."

Most of the extant sources for the *Lives* are fragments from a now-lost work, the *MHC,* compiled by Wang Yen after 479.[16] In the *MHC* we find the most fragments of possible sources for the *Lives.* Of the sixty-five biographies, five appear in the *FYCL*. All these five, biographies 10, 16, 22, 37, and 39, are taken from the *MHC* as quoted in the *FYCL,* and a different version of biography 10 is found in the *Chin nan-ching ssu chi* (Notes on the convents and monasteries of the southern capital of the Chin dynasty), a book no longer extant but quoted in the *FYCL.*[17]

A detailed comparison of the different versions of the biographies of the same nun reveals how Pao-ch'ang used and changed his sources. The five, and possibly six, biographies that have more than one extant version are biography 10, Tao-jung, with four versions;[18] biography 16, Hui-yü, with three versions;[19] biography 22, Hui-mu, with two versions (both have been translated to demonstrate the differences);[20] biography 37, Fa-yüan, with two versions;[21] biography 52, Ching-hsiu, with three versions.[22] The sixth biography, Hui-ch'iung (no. 20), is distantly connected to that of a certain Fa-ch'iung in the collection *Kuang hung ming chi* (The extended collection making known the illustrious) (hereafter *KHMC*).[23]

The two most interesting of these few biographies are Tao-jung (10) and Ching-hsiu (52). The first interests us because it has four versions. No two versions are identical, but the fact that there is much overlapping strongly suggests a common, and much longer, source. Ching-hsiu's biography interests us because we have the original source used by Pao-ch'ang. Ching-hsiu's original biography was written by Shen Yüeh, a famous man of letters.[24] He wrote a lengthy biography of the nun, which is included in Tao-hsüan's collection, the *KHMC.*[25] A comparison of the two versions indicates that Pao-ch'ang used, condensed, and edited Shen Yüeh's writing as the original source.

Shen Yüeh also must have had contact with other nuns because he wrote a eulogy for Seng-ching (no. 39). That eulogy, although not included in the *Lives* with the biography, is preserved in the *KCTSCC,* vol. 506, p. 14b. The translated eulogy is appended to Seng-ching's translated biography.

Literary Prototypes

The *Lives,* unique in content, is part of a long tradition of biographical writing in China composed not merely for the sake of history itself but for edification, example, and instruction. Within the biographical form it is possible to evaluate individuals and their actions, whether for good or ill, as statements of admonition and encouragement.[26]

The most obvious of the prototypes for the women in the *Lives* is the *Lieh nü chuan* (Lives of women) (hereafter *LNC*)[27] compiled some time between 77 B.C. and 6 B.C. by Liu Hsiang, a scholar of the Former Han dynasty (206 B.C.–A.D. 8).[28] The *LNC* is intended to be a vehicle for moral instruction and memorials for women by relating the lives of those who are worthy of emulation and serve as models of righteouness and upright conduct. The moral qualities of these women, paragons of traditional society, are the apex of what is expected and admired in women within the traditions of that society.

The *Lives* contains this type of biographical documentation. The two collections, however, have a different structure, the *LNC* being arranged categorically, including types such as the virtuous and wise, the chaste and obedient, or those able in reasoning. The eighth category, possibly not by Liu Hsiang, contains warnings about the pernicious and depraved.[29] The type of women in this last category does not appear in the *Lives* and would be contrary to Pao-ch'ang's purpose. All the other Buddhist biographies, as well as the *LNC,* divide their material by categories, and Pao-ch'ang did likewise in his *MSC.*

The *Lives* is divided chronologically. Pao-ch'ang in his preface, however, singles out four types of women whom he especially admires: the ascetics (Shan-miao, no. 26, and Ching-kuei, no. 47); the contemplatives (Fa-pien, no. 31, and Seng-kuo, no. 27); the faithful and steadfast (Seng-tuan, no. 24, and Seng-chi, no. 8); and the teachers of great influence (Miao-hsiang, no. 4, and Fa-ch'üan, no. 44). Reading these biographies, we see that Pao-ch'ang has chosen extreme examples, the most spectacular being the ascetics who commit suicide by fire in honor of the Buddha; the steadfast are those who refuse marriage by using daring means to escape. The contemplatives go into trances so deep that they are like wood and stone. The teachers have hundreds of disciples and followers.

The *Lives* also serves as a model or exemplar for Buddhist women, but in this case the values are Buddhist. Nevertheless, in the *Lives,* when the biographer records secular values such as filiality, obedience, and upholding tradition, we see attempts on the part of the compiler to show clearly that Buddhist values and way of life did not fundamentally go against the traditions of society, or against Confucian ethics and morals. One difference is that the women of the *LNC* are praised or blamed because of their effect on father, husband, or son, the three men to whom a woman is to be obedient throughout her life. The nuns, on the contrary, are in most cases praised and honored for their own worth, for their own self-development, often in the face of opposition.

The vocabulary of praise and blame are different—with some overlapping—between the *LNC* and the *Lives*. The emphasis changed from Confucian-inspired ideals, such as *i* (righteousness) or *jen* (human heartedness), to Buddhist ideals such as keeping the precepts or teaching the Buddhist law. Women in the *LNC* commit suicide for more passive reasons, as, for example, to preserve their reputation or that of their families—a Confucian ideal woman. In the *Lives* women who commit suicide do it for religious reasons, a very positive attitude of doing something in honor of the Buddha, his law, and his monastic assemblies.

The terminology of praise in the *Lives* often conforms to Buddhist texts as models. For example, the text known as the *Mahāprajāpatī Scripture* provides a compact example for the women to follow.[30] Much of the content of the nuns' experiences has direct prototypes in the Buddhist scriptures. The biographies demonstrate and give proof of the efficacy of the Buddhist Way. The two clearest examples are the sacrifice of one's life by fire as advocated in the *Flower of the Law Scripture* and the protection given by the bodhisattva Kuan-yin as promised in the *Kuan-yin Scripture*. Many rituals and practices derive directly from the scriptures.

Despite the Buddhist inspiration of most of the biographies, there are several that seem to have a secular background. The biography of Miao-yin (no. 12), for example, illustrates a nun highly involved in the secular world, carrying on actions specifically prohibited to nuns.[31] Miao-yin is an adviser to the emperor, and she hobnobs with all the famous people of her day. Everyone flocks to her because of her influence. She is literate and clever; she is a famous person, the type of cleric whom Pao-ch'ang admired.

APPENDIX B: THE *MĀNATTA* RITUAL

A description of the ritual taken from the *Wu fen lü,* or *Mahīshāsaka-vinaya, T.* 22:186.b–c:

"We now ask for the semimonthly *mānatta* ceremony. We wish that the Assembly of Monks will give us the semimonthly *mānatta* ceremony." Request in this manner three times, and in response a monk will recite: "Listen, Great Assembly of Monks. This nun N. N. has committed a serious offense [Sanskrit: *sanghāvashesa;* or Pali: *sanghā-disesa*] and from the Assembly of Monks asks for the semimonthly *mānatta* ceremony. The monks' assembly is now giving the *mānatta* ceremony." If it is suitable, then they will permit it. He speaks thus: "Listen, great Assembly of Monks. This nun N. N. has committed a serious offense and from the Assembly of Monks asks for the semi-monthly *mānatta* ceremony. The Assembly of Monks is now giving the *mānatta* ceremony. All elders who are willing to permit it remain silent. Those who do not, speak up." This is repeated three times. "The monks' assembly has granted the semimonthly *mānatta* ceremony. Because the monks' assembly has kept silent, perform it thus: The monks' assembly has permitted the *mānatta.* You should rise in the morning and sweep and sprinkle everywhere in the nuns' residence —all cells, ponds, walls, and ground. You should fill up all those places that require water. You should do everything that can be done. If a guest nun comes or a nun leaves, you should address her. Further-more, you should take a nun as a companion and go to the monks' res-idence, and there everything that should be done you should do as above. If a guest monk comes or a monk leaves, you also should address him. At dusk you return to the nuns' residence. Do this for half a month. In the presence of twenty monks and twenty nuns per-form the ritual for expiating offenses according to the monks' method."

NOTES

Introduction

1. The translation of the *Lives* is based on the Japanese edition of the Chinese Buddhist canon, the *Taishō-shinshū-daizōkyō*. The *Lives* is no. 2063 in vol. 50. All further references to the *Taishō* edition will be abbreviated *T.*

2. Shih Pao-ch'ang, biography in *Hsü kao seng chuan* (Further lives of eminent monks), *T.* 50, no. 2060, 426.b.13–427.c.20. For more about Shih Pao-ch'ang, see Wright, "Biography and Hagiography."

3. See appendix A for details about the history of the text.

4. Buddhism separated into two main branches about three to four hundred years after its founding, the Hīnayāna and Mahāyāna, or Small Vehicle and Great Vehicle. The adherents of the Great Vehicle assigned the title Hīnayāna to their opponents. We prefer to use the term *Disciples' Vehicle* rather than Hīnayāna. The adherents of the Disciples' Vehicle ignored their opponents. The only remaining school of the Disciples' Vehicle is the Theravāda school found mostly in Southeast Asia. See Robinson and Johnson, *Buddhist Religion*, pp. 65–69; Ch'en, *Buddhism in China*, pp. 11–16. (See also chap. 1 n. 50, below.)

5. See Tsai, "Chinese Buddhist Monastic Order," pp. 2–3, for a much more detailed discussion of this problem. Also see Paul, *Women in Buddhism*, which has a different approach and understanding.

6. *Cullavagga*, X, 1.4, 6; and among others in the Chinese Buddhist canon the *Ssu fen pi-ch'iu-ni chieh mo fa* (Dharmaguptaka nuns' rites and rule book) *T.* 22, no. 1434, 1066.c.18–19; and also *Ssu fen pi-ch'iu-ni chieh pen* (Dharmaguptaka nuns' rule book), *T.* 22, no. 1431, 1037.c.20–21.

7. Robinson and Johnson, *Buddhist Religion*, p. 7ff.

8. *Hou han shu* (History of the Latter Han dynasty), chaps. 42, 88.

9. Taoism was never a single set of practices or beliefs. That Buddhism superficially resembled Taoism in so many aspects contributed in some measure to the initial spread of Buddhism. Recently much scholarly work has been done in the study of Taoism. Two good introductory books are Welch, *Taoism: The Parting of the Way;* and Kaltenmark, *Lao Tzu and Taoism.* Two important collections of articles are *Facets of Taoism in Chinese Religion,* ed. Holmes Welch and Anna Seidel; *Symposium on Taoism,* in *History of Religions.* A very important article, a combination of a bibliography and an encyclopedic entry, is Seidel's, "Chronicle of Taoist Studies." This issue of *Cahiers*

is a double issue devoted entirely to Taoist studies. The *Encyclopaedia Britannica,* fifteenth ed., has excellent articles on both Taoism and Buddhism.

10. Maspero, "Les origines," esp. pp. 92–93.

11. The decision to translate the Buddhist texts into Chinese was of monumental importance for the history of Buddhism in China. It is not an automatic assumption that sacred scriptures should be translated. Other religions often keep their holy books in ancient and original tongues. The texts most popular in China were usually the ones most similar to the taste of literate Chinese.

12. Ch'en, *Buddhism in China,* pp. 48–53; Zürcher, *Buddhist Conquest,* pp. 26–27; Link, "Taoist Antecedents of Tao-an's Ontology," pp. 181–215.

13. Zürcher, *Buddhist Conquest,* p. 57.

14. Prip-Møller, *Chinese Buddhist Monasteries,* preface.

15. See Wright, "Fo-t'u-teng," pp. 325–326.

16. The story is from *Yün chi ch'i ch'ien* (Seven tallies in a cloud satchel), *chüan* 115–116, p. 1614. This is a Sung-dynasty collection of about A.D. 1025 of major Taoist writings.

17. Zürcher, *Buddhist Conquest,* pp. 273, 286–287; Ch'en, *Buddhism in China,* pp. 184–185.

18. Ch'en, *Buddhism in China,* pp. 76–77; Gernet, *Aspects économiques,* pp. 25–26, passim.

19. Zürcher, *Buddhist Conquest,* pp. 28–29.

20. Ibid., pp. 188–189

21. Tao-an (312–385), biography in *Kao seng chuan* (Lives of eminent monks), *T.* 50, 351.c.3ff; *Ch'u san-tsang chi chi* (Collected notes on the translation of the Buddhist scriptures into Chinese), *T.* 55, 43.c., 44.b–46.b; 108.a–109.c; Zürcher, *Buddhist Conquest,* pp. 187–189; biography translated by Link, "Biography of Shih Tao-an."

22. Hui-yüan (344–416), biography in *Kao seng chuan, T.* 50, 357.c.23ff; and in *Ch'u san-tsang chi chi, T.* 55, 110.b.ff. Ch'en, *Buddhism in China,* pp. 76–77; Robinson, *Early Mādhyamika in India and China,* pp. 96–114. Biography translated in Zürcher, *Buddhist Conquest,* pp. 240–253.

23. Zürcher, *Buddhist Conquest,* p. 28.

24. *Lo-yang ch'ieh-lan chi* (A record of monasteries and convents in Lo-yang), *T.* 51, no. 2092, 1004.c.15–16, 1005.c.16–17, 21; and reprinted by Shih-chieh Publishing, 1962, map insert between pp. 8–9.

25. *Kao seng chuan,* by Hui-chiao, a contemporary of Pao-ch'ang, *T.* 50, no. 2059. See appendix A.

26. Zürcher, *Buddhist Conquest,* pp. 231–239.

27. See, for example, *Ssu fen lü* (Dharmaguptaka-vinaya), *T.* 22, no. 1428, 924.c.17–18; *Ssu fen pi-ch'iu-ni chieh pen* (Dharmaguptaka nuns' rule book),

T. 22, no. 1431, 1037.c.20; *Mo-ha-seng-shih pi-ch'iu-ni chieh pen* (Mahā-sānghika-bhikshunī-prātimoksha), *T.* 22, no. 1427, 557.b.12.

28. One may learn the causes and conditions of why modern women become Buddhist nuns and teachers in Friedman, *Meetings with Remarkable Women,* especially the story of Karuna Dharma, pp. 193–211.

29. Zürcher, *Buddhist Conquest,* p. 7.

30. Gernet, "Les suicides," pp. 537, 548; also *Le lie-sien tchouan,* pp. 36 n. 1, 54 n. 2, 81, passim.

31. The collection of Buddhist texts, compared to, for example, the Bible of the Christians, or the Koran of the Muslims, is vast. Of the major collections of Buddhist texts, which are classified by language, the Chinese collecton is the largest. The Chinese Buddhist canon, the *Ta tsang ching* (Great storehouse of scriptures), consists of fifty-five volumes of texts, plus a forty-five-volume supplement. Each volume has about one thousand pages, and each page has about one thousand characters.

32. The monk Seng-chao, in his commentary to the *Vimalakīrti,* the *Chu wei-mo-chieh ching, T.* 38, no. 1775, 344.c.1ff.

33. Needham, *Science and Civilisation,* 5, no. 2:294–304.

34. In the "Medicine King" chapter in *Miao fa lien hua ching,* 53.b–54.a; *Cheng fa hua ching,* 125.b–126.a. See *Flower of the Law Scripture* in Bibliography.

35. *Le lie-sien tchouan,* p. 37, passim.

36. Ibid., pp. 112, 153.

37. Demiéville, "Momies," pp. 148–149. He suggests that mummification was rare in Taoism; Needham, in *Science and Civilisation,* 5, no. 2:300, believes it was more common.

Shih Pao-ch'ang's Preface to *Lives of the Nuns*

1. Literally, "The man who longs to emulate Yen will be the same kind of person as Yen." Yen Hui was a disciple of Confucius. The full quotation is found in *Chin shu,* chap. 82, biography of Yü P'u. Shih Pao-ch'ang has reversed the two phrases.

2. Sages, of whom the most famous is Lao-tzu in *Lao-tzu tao teh ching,* chap. 56: "Those who know do not speak; those who speak do not know." Another sage is Chuang-tzu, in chap. 22: "Perfect speech is giving up speech." ("Perfect speech is the abandonment of speech," Burton Watson, *Complete Works of Chuang Tzu,* p. 247.)

3. The Three Ages are the periods of the first age of the True Dharma (Law) lasting five hundred or one thousand years; the second age, the counterfeit age, lasting five hundred or one thousand years; the third age is the decay of

the Dharma. The time span for these ages varies according to the source, depending on the length of ages the Chinese used to determine the birth date of the Buddha (Ch'en, *Buddhism in China,* pp. 297–298).

1. The Chin Dynasty

1. The early Buddhist missionaries from India and central Asia were given surnames in China that indicated the country of their origin: Chu for India, An for Parthia, K'ang for Sogdia, and Chih for Scythia. For several centuries their Chinese disciples took religious surnames from their masters until the custom arose of using the first character of the Buddha's own name, Shā-kyamuni—or Shih-chia-mou-ni in Chinese transcription—thus giving rise to the practice of all monks and nuns taking the religious surname of Shih.

2. Ching-chien's biography has been translated in *Buddhist Texts through the Ages,* pp. 291–292.

3. P'eng-ch'eng was in the present-day region of northwest Chiangsu Province and southern Shantung Province. P'eng-ch'eng was a very early and important center of Buddhism in China, with evidence for Buddhist practice, of a sort, dating to mid–first century A.D. It remained a flourishing center lying as it did in a pivotal section of a trade route that connected the Silk Road, with P'eng-ch'eng lying at the extreme eastern end, and southern China, the areas of Kuei-chi and modern-day Nanjing, the capital, under different names, of the succession of Southern dynasties beginning with the Eastern Chin dynasty (A.D. 317). See Maspero, "Les Origins," pp. 87–92.

4. Present-day Wu-wei County in central Kansu Province. See map.

5. Lo-yang served as the capital of the Chin dynasty until the fall of Western Chin in 317. See map.

6. This means only that the nuns have more rules than the monks. The number of rules for nuns in the various schools: Dharmaguptaka, 348; Mahī-shāsaka, 373; Sarvāstivāda, 354; Mahāsāmghika, 290; Pali canon, 311; Tibetan canon, 364; Mūlasarvāstivāda, 309. See Mochizuki, *Bukkyō-daijiten* 5:4292.

7. These are the ten basic rules that the novice in training is to observe—namely, to refrain from (1) harming living beings; (2) stealing; (3) wrong sexual conduct; (4) false speech; (5) intoxicating substances; (6) wearing perfumes or garlands; (7) participating in entertainments or going to observe them; (8) using a high or wide bed; (9) eating at improper times; and (10) carrying or using silver, gold, or other precious objects (which prohibits the use of money).

8. Chih-shan from Kashmir: The table of contents to the *Ming seng chuan* (Lives of famous monks) (of which only fragments remain) lists in chap. 19 a Chih-shan in the category of foreign meditation masters. Because he is listed

as having been active in the Sung dynasty (420–479), it is questionable whether he is the same as Ching-chien's instructor. The book *Lives of Famous Monks* was also compiled by Pao-ch'ang. See appendix A.

9. This is the most likely date because it refers to the *chien-wu* reign period of Chin (317), rather than to the *chien-wu* reign period of the Latter Chao (335). The biographies are dated according to the reign periods of the Southern dynasties. This means he left the same year that the Chinese dynasty of Chin had to flee south from the non-Chinese invaders.

10. According to the records Chu Fo-t'u-teng lived from the year 232 to the year 348. He has a biography not only in the Buddhist collection of biographies, *Kao seng chuan,* vol. 50, chap. 9:383.b–387.a, but also in the official history of the dynasty, the *Chin shu,* chap. 95. His biography from *Kao seng chuan* has been translated by Wright, "Fo-t'u-teng." Fo-t'u-teng, a central Asian of Indian ancestry and hence surnamed Chu, carried out his missionary work in northern China, arriving from Kucha in A.D. 310 in time for the calamitous loss of north China to invading non-Chinese tribes. He remained in north China using his considerable magical powers to ameliorate the harsh rule of the barbarian emperors. His Chinese disciples, in particular the monk Shih Tao-an (whose biography appears in *Kao seng chuan,* 5:351.c–354.a, and has been translated into English by Link, "Biography of Shih Tao-an"), established the intellectual and institutional foundations not merely of Buddhism in China but also of Chinese Buddhism.

11. The allusion is to *Mencius,* book 3, part A: "The virtue of the gentleman is like the wind. The virtue of the common man is like the grass. When the wind blows the grass will surely bend." See also the translation by Lau in *Mencius.*

12. In the year A.D. 317 barbarians took control of north China, forcing the imperial court to flee south where it set up another capital city at Chien-k'ang (present-day Nanjing), on the south bank of the Yangtze River. Many refugees, especially among the upper classes, fled south at the same time. Ching-chien, however, was not among them, remaining instead in or near Lo-yang. The city of Lo-yang had been sacked in A.D. 311 (Ch'en, *Buddhism in China,* p. 57; Zürcher, *Buddhist Conquest,* pp. 59, 84).

13. Land of the Scythians, lit. Yüeh-chih people, in present-day Kashmir, Afghanistan, and Pamir. The Yüeh-chih are known in the west as Scythians. The Yüeh-chih Buddhist missionaries were very active in bringing Buddhism to China, and colonies of Yüeh-chih lived in the northwest section of China, e.g., Kansu and the Tun-huang region. The translator monk Dharmaraksha, the "bodhisattva from Tun-huang," for example, was of Yüeh-chih ancestry. The importance of central Asians of several groups such as the Kucheans, Khotanese, and Sogdians in transmitting the Buddha's law from India to China cannot be overemphasized.

14. We have used the variant reading as it appears in the Sung, Yüan, and Ming editions of the Buddhist canon. This makes our interpretation somewhat different from others. For example, Tsukamoto Zenryū, *Chūgoku-bukkyō-tsūshi*, p. 438, states, "The foreign monk T'an-mo-chieh-to set up an ordination platform in Lo-yang using the *Mahāsānghika Ritual and Rule* book brought back from Yüeh-chih by Seng-ching." In Mochizuki, *Bukkyō daijiten*, p. 4292b., we read, "In the *hsien-k'ang* period of Latter Chin, Seng-ching got the *Mahāsānghika Ritual and Rule* book, and in the first year, second month of the *sheng-p'ing* period requested T'an-mo-chieh-to to set up a *bhiksunī* ordination platform." We do not see any way to reconcile these differing versions, and we have chosen our interpretation for the reason that the date of the completion of the translation is given.

15. The eighth day of the second month (or, according to some sources, the fifteenth day of the month) was celebrated as the Buddha's nirvana day; i.e., the day he passed into final nirvana. See, e.g., *Fa yüan chu lin* [Forest of pearls in the garden of the law] *T.* 53, 371.c.–372.c.; and *Nirvāna Scripture, T.* 12, 365.c.8–9.

16. The Chinese text for the phrase "scriptures on the origins of monastic rules" could also be interpreted as the title of a specific book. There is such a book, the *Origin of Monastic Rules Scripture,* translated in the northern capital of Ch'ang-an (see map) between 379 and 385. This date, however, places the translation too late for use by the monk Shih Tao-ch'ang because the nun Ching-chien died no later than 361. It is always possible that an earlier, but now-lost, translation that used the same title could have been available. A text called *Pi-nai-yeh* (i.e., *Vinaya*) in ten *chüan* was translated by Chu Fo-nien of the Yao Ch'in. He went to Ch'ang-an in the *chien-yüan* reign period (365–384) and was part of the translation team headed by Tao-an who had been taken by force to Ch'ang-an in 379. The text was translated between 379 and 385. See Hirakawa Akira, *Ritsuzō-no-kenkyū*, pp. 155–160, for a discussion of the date of translation. This date means that the text was translated some years after Ching-ch'ien's full ordination and therefore could not be the one specified in the biography. It is possible that the words *chieh yin-yüan ching* refer to *Vinaya* texts in general because in the body of these texts the circumstances that lead to the creation of a new rule are referred to as *yin-yüan*. See, e.g., *T.* 22, no. 1425, 522.a.10, 522.c.17. Waley, in *Buddhist Texts through the Ages,* p. 292 n.3, suggests that it is referring to the *Ta-ai-tao pi-ch'iu-ni ching* (The scripture of Mahāprajāpatī's *Vinaya*). But the date of translation of this text is approximately 412–439, thus being too late. See *Répertoire,* p. 126. Another possibility is that it is the title for a text now lost.

17. This sentence is admittedly difficult to interpret. Tsukamoto Zenryū in his book *Chūgoku bukkyō tsūshi*, p. 438, says that Ching-chien and her companions received the precepts on an ordination platform on the boat.

Although this practice of using a floating ordination platform was carried out at times, the circumstances in this instance seem not to warrant that interpretation. The Ssu River was not located conveniently near Lo-yang. Waley, in *Buddhist Texts through the Ages*, p. 242, says that the foreign monk went south on the river. Regardless of who went south, the goal of such a trip might well have been P'eng-ch'eng, a thriving center of Buddhism since at least the first century (see Zürcher, *Buddhist Conquest*, pp. 26–28), or even Chien-k'ang. The lower reaches of the Ssu River were "stolen" when the Yellow River changed course in the late twelfth century and flowed into the Yellow Sea south of the Shantung peninsula until the mid-nineteenth century when the Yellow River once again changed course to flow north of the Shantung peninsula. The Ssu River was not restored.

18. Rising bodily to the sky is a Taoist way of death. See *Le Lie-sien tchouan*, p. 112; *Yün chi ch'i ch'ien* (Seven tallies in a cloud satchel), e.g., pp. 1619–1620.

19. Thus she was in her late twenties when she received the ten precepts and in her late sixties when she finally received full admission to the Assembly of Nuns.

20. This biography has been translated by Wright, "Biography of the Nun An Ling-shou."

21. Non-Chinese—lit. "illegitimate dynasty of Latter Chao."

22. The traditional conception of a woman's duty was to obey first her father or elder brother, then her husband, and finally her son. See Wright, "Biography of An Ling-shou," p. 195, where he quotes James Legge's translation of the *Li Chi:* ". . . In her youth, she follows her father and elder brother, when married, she follows her husband; when her husband is dead, she follows her son." This describes an ideal situation. An Ling-shou was obeying a higher authority that included her duty to her parents.

23. Buddhist monastic life ran counter to traditional values and was the biggest obstacle to Chinese acceptance of Buddhism. This is standard Buddhist apology. The theme is central to Dudbridge, *The Legend of Miao-shan*, pp. 89–91.

24. Kucha was an oasis city kingdom of central Asia along the Silk Road some distance from northwest China.

25. See biography 1. In reading his reply to Chung, one must keep in mind that he was a magician as well as a monk and used this very successful expedient means to influence the rulers in north China at the time, Shih Lo and Shih Hu. Evidence indicates that he ameliorated some of the very harsh aspects of the rule of these two. See Wright, "Fo-t'u-teng."

26. See Wright, "Fo-t'u-teng," pp. 337–338. Fo-t'u-teng could also hear prophesies from the sound of bells and could interpret dreams. The early Buddhist missionaries to China often were wonder workers and healers.

27. Traditionally a garment made from rags collected from the dustheap and patched together. The Chinese passage could also be interpreted to mean that the vestment and the robe were the same garment.

28. There is also a vestment tie known as a *hsiang-pi* (elephant trunk), which would make the sentence read "elephant-trunk tie, and a water ewer." The interpretation in the translation was chosen because of the structure of the sentence.

29. Emperor Shih Lo (*Chin shu,* chap. 104; *Wei shu,* chap. 95).

30. The Latter Chao, 319–350, was one of many non-Chinese dynasties that rose and fell in the north after the legitimate Chinese dynasty was forced to flee south in A.D. 317. This dynasty, under Shih Lo, and especially under his nephew Shih Hu,(who killed Shih Lo's son) has been described as a reign of terror and Shih Hu in particular as a psychopath. Their capital sites were Hsiang-kuo and Yeh in north China. See Zürcher, *Buddhist Conquest,* pp. 85, 181.

31. *Ching-sheh* was not originally a Buddhist term. It derived from Han times and was used by both Confucianists and Taoists. There are several alternate combinations of characters. See Stein, *"Remarques,"* p. 38.

32. Shih Hu (r. 335–349) (*Chin shu,* chap. 106; *Wei shu,* chap. 95).

33. Ch'ing-ho, in present-day Hopei Province, Ch'ing-ho County. See map.

34. Ch'ang-shan, in present-day Hopei Province, Cheng-ting County. See map.

35. Fu-liu County, in present-day Hopei Province, Chi County.

36. It should be noticed that in the biographies Confucianism as such is never the subject of polemics. Huang-Lao Taoism evolved during the Han dynasty and concerned obtaining long life and immortality. It is possible that the administrator of the commandery was a consciously practicing Huang-Lao devotee, but he was more likely to be a Confucian.

37. See Zürcher, *Buddhist Conquest* 2:414 n. 27, where he lists five instances of the investigation of the assemblies of the monks and nuns, one of which is mentioned here.

38. In 357. His uncle Fu Chien (different character) (r. 351–355) declared himself emperor in 351, founding the Former Ch'in dynasty, one of the Sixteen Kingdoms of non-Chinese rulership in north China, 304–463. Former Ch'in (351–394) united north China during Fu Chien's reign (357–385). He was strangled to death in 385. The seat of the Former Ch'in government was at Ch'ang-an within the province of Ssu-li, and this is probably the Ssu Province given as the location of Chih-hsien's convent home. She presumably moved from her hometown in Hopei to the capital, or the biography is giving her ancestral home, a common practice in Chinese Buddhist biographical writing. She is thus located in Ch'ang-an during approximately the same time as Ching-chien (biography 1). On Fu Chien, see Rogers, *Chronicle of Fu Chien; Chin shu,* chap. 113–114; *Wei shu,* chap. 95.

39. Ssu-li Province. See n. 38 above.

40. The Chinese title indicates that Chih-hsien used the translation by Dharmaraksha (Chu Fa-hu), done in the year A.D. 286 in Ch'ang-an in northwest China. *T.* 9, no. 263. See *Répertoire*, p. 36.

41. This is a *tour de force* in terms of the length of the text. It would require chanting about fifty words per minute nonstop for a twenty-four-hour period. If she took any rest, she would have to have chanted much faster.

42. Concourse with animals is frequently the indication of a holy person of whatever tradition. See Eliade, *Shamanism,* p. 99, passim. One is reminded of St. Francis of Assisi, who preached to the animals, and St. Seraphim of Sarov, who associated with the bear and other animals.

43. Ritualized walking, *ching hsing*, a Buddhist term referring to a ritualized walking exercise often used as a break to punctuate the hours of sitting in meditation. See Oda, *Bukkyō-daijiten*, p. 249.c.

44. Hung-nung in north China. Probably the town located on the Yellow River to the west of Lo-yang, halfway between Lo-yang and the north bend of the Yellow River. See map.

45. Chang Mao, otherwise unknown. He is not likely to be one of the four persons whose names appear in the dynastic histories because the locations do not conform to the biography. *Chin shu*, chaps. 30, 78, 86, 107, refer to the four different individuals, and there is no evidence identifying any of them as Miao-hsiang's father.

46. Pei-ti, north of the capital of Ch'ang-an. See map.

47. Grand secretariat of the right. See des Rotours, *Traité*, p. 595. "Les quatre secrétaires du grand secrétariat de droit de l'héritier du trone (T'ai-tseu-cho-jen) etaiant mandarins du sixiéme degré, primiére classe."

48. Confucian propriety, i.e., observing all the rules and rites associated with the death of a parent. A clear explanation is given in Waley, *Analects of Confucius*, pp. 62–64; Thompson, *Chinese Religion*, pp. 51–52.

49. Kao-p'ing, in present-day Shantung Province. See map.

50. This refers to Mahāyāna, or Great Vehicle, Buddhism, the type of Buddhism prevalent in East Asia. Great Vehicle Buddhism teaches that the religious ideal is the bodhisattva, or Buddha to be, who helps living beings attain final nirvana ahead of them by accumulating vast stores of spiritual merit and donating that merit to any and all who ask. The followers of the Great Vehicle contrast this ideal with that of the Small Vehicle, which holds that the religious ideal is the arhat or enlightened individual who, after death, will be reborn no more, having attained final nirvana, and who is not, according to the teachings of the Small Vehicle, able to grant spiritual merit to another. These two main branches of Buddhism are distinguished by many other features, an important one of which is the collections of scriptures. Great Vehicle Buddhism has vast numbers of texts claiming to be the word of the Buddha as compared to the relatively modest number of texts belonging to the Small

Vehicle. Adherents of the Small Vehicle, or Disciples' Vehicle, naturally enough do not consider their Buddhism to be a lesser teaching at all, and the Great Vehicle is something that, traditionally, they simply ignored. The one remaining Disciples' Vehicle school, the Theravāda (Way of the Elders), is prevalent in Sri Lanka, Burma, and Thailand. See, e.g., Robinson and Johnson, *Buddhist Religion,* pp. 65ff.

51. These are the Buddha, his teaching, and the monastic assemblies.

52. These five are refraining from harming any living beings, from lying, from wrong sexual conduct, from stealing, and from intoxicating substances. Robinson and Johnson, *Buddhist Religion,* pp. 59–60. Also, e.g., *Tseng i a-han ching* (Ekottarāgama), T. 2, no. 125, pp. 576–577.

53. This scripture is chap. 25 of Kumārajīva's translation of the *Lotus Flower of the Wonderful Law* (Saddharma-pundarīka-sūtra) (Miao fa lien-hua ching), T. 9, no. 262; and chap. 23 of Chu Fa-hu (Dharmaraksha), *Cheng fa hua ching* (Flower of the true law scripture), T. 9, no. 263. It is also known as the Universal Gate chapter *(P'u men p'in),* and it enjoyed wide circulation and popularity as a separate text. Chu Fa-hu's version is the one she would have had as Kumārajīva's was not translated until about half a century later. See Bibliography, *Flower of the Law Scripture.*

54. This date cannot be reconciled with the dates of Ho Ch'ung. In the biography of Hui-chan (biography 7), the date given for the nuns crossing the Yangtze River is 344.

55. Ho Ch'ung (292–346) (*Chin shu,* chap. 77). Ho Ch'ung was an upper-class influential man who promoted Buddhist interests, and he was likely a Buddhist himself. See Zürcher, *Buddhist Conquest,* p. 86, passim, especially pp. 96–97.

56. "For the first time" probably means that this is the first time since the flight of the Chinese court to the south in A.D. 317 that there were nuns in the south. Ming-kan's arrival in the south is at least a decade before Ching-chien (biography 1) was *fully* admitted to the assembly in 357 in Lo-yang. Ming-kan is treated as one who has received all the rules for a member of the Assembly of Nuns.

57. *Dharma* is a Sanskrit word that means law, or pattern, that must be followed. The Way of Buddhism, for example, is called the Buddha's Dharma. The Chinese translated the word by their word *fa,* but they also often transliterated it as *T'an-mo.* When the transliterated form was used as part of a name, as in the case of T'an-pei, the second syllable was usually dropped.

58. City of Chien-k'ang, the capital of Eastern Chin; located in present-day Chiangsu Province at Nanjing. See map. This is the first biography of a nun native to the south.

59. Emperor Mu (*Chin shu,* chap. 8; *Wei shu,* chap. 96).

60. Niece of Ho Ch'ung (see n. 55 above; biography 5). Empress Chang,

consort of Emperor Mu, had no sons (*Chin shu,*, chap. 32). She died at the age of sixty-six in A.D. 402 or 404, having survived her husband by forty-four years. She was in her early twenties when the emperor died.

61. At this time Emperor Mu was eleven years old.

62. Shākyamuni Buddha, who was born in India in the sixth century B.C., was the most recent in a very long series of Buddhas. Soper, *Literary Evidence,* p. 13, believes that such halls were intended for the seven Buddhas of the past who are Vipashyin, Shikhin, Vishvabhū, Krakucchanda, Kanakamuni, Kāshyapa, and Shākyamuni. Oda, *Bukkyō-daijiten,* 739.c–740.a.

63. The part of the sentence beginning "as proof" and ending "in times of distress" does not appear in the Chinese text. Nevertheless, this exact circumstance, i.e., one who is about to be harmed by a robber wielding a knife or staff calls on the name of the bodhisattva Kuan-yin and is kept safe from harm because the robber cannot then raise up his hands, is described in the *Flower of the Law Scripture,* the earlier translation by Chu Fa-hu (d. 310+) of the Western Chin dynasty (*T.* 9, no. 263, 129.a.11ff). The other translation of this scripture (*T.* 9, no. 262), that by Kumārajīva (d. 409 or 413), does not include the detail that the robber would be unable to raise up his hands against his victim (*T.* 9, no. 262, 56.c.16ff).

64. *Chien-yüan* reign period (344) is a more likely date than 348 given in biography 5 because Ho Ch'ung died in 346. See n. 55, above.

65. Sangha: *Seng* is the first syllable of the Chinese transliteration, *Seng-chia* (in ancient times *Seng-ka*), for the Sanskrit *Sangha,* which means the assemblies of monks and nuns. The character *seng* may also mean the individual Buddhist cleric as well as the assembly as a whole.

66. Chi-nan, in the western part of Shantung Province, Li-ch'ang County. See map.

67. Emperor K'ang (*Chin shu,* chap. 7; *Wei shu,* chap. 96).

68. Empress Ch'u (324–384) (*Chin shu,* chap. 32).

69. She was probably older. If she were only sixty-eight when she died, then she would have been fourteen years old when the consort built the convent for her, and this is not likely because the biography states specifically that she was already twenty-one when she became a nun.

70. The word *way* translates the Chinese *tao.* Although it is used frequently in these biographies to mean Buddhism, it is not always so used. Whenever the word is used, the translation will make it clear as to which particular way is meant.

71. T'ai-shan in northern China, in present-day Shantung Province. See map.

72. *Flower of the Law.* Because she was in the north, she could possibly have used Kumārajīva's translation.

73. *Vimalakīrti.* There are at least two versions she may have used: (1) *T.*

14, no. 474, by Chih-ch'ien, of Indo-Scythian background and a layman, who did his translation work from A.D. 220–252 in Nanjing. See Zürcher, *Buddhist Conquest,* pp. 48–50. (2) *T.* 14, no. 475, by Kumārajīva, a native of Kucha who worked on translating scriptures in the northwest of China during the years 385–409/413. See *Répertoire,* p. 267. The *Vimalakīrti* is about the householder bodhisattva who bests in argument all the great bodhisattvas and disciples of the Buddha. It is very congenial to Chinese literary taste. The climax of this book is silence, the method of the sage's communication.

74. Pure Talk was a type of discussion or argument both witty and arcane that was cultivated among the educated elite. More popular and more widespread than Pure Talk was the Way of the Yellow Emperor and Lao-tzu, a system of physical and mental techniques for the prolongation of life and health with the hope of attaining immortality.

75. *Smaller Perfection of Wisdom* (Ashtasāhashrikā-prajñā-pāramitā-sūtra). It is not clear exactly which text is meant. If the nun Tao-hsing died during the *t'ai-ho* reign period (366–371), the name cannot refer to Kumārajīva's translation done in 408 (*T.* 8, no. 227). The *Ch'u san-tsang chi chi* (Collected notes), a sixth-century catalogue (see appendix A) lists a translation by Chu Shih-hsing, the *Fang kuang ching,* done in 291. Seng-yu (compiler of the *Collected Notes*) appends a notice that says, "It had ninety chapters *(p'in)* and was once called the *'Old Smaller Prajñā-pāramitā.'* It is now lost." (See the *Collected Notes,* 7.b.7.) The *Collected Notes* also lists another text, *Keng ch'u hsiao p'in,* now lost with no date of translation (*Collected Notes,* 8.c.13). Again the *Collected Notes* lists a *Hsiao p'in* and the appended note says that the scripture was translated by both Kumārajīva and Dharmaraksha (Chu Fa-hu) who was in Ch'ang-an in 265–313 (*Collected Notes,* 15.a.22.) Dharmaraksha's *Kuang tsan ching* is extant (*T.* 8, no. 222). Prajñā-pāramitā means perfection of wisdom and designates a cluster of texts exploring the concept of emptiness. Its tricky logic appealed to many of the Chinese Buddhist literati.

76. A method for lengthening life. See, e.g., "Les procédés de nourrir le principe vital," pp. 470–496 in Maspero, *Le Taoïsm,* esp. p. 485. See also Ngo, *Divination,* p. 205.

77. Li-yang in present-day Anhui Province. See map.

78. Emperor Ming (*Chin shu,* chap. 6; *Wei shu,* chap. 96).

79. See introduction. It could also imply the suggestion of the Buddha seated on a lotus blossom.

80. Because Chien-wen, youngest son of Emperor Yüan (276–322–323), was never a crown prince, he is referred to merely as the future emperor. At the death of his predecessor he was chosen by a group of officials to be the emperor. Even when he was young, he was especially beloved of his father, one of whose officials had said that Chien-wen was a man capable of restoring the fortunes of the Chin dynasty. His third son and successor, Hsiao-wu,

while in a drunken stupor died by suffocation at the hands of a consort (*Chin shu*, chap. 9; *Wei shu*, chap. 96).

81. The text is ambiguous as to whether Pure Water is a place-name, for there is such a place, or is a type of Taoist practice. "Pure water" *(Ch'ing shui)* can also refer to saliva. See Maspero, *Le Taoïsme*, p. 527, n.2.

82. Ch'ü An-yüan. See *Kao seng chuan* 5:356.c.19–20; and *Chin shu*, chap. 76, where he is described as a wonder worker *(pu shu chih jen)*.

83. A common list of the eight is the five precepts described above (in n. 52), plus the sixth, refraining from applying perfume to the body, wearing adornments, watching entertainments or listening to singing; the seventh, refraining from sitting or lying on a high and wide bed; and the eighth, refraining from eating at proscribed times, i.e., after noon.

84. A Taoist way of death is to disappear and leave behind a sandal or a robe. See Maspero, *Le Taoïsme*, p. 335.

85. Kao-p'ing, in present-day Shantung Province. See map.

86. Invading nomadic tribes: lit. slaves.

87. These are the Buddha, his teaching or law, and the monastic assemblies.

88. Universal Gate chapter is also known as the Bodhisattva Kuan-shih-yin chapter, found in the *Flower of the Law Scripture*.

89. Province of Chi, in the present-day Hopei and Shansi provinces and Honan north to the Yellow River. See map.

90. Meng Ford, a crossing of the Yellow River, is a good distance west of her home and suggests that she returned by a very circuitous route. See map.

91. The white deer is an auspicious omen, often associated with Taoists. Lao-tzu is said to have ridden a white deer. (*T'ai-p'ing yü lan, chüan* 906, p. 5). The interaction between animals and people indicates the holiness of the person, or his own immortality. Tigers also often help people who are holy and sincere.

92. As on dry land. This, too, is in response to her faith and can be attributed, at least in part, to the bodhisattva Kuan-shih-yin. (See *T*. 9, no. 263, 128.c.29–129.a.l.)

93. Emperor Hsiao-wu (*Chin shu*, chap. 9; *Wei shu*, chap. 96). Third son of Emperor Chien-wen.

94. Sumeru is the central axis of the cosmos in Indian and therefore in Buddhist cosmology.

95. The text does not specifically say Amita, but he is implied because as the Buddha of Infinite Light, Amitābha, or Infinite Life, Amitāyus, he presides over the Western Paradise, a place from which it is impossible to fall again into rebirth. One who achieves birth in this paradise waits there, seated in a lotus blossom, for his final nirvana, but in the popular mind, the Western Paradise is in itself the final goal. No women come to birth in the Western Para-

dise because, if they have attained enough merit to gain such a birth, they also have attained enough merit to be born there in a male body.

96. One of the several picturesque expressions used in the Chinese Buddhist biographies to say that a person died. This expression is also Taoist, the character *ch'ien* having as one of its components the flapping of wings like a bird, and one who gets wings and can fly is an immortal. In the early Han dynasty an immortal is one who becomes a bird. See Kaltenmark's preface to his translation of *Le Lie-sien tchouan*, p. 10.

97. In the lineage of Kushanan or Indo-Scythian missionaries.

98. Grand tutor, Tao-tzu, prince of Kuei-chi (*Chin shu*, chaps. 64, 84, *passim*).

99. Wang Ch'en (d. 392). See Zürcher, *Buddhist Conquest*, p. 199; *Chin shu*, chaps. 5, 75; Liu, *Shih-shuo hsin-yü*, pp. 583–584.

100. Wang Kung (d. 398). See Zürcher, *Buddhist Conquest*, p. 151; *Chin shu*, chap. 84; Liu, *Shih-shuo hsin-yü*, p. 590.

101. Huan Hsüan (369–404). *Chin shu*, chap. 99; Liu, *Shih-shuo hsin-yü*, p. 535.

102. Yin Chung-k'an (d. 399/400) (*Chin shu*, chaps. 84, 85; Liu, *Shih-shuo hsin-yü*, p. 604).

103. The province of Ching included the territory of the ancient kingdoms of Ching and Ch'u—hence, Miao-yin's use of the two names.

104. This intrigue is corroborated in the dynastic histories. Factionalism among the powerful families of the Eastern Chin dynasty eventually destroyed the dynasty and led to the establishment of the Sung dynasty in A.D. 420. The nun Miao-yin, one of the very few nuns mentioned in official dynastic histories, obviously played a crucial role in some of the intrigues because of her access to the ears of those both within and without court circles. That a nun who meddled in worldly politics—and very sordid politics at that—was included in a collection of exemplary women seems at first glance ironic, but it merely reflects the editor's bias in favor of the famous and influential. See Liu I-ch'ing, *Shih-shuo hsin-yü* (translated by Richard Mather in *A New Account of Tales of the World*), and E. Zürcher, *Buddhist Conquest*, for clear expositions of these intrigues and their consequences. The grand tutor, Ssuma Tao-tzu, was a scheming profligate who, together with his faction, terrorized the court and others. Wang Kung's faction was in opposition to the grand tutor. The emperor, in consulting with Miao-yin, was attempting to arrange for help from Wang Kung's faction, but even within that faction there were rivalries, with Huan Hsüan fearing Wang Kung and wanting to keep his power and influence in check. Huan Hsüan therefore had asked Miao-yin to use her influence to select the new governor of Ching.

105. Within and without Buddhist circles. Miao-yin is one of the very few

Buddhist nuns mentioned in the dynastic histories; she is mentioned, e.g., in *Chin shu,* chaps. 64, 75.

106. Lou-fan, in present-day Shansi Province.

107. This famous nephew of the nun Tao-i was born in A.D. 334 and died in A.D. 416 (some records give the variants 415 and 417). His biography appears in the Chinese collection of biographies of Buddhist monks, *Kao seng chuan* 6:357.c–361.b, and has been translated by E. Zürcher in *Buddhist Conquest,* pp. 240–253. Hui-yüan contributed to the intellectual development of Buddhism in China, defended the monastic system against anticlerical officials, and is popularly credited with founding the Pure Land school of Chinese Buddhism because he led monks and laymen in making a vow to be reborn in the Western Paradise of the Buddha Amitābha. Although in fact he did not found that school, he did do much to promote the growth of the Amitābha cult in China. He was acquainted with the persons involved in the intrigue described in biography 12. Hui-yüan had a younger brother who also became a monk and who took the name of Hui-ch'ih and whose biography is also in *Kao seng chuan* 6:361.b. In Hui-ch'ih's biography we learn that it was he who brought his aunt to the capital from Chiang-hsia that lay along the western reaches of the Yangtze River.

108. Hsün-yang Commandery, in present-day Chiangsi Province, Chiuching County.

109. *Flower of the Law Scripture.* It cannot be determined with any certainty which translation was used. Chu Fa-hu worked in north China as did Kumārajīva.

110. *Vimalakīrti.* Again it cannot be determined which translation the nun would have used. Kumārajīva worked in the north and Chih Ch'ien in the south.

111. *Smaller Perfection of Wisdom (Hsiao p'in).* The abbreviation of the title to *Hsiao p'in* points to Kumārajīva's translation. *T.* 8, no. 227.

112. Without having to rely on teachers. This is possibly a divine revelation of texts. See Tsai, "Chinese Buddhist Monastic Order," p. 16 n. 51. Divine revelations of texts occurs among both the Buddhists and the Taoists. Sengyu's *Ch'u san-tsang chi chi,* p. 40.b, gives notice that a nun of Green Garden Convent (home to several of the nuns in the *Lives*) chanted "revealed" texts. These are listed in the section for "suspect" texts.

113. Empress Ho Convent, the same convent as Everlasting Peace Convent in biography 6. See also Zürcher, *Buddhist Conquest,* p. 210, and the biography of Hui-ch'ih, Hui-yüan's younger brother in *Kao seng chuan* 6:361.b.21ff.

114. Begging bowl and staff: early Buddhism required monks and nuns to rely on the goodwill of alms givers because in the very early days of Buddhism, the monks and nuns lived a truly homeless life. The Chinese nuns lived a settled life.

2. The Sung Dynasty

1. Huai-nan, in present-day Anhui Province, Hsün County. See map.

2. Buddhist monks and nuns are not allowed to wear silk because its manufacture involves the killing of silkworms.

3. Ch'ing Province, in present-day Chiangsu Province. See map.

4. Pei-ti, in present-day Shensi Province. See map.

5. T'an-tsung, contemporary with Pao-ch'ang and living in the same monastery with him. See *Kao seng chuan* 7:373.b.6.

6. Gunavarman, biography in *Kao seng chuan* 3:340.a.15; and in *Ch'u san-tsang chi chi* (Collected notes on the translation of the Buddhist scriptures into Chinese), *T.* 55, 104.b, which says essentially the same thing, and in *Fa yüan chu lin* (Forest of pearls in the garden of the law), *T.* 53, 616.c., which quotes from *Ming hsiang chi* (Records of mysterious omens), and *Fo tsu t'ung chi* (Thorough record of the Buddha's lineage), *T.* 49, 344.c. Gunavarman was a member of the royal family of the central Asian kingdom of Kashmir. He came to the southern capital of China in 431 and died there the same year.

7. Much additional material is added to this biography to clarify the discussion between Hui-kuo and Gunavarman.

8. Mountains create a barrier. See *Fa yüan chu lin* (Forest of pearls in the garden of the law), *T.* 53, 944.c.9–945.b.1.

9. This name, Hui-i, is added from the Sung, Yüan, and Ming editions.

10. Sanghavarman, biographies in *Kao seng chuan* 3:342.b, and in *Ch'u san-tsang chi chi,* 104.c. He arrived in the southern capital in 433 and returned to the west, presumably to his homeland of India, in 442. The date of his arrival and the date of the nuns' reception of the full monastic obligation in 432 obviously do not match. Biography 27 says that this event took place in the year 433. Biography 34 says 434. All agree that the monk Sanghavarman performed the ceremony. In *Fo tsu t'ung chi* (Thorough record of the Buddha's lineage) by Chih-p'an (1258–1269), *T.* 49, no. 2035, 344.c.11–12 is a reference to Sanghavarman readministering the full obligation to the nuns on a raft or a boat in the tenth year of the *yüan-chia* (433) reign period. This statement is repeated (*T.* 49, no. 2035, 462.c.14–15).

11. Ch'ing-ho, in present-day Hopei Province, Ch'ing-ho County. See map.

12. Chin-ling, present-day Nanjing, the capital of the Sung dynasty. See map.

13. This is the first use of the title, master of the law, in the biographies of the nuns.

14. The name Amita Buddha is implied but not specifically stated in the biography.

15. Western Paradise, the abode of Amita Buddha. There is also the Eastern Paradise of Buddha Akshobhya.

16. *Tathāgata* is the Sanskrit word that the Chinese translated as *ju-lai* (thus come) as the former Buddhas had come. It is an epithet of the Buddha. This sentence has been expanded in the translation to include the names of the Buddha and the two bodhisattvas who attend him. After Amita Buddha enters final nirvana, Kuan-shih-yin (Avalokiteshvara) will become the next Amita Buddha, and after his entry into final nirvana, Ta-shih-chih (Mahāsthama-prāpta) will become Amita Buddha. The devotional Buddhism that eventually flowered into the Pure Land school has its roots in these early years. See *Infinite Life Scripture (Wu liang shou ching) (Sukhāvatīvyūha)* T. 12, no. 360, 273.a.–274.bff.

17. See chapter 1, n. 50, in biography 5.

18. Yü-chang, in present-day Chiangsi Province, Nan-ch'ang County.

19. Chang Pien, *Kao seng chuan* 12:405.a.24; *Sung shu,* chap. 53.

20. Wu Commandery, in present-day southeastern part of Chiangsu Province, Wu County. See map.

21. Chiang-ling, in present-day Hupei Province, Chiang-ling County.

22. *Flower of the Law Scripture;* see n. 63 on the translation, "as proof of the power," in chapter 1, biography 7: Hui-chan.

23. *Shūrangama[-samādi-]Scripture* (Shou-leng-yen san-mei ching) T. 15, no. 642, translated by Kumārajīva.

24. Another example of speed chanting, a mark of singularity.

25. Western Shan, following the Sung, Yüan, and Ming editions.

26. The six prohibitions are against killing, stealing, sexual misconduct, false speech, intoxication, and pointing out the faults of anyone in the four groups: monks, nuns, laymen, and laywomen.

27. The traditional classics and histories written or compiled mostly by Confucian scholars.

28. The empress during 376–396, the reign of Emperor Hsiao-wu of Chin. One empress died in 380 at age 21. The empress dowager died in 402, after the death of Emperor Hsiao-wu of Chin in 396. We do not know to which empress the biography is referring.

29. In Great Vehicle Buddhism, with its doctrine of bodhisatttvas who work to save all beings, the idea of transferable merit arose. The bodhisattvas can give merit to devotees. Devotees can gain merit for themselves as well, but it is more meritorious to gain merit for all living creatures. In this case, the empress is gaining merit for herself probably so that she might be reborn into a better life, or into one of the heavens or paradises.

30. The four monasteries or convents were all located in the capital. The Pottery Office Monstery was very prominent, having been founded by Emperor Ai of Chin (see *Fa yüan chu lin* [Forest of pearls in the garden of the law], T. 49, no. 2035, p. 463.c.1.). Establishing Blessings Convent was the home of six of the nuns in the *Lives.*

31. The Buddha entering nirvana.

32. This mark, a tuft of white hair curled clockwise that frequently emits a light, is one of the thirty-two marks of a great, holy man such as the Buddha. That the statue, too, emitted such a light was indeed cause for amazement and joy.

33. Yüan empress consort during the Sung dynasty, otherwise unknown.

34. This convent is named after the Jeta Grove given to the Buddha by a wealthy devotee to use as the site of a monastery.

35. Chanted the *Flower of the Law* three thousand times. Kumārajīva's version in the *Taishō* edition has sixty-two pages, and Chu Fa-hu's seventy. Considering the length of the text, it could have taken her eight years, nonstop, one second per word to chant the *Flower of the Law* three thousand times.

36. This suggests that she was to be compared with the Buddha.

37. Lu An-hsün. A textual note within the biography adds that the book *Hsüan yen chi* (Records of encompassing examination) says, "This is An Hsün." Lu Hsün in *Ku hsiao-shuo kou ch'en* (A study of ancient fiction) 2:436, also records this tale in which it is An-hsün himself who is cured, rather than his daughter. The best evidence that it is the story of a nun is (1) that it appears in the *Lives;* (2) that the same convent is home to another nun (biography 29) in the *Lives;* and (3) that Lu Hsün himself, in an appended note, refers to the textual note in the *Lives.* The book *Hsüan yen chi* is now lost.

38. The Three Treasures are the Buddha, his teaching, and the monastic assemblies.

39. See introduction. It is interesting to note the eclectic nature of Buddhist worship at this time.

40. Tushita Heaven, presided over by Maitreya, the next Buddha, is a temporary location for those born there because they are subject to rebirth on earth as soon as their stock of good merit has been exhausted. The hope is to be reborn on earth from that heaven at the same time that Maitreya is born on earth as the Buddha.

41. Literally, "It is not known where she went." This is frequently the Taoist description of death.

42. Kuang Province, in present-day Kuangchou. See map.

43. See n. 2 above. In the Confucian tradition one of the indications of a peaceful and well-ordered country is that the aged have meat to eat and silk to wear. See *Mencius,* chapter 1, sections 3 and 7 (pp. 52, 57).

44. Kuang-ling, in Chiangsu Province, Chiang-tu County. See map.

45. *Sung shu,* chap. 61.

46. Prince of Chiang-hsia (*Sung shu,* chap. 61; *Nan shih,* chap. 13).

47. Founder of the Sung dynasty, Emperor Wu (*Sung shu,* chaps. 1–3; *Nan shih,* chap. 1).

48. Hsiao Ch'eng-chih (*Sung shu,* chap. 78 in biography of Hsiao Ssu-hua).

49. Lan-ling in present-day Chiangsu Province, Wu-chin County.

50. Hui-chih, not known in the *Kao seng chuan,* but whose name is found in the table of contents of the *Ming seng chuan* (Lives of famous monks) (about which see appendix A).

51. Twenty-fourth year–date according to Sung, Yüan, and Ming editions.

52. Meng I, prefect of Mou-hsien in present-day Chechiang (*Sung shu,* chap. 66; *Nan shih,* chap. 19; *Chin shu,* chap. 96; *Kao seng chuan,* 13:410.a.5).

53. Kuei-chi, in present-day Chechiang Province, Tai-wu County. See map.

54. During the time that Buddhism was being introduced into China this method of disposing of a corpse was totally repugnant to Chinese sensibilities and contrary to all tradition.

55. Chü-jung County, in present-day Chiangsu Province, Chü-jung County. See map.

56. Mummification, see introduction.

57. Eminent Dais Monastery, in the capital.

58. Perhaps reflecting the origin of the pagoda as a shrine for the relics of the Buddha.

59. P'o-hai, in present-day Hopei Province, Nan-pi County. See map.

60. Kuang-ling, in Chiangsu Province. See map.

61. *Flower of the Law Scripture.* By this time it is possible that Kumāra-jīva's translation was available.

62. At the rate of three scrolls a day. Another example of rapid chanting as a mark of spiritual eminence.

63. The theme of dying and reviving is a classical theme as well as a Buddhist one. It is also pre-Taoist. See de Groot, *Religious Systems* 1:241–245.

64. Liang Commandery, in present-day Chiangsu Province, Tang-shan County. See map.

65. *Larger Perfection of Wisdom:* this scripture is called the *Ta-p'in* in the *Lives.* Therefore it is possibly Kumārajīva'a translation, the *Mo-ho-pan-jo po-lo-mi ching* or *Mahā-prajñāpāramitā-sūtra,* also known as the *Ta-p'in.* See *Répertoire,* p. 33.

66. This scripture, too, was read with amazing speed. She would have had to recite twenty thousand words per day, or approximately 833 per hour.

67. This implies that she transgressed the rule of not eating meat. The alternate biography (22a), however, says that she transgressed the rule of not eating after noon.

68. The Dharmaguptaka sect was one of four Disciples' Vehicle sects whose books of monastic rules were being translated into Chinese at this time. The texts of monastic rules were not translated so quickly as the scriptures, or Buddha word, and, as a result, sound organizational foundation for the

monastic institutions was delayed for several centuries after the first appearance of Buddhism in China.

69. *Dharmaguptaka Monastic Rules in Four Divisions;* and *Rituals for Entering Monastic Life.* The exact text of the *Dharmaguptaka Vinaya* used by the nuns cannot be pinpointed with certainty. See *Répertoire,* p. 122; *Ssu fen pi-ch'iu-ni chieh pen,* trans. Buddhayashas, *T.* 22, no. 1431; and *Ssu fen pi-ch'iu-ni chieh-mo fa,* trans. Gunavarman, *T.* 22, no. 1434.

70. *Ming hsiang chi* (Records of mysterious omens). Collected fragments are found in Lu Hsün, *Ku hsiao-shuo kou ch'en* (A study of ancient fiction), taken from the book *Ming hsiang chi* (Records of mysterious omens), by Wang Yen, late fifth century, now lost except for the fragments.

71. He has not seen or heard any evidence indicating her spiritual accomplishments.

72. "Origins are unknown." We have added this phrase from the Sung, Yüan, and Ming editions without eliminating the original reading.

73. Wu County, in present-day Chiangsu Province, Wu County. See map.

74. Assembly. The word can also be interpreted to mean, "everyone."

75. Ho-nei, present-day Honan Province, Ch'in-yang County.

76. P'i-ling, in present-day Chiangsu Province, Wu-chin County.

77. The implication here is that they are preparing to offer her honor and worship because she is soon to become either a bodhisattva or a Buddha.

78. *Bodhisattva Kuan-shih-yin Scripture.* See chapter 1, n. 53, for biography 5.

79. *Great Nirvāna Scripture, T.* 12, probably one of the three listed as no. 374, trans. T'an-wu-ch'an; no. 375, trans. Hui-yen; or no. 376 trans. Fa-hsien. See *Répertoire,* p. 47.

80. Assuming that she chants twenty-four hours per day, she is chanting at the rate of 7.5 words per second.

81. Wu-hsing Commandery, in present-day Chechiang Province, Wu-hsing County. See map.

82. Eating only pine resin. See introduction.

83. His biography, *Kao seng chuan* 9:399.a, says that Fa-ch'eng himself gave up eating the five grains and instead lived on a diet of pine resin.

84. Here we have followed the Sung, Yüan, and Ming editions. The main edition reads, "eighteenth day."

85. Fan County, in present-day Ssuch'uan. See map.

86. First fruit: *srotāpanna-phala,* entering the stream toward bodhisattva- and Buddhahood, therefore no longer reborn in the lower destinies of hell, hungry ghosts, or animals.

87. Chi Commandery. See map.

88. Another example of both karma and holiness.

89. As lifeless as dry wood: this type of meditation in which one is insensi-

ble to the world was condemned as inferior by others in the Chinese Buddhist tradition who said that it was the "trance of cessation" of the Disciples' Vehicle, but Pao-ch'ang seems to have approved of it. See Seng-chao's *Chu wei-mo-chieh ching* (Commentary to the Vimalakīrti scripture) *T.* 38:344.c.

90. Nan-t'i, the Sri Lankan boat captain also mentioned in the biography of Gunavarman in *Kao seng chuan.*

91. This paragraph is here attributed to the nuns from Sri Lanka. There is nothing in the text itself, however, to indicate a change of speaker at this point, and it is not impossible that the quotation should be continued as part of Seng-kuo's previous speech. From the biography of the nun Hui-kuo (biography 14), we know that the Chinese nuns had a general understanding of the problem, so one may imagine that Seng-kuo herself also understood the problem and is restating it. The following sentence beginning "Although Seng-kuo agreed . . ." is sufficiently ambiguous that one may not use it to make a categorical decision about the identity of the speaker of the previous paragraph. It is also possible that the long quotation here attributed to the nuns from Sri Lanka should be broken off from Seng-kuo's first speech at some other point that the one chosen here.

92. Eight special prohibitions: First, a nun, even if she has one hundred years' seniority, must pay respects and offer a seat to a monk, even if he is newly received into the monastic life. Second, a nun is never to curse or slander a monk. Third, a nun is never to speak of a monk's transgressions, but a monk may speak of hers. Fourth, a novice, after having trained in the six precepts of a novice, must receive all the monastic precepts from the monks. Fifth, if a nun has transgressed any of the monastic rules, she must make her confession at the semimonthly confession ceremony in front of both assemblies, i.e., of monks and of nuns. Sixth, a nun must seek out an instructor in the precepts from among the monks every half month. Seventh, a nun must not spend the summer retreat in the same location as the monks. Eighth, after the summer retreat a nun must find a confessor from among the monks (Horner, *Women,* pp. 119–120; *Cullavagga,* X, I, 4, no. 6).

The Buddha himself said that, if women had not entered the homeless life, the True Law would have lasted a thousand years, but because they had, the True Law would last only five hundred years. The Buddhists say that there are three ages of Buddhism, that of the True Law lasting five hundred years, the Counterfeit Law lasting five hundred or a thousand years (depending on the sources), and the age of decay and dissolution lasting ten thousand years. Buddhist tradition holds Ānanda, a cousin and disciple of the Buddha, responsible for persuading the Buddha to allow women to enter the homeless life. Ānanda, a very likable figure, was held responsible for many of the internal problems or quarrels that beset Buddhism from the first. Another of Ānanda's supposed failures is that, when the Buddha told him that he, the Buddha, could, by his magic powers, remain alive for innumerable years, Ānanda did not request him to do so. Therefore, the Buddha died. Yet another of Ānanda's faults is that after the death of the Buddha, Ānanda showed the Buddha's concealed penis to women. (One of the thirty-two marks of a great holy man is that his penis is concealed within a sheath like that of a horse.) Ānanda defended his action saying that he did it in the hope that the women would therefore be ashamed of their own female body and would aspire to attain a masculine body in a future rebirth. Because Ānanda is often contrasted unfavorably with another of the Buddha's disciples, one must suspect sectarian rivalries among followers of the Buddha. (*Ta chih tu lun* [Great perfection of wisdom commentary]) *T.* 25, no. 1059, and the French translation by Lamotte, *Traité* 1:96–97.)

93. Gunavarman, lit. *San-tsang* (three baskets) of Buddhism: doctrine, commentary, and monastic rules. *San-tsang* is used as an address of honor. Gunavarman arrived in the southern capital in 431 and died there the same year. See *Répertoire*, p. 252. Biography in *Kao seng chuan* 3:340.a.ff; and *Ch'u san-tsang chi chi* (Collected notes on the translation of the Buddhist scriptures into Chinese), 104.b.11ff.

94. This is a tentative reading for the Chinese transcription *T'ieh-sa-lo.* Another possible choice is *Dewasara.*

95. Sanghavarman arrived in the southern capital in 433 (or 423) and worked until 442 when he returned to the west. See *Répertoire,* p. 281. Biography in *Kao seng chuan* 3:342.b; and in *Ch'u san-tsang chi chi* (Collected notes), 104.c.5.

96. This type of meditation in which one is insensible to the world was criticized as inferior by others in the Chinese Buddhist tradition who said that it was the trance of cessation of the Disciples' Vehicle, but Pao-ch'ang seems to have approved of it. See Seng-chao's *Chu wei-mo-chieh ching* (Commentary to the Vimalakīrti scripture), *T.* 38:344.c. See Biographies 27, 29, and 31. This type of trance was approved by the Taoists. See Watson, *Complete Works of Chuang Tzu,* pp. 36 (ch.2), 116 (ch.11), and 237 (ch.22).

97. Ch'iao Commandery, in present-day Anhui Province. See map.

98. Po-p'ing, there are two possible locations. See map for both.

99. See *Lun yü,* chap. 14; and Confucius, *The Analects,* p. 124; and *The Analects of Confucius,* p. 180.

100. Tun-huang, an important town along the Silk Road, in present-day Kansu. See map.

101. Fuh clan, spelled *Fuh* to distinguish from the Fu of Fu Chien. They are two different characters.

102. Fu Chien lost an important battle in 383 when he tried to invade the territory of Eastern Chin. He was strangled to death in 385 by a rival (Rogers, *Chronicle of Fu Chien,* p. 190; *Chin shu,* chaps. 113–114; *Wei shu,* chap. 95).

103. See introduction and biographies 27 and 31.

104. Emperor Wu of Sung (363–420–422) (*Sung shu,* chaps. 1–3; *Nan shih,* chap. 1).

105. Emperor Wen of Sung (407–424–453) (*Sung shu,* chap. 5; *Nan shih,* chap. 2).

106. The Three Refuges are the Buddha, his teaching, and the monastic assemblies.

107. Wang T'an-chih (330–375), an important lay Buddhist during the Southern dynasties (biography in *Chin shu,* chap. 7). Wang Ching-shen was perhaps a distant relative or descendent of Wang T'an-chih.

108. Such as onions and garlic, prohibited by the monastic rules. For example, the *Mi-sha-se pu ho hsi wu fen lü (Mahīshāsaka-vinaya),* T. 22, no. 1421, 86.c.7ff and 176.a.11ff.

109. Yü, Lang-yeh prince, governor of Yang Province. No biography in the dynastic histories.

110. Kālayashas (biography in *Kao seng chuan* 3:343.c). He was known for his prowess in meditation because every time he sat down in contemplation he remained there for a week.

111. Ch'ao-pien (biography in *Kao seng chuan* 12:408.b). The second character of the name is supplied by the Sung, Yüan, and Ming editions.

112. The six perfections are the six practices that are to be perfected by the individual aspiring to supreme, perfect enlightenment. They are (1) charity or donation; (2) morality; (3) patience or forbearance; (4) vigor, energy, or diligence; (5) concentration or meditation; and (6) wisdom or insight. The six are supposed to be cultivated simultaneously. See Robinson and Johnson, *Buddhist Religion,* pp. 77–78.

113. Appointed court scholar of Sung, Liu Ch'iu: Liu Ch'iu was appointed court scholar in the year 495, during the Ch'i dynasty but did not serve and died later that year. He was twenty-five years old when Tao-tsang died. It is possible that he composed his verse in her praise many years after her death. He withdrew from society and quit eating cereals; he fed himself on hemp and sesame alone. He also revered the Buddhist Way and wrote a commentary to the *Flower of the Law Scripture* (biography in *Nan ch'i shu,* chap. 54; and *Nan shih,* chap. 50).

114. Behavior forbidden by monastic rules. See *Ssu fen lü* (Dharmaguptaka-vinaya), T. 22:925.c.3.

115. Chiang-hsia prince, I-kung (413–465), fifth son of Emperor Wu (biography in *Sung shu,* chap. 61; and *Nan shih,* chap. 13).

116. [Seng-]hua. The first syllable taken from the Sung, Yüan, and Ming editions.

117. Ch'en Commandery, in present-day Honan Province, Hsiang-ch'eng County. See map.

118. Mourning period. The woman was carrying out the Chinese mourn-

ing ritual, but her observance was extreme and included some unusual elements, such as giving up cereals and eating only arrowroot and taro, a practice that indicates Taoist influence. See Thompson, *Chinese Religion,* pp. 51–52, quoting the *I Li* (Ceremonial and ritual), and *Lun yü* (Analects).

119. Emperor Wen, third son of the founder of the dynasty, Emperor Wu (biography in *Sung shu,* chap. 5; and *Nan shih,* chap. 2).

120. Hsiao-wu, third son of Emperor Wen (biography in *Sung shu,* chap. 6; and *Nan shih,* chap. 2).

121. Emperor Ming, eleventh son of Emperor Wen (biography in *Sung shu,* chap. 8; and *Nan shih,* chap. 3).

122. The office of the rector of the assembly originated in China during the Yao Ch'in dynasty (384–417) for the purpose of controlling the monastic assemblies that had by then grown to considerable size. Pao-hsien would have been in charge of the Assembly of Nuns only. See *Ta sung seng shih lüeh* (Great Sung dynasty compact history of the Buddhist assemblies), *T.* 54, no. 2126, 242.c.14–243.a.12–18.

123. Gunavarman; see biographies 14, 27.

124. Tessara; see biographies 14, 27.

125. Sanghavarman; see biographies 14, 27.

126. Fa-ying, reversing the characters *lü* and *ying* in the text. Fa-ying has a biography in *Kao seng chuan* 11:402.a. After he had come to the Sung capital from the far northwest he became so well known for his expertise in monastic rules and organization that he was named the rector of the assembly of the capital by the Emperor Hsiao-wu, a position that he later resigned. He is recorded as having edited the text of monastic rules about which he gave the lecture mentioned above.

127. *Sarvāstivāda Monastic Rules in Ten Recitations.* The Sarvāstivāda is one of the Disciples' Vehicle sects whose texts of monastic rules were being translated into Chinese during the fifth century. See *Répertoire,* pp. 123–124; and *T.* 23.

128. Emperor Ming. See chap. 2 n. 121, biography 34.

129. The director of conventual affairs or precentor was in charge of the routines of the convent. Only the Assembly of Nuns was under Fa-ching's authority.

130. These are the Buddha, his teaching, and the assemblies of monks and nuns.

131. Liu Liang, governor of I Province in western China, the territory of Shu, died in 472 after eating Taoist medicines of immortality and was afterward seen riding a white horse going off to the west. In other words, he became a Taoist immortal (*Sung shu,* chap. 5; *Nan shih,* chap. 2).

132. The Lantern Festival is a Buddhist festival of Chinese origin. Accord-

ing to tradition, when Buddhism first came to China, there was a trial with the Taoists and other worshippers who offered sacrifices to local gods. The scriptures of the Buddhists and Taoists were placed on two separate altars and the offerings to the spirits placed on a third. All were set on fire, but only the Buddhist scriptures were not consumed. The date for this trial was the fifteenth day of the first month, and every year afterward the people would light lamps to honor the light of the Buddha's teaching. See *Fo tsu t'ung chi,* p. 318.c.25–29; *Ta sung seng shih lüeh,* p. 254.b–c (which gives the *Han fa nei pen chuan* as its source); *Kuang hung ming chi,* 98.c.–99.b; and others. It would not be surprising that the *Han fa nei pen chuan* were the source of all subsequent versions. For a description of this festival during T'ang times, see *Ennin's Diary,* pp. 71–73.

This contest reminds one of the contest between the prophet Elijah and the priests of Baal (I Kings 18:31–39).

133. *Sharīra* are little pellets thought to be found in the ashes of holy persons who have been cremated. The holier the person, the more *sharīra* will be found. Most Chinese Buddhists, however, were not cremated. Relics of the Buddha himself are found throughout the Buddhist world, similar to the widespread distribution of the relics of the True Cross throughout the Christian world.

3. The Ch'i Dynasty

1. Tung-kuan, Tseng-ch'eng in present-day Kuangtung Province. See map.

2. Full-moon day, see introduction on phases of the moon.

3. See biography 36, chap. 2 n. 132, on Lantern Festival.

4. Kuei-chi, in present-day Chiangsu Province. See map.

5. Eight precepts of the householder; see biography 10, chap. 1 n. 83.

6. Ling-nan, the general region of the two Kuang provinces.

7. Ch'ao-t'ing, in present-day Kuangtung Province.

8. Emperor Ming; see biography 34, chap. 2 n. 121.

9. Tan-yang, the immediate vicinity of the capital.

10. Emperor Wen-hui (of Ch'i) (biography in *Nan ch'i shu,* chap. 21; and *Nan shih,* chaps. 5, 44); and Prince of Ching-ling, Wen-hsüan Wang (biography in *Nan Ch'i shu,* chap. 40; and *Nan shih,* chaps. 5, 44).

11. Northeast of the capital, the present city of Nanjing. It was a famous and thriving center of Buddhism and the site of many temples.

12. Shen Yüeh (441–513); see appendix A, notes.

13. Although an inscription written by Shen Yüeh in honor of this nun is not found in her biography, one is found in another collection, the *Ku chin t'u shu chi ch'eng* (Complete collection of records ancient and modern), vol. 506. It reads,

She left a legacy in words and the Way,
    in standards of affection and wonderful enlightenment.
She dismissed thought to rely upon emptiness,
    and trained her mind to complete her study.
Days, endless days;
    years, faraway years;
The wind shifts, the lightning flickers,
    but the principle of change does not waver.
In spirit she reached a distinguished goal;
    in form she died the same as all.
At the time of her death we joined in bitter mourning,
    in sorrow that the light is gone.
And among the stately pines, whirlwinds overturn parasols;
    among the majestic mountains storms fling aside cloaks.
I inscribe a record of her chaste rule, seeking to make
    known this remarkable nun.

14. Nan-yang, in present-day Honan Province, Teng County. See map.

15. Yen-kuan, in present-day Chechiang Province, Hai-ning County. See map.

16. Yü-hang, in present-day Chechiang Province, Yü-hang County.

17. The text says specifically that she died rather than merely fainted or went into a coma.

18. If her age at death and the date of death are correct, then she was fifteen when she left home to become a nun.

19. Chang Tai (413–483), made governor of I Province (present-day Ssu-ch'uan Province) about 475, held the post for four years, and served in other offices afterward (biography in *Nan Ch'i shu,* chap. 32; and *Nan shih,* chap. 31).

20. The dwelling place of the immortals is one of the names referring to Deer Park where the Buddha first turned the Wheel of the Law. See Mochizuki, *Bukkyō-daijiten* 5:5079.a.

21. Concourse with animals is not unique to Buddhism but is a characteristic of shamans and holy men of all traditions.

22. Chinese Buddhist writings often use the term *great conversion* to refer to the teachings of the Buddha.

23. This is the teaching that the external world consists only of dharma marks or the defining characteristics of dharmas, the elements of the universe.

24. Emperor Wu of Ch'i (*Nan Ch'i shu,* chap. 3; *Nan shih,* chap. 4).

25. *Shrīmālā-devī-simhanāda-sūtra* (Sheng-man shih-tzu hou i sheng ta fang pien fang kuang ching), or *The Lion's Roar of Queen Śrīmālā, T.* 12, no.

353, by Gunabadhra, who worked in the south 443–468. See *Répertoire.* Also see bibliography for reference to translation into English.

26. *Vimalakīrti's Preaching Scripture.* See biography 9, chap. 1 n. 73.

27. Wen-hsüan of Ch'i (*Nan Ch'i shu,* chap. 40; *Nan shih,* chap. 44).

28. Wang Lun (in biography of Wang Yü-chih in *Nan Ch'i* shu, chap. 32; *Nan shih,* chap. 24).

29. The text literally says "the four classes of society." These are, in descending order of importance in the traditional view, the gentry, including officials and scholars; peasants; artisans; and merchants.

30. *Great Final Nirvāna Scripture* (Ta pan nieh-p'an ching) (Mahāparinirvāna-sūtra), *T.* 12, nos. 374, 375, 376. See *Répertoire,* p. 47. The nun could have used any one of these three versions. A fourth version is a much later translation. The *Nirvāna Scripture* is not a short text.

31. This is the only mention of a nun writing commentaries.

32. Seng-tsung (438–496) (biography in *Kao seng chuan* 8:379.c); and T'an-pin (d. 473/477) (biography in *Kao seng chuan* 8:373.a–b); Hsüan-ch'ü (subbiography in *Kao seng chuan* 8:375.c).

33. Wen-hui; see biography 39, chap. 3 n. 10.

34. Wen-hsüan; see biography 39, chap. 3 n. 10.

35. In the developed doctrine of the Great Vehicle, there are ten fundamental bodhisattva precepts: abstention from killing or harming living beings; from theft or taking what is not given; from engaging in illicit sensual pleasures; from telling lies; from slander and gossip; from harsh speech; from frivolous and senseless talk; from covetousness; from ill will and malice; and from wrong views or heretical opinions. Four of the ten concern misuse of speech.

36. Seng-yüan, biography in *Kao seng chuan* 8:377.c.8.

37. Brought forth a response to her holiness, see introduction, about devotion to Kuan-yin or other Buddhist deities.

38. According to Buddhist tradition, Pindola, one of the Buddha's disciples, exhibited his supernatural powers, acquired as a result of meditation, in front of non-Buddhists. It is an offense against the discipline to exhibit one's supernatural powers, and as a punishment the Buddha ordered him to refrain from entering nirvana so that he could provide a field of merit for those who would live during the last degenerate age of Buddhism. The cult of Pindola flourished in China, and in some instances is associated with the cult of Maitreya, the next Buddha, and his heaven, Tushita. See Lévi and Chavannes, "Les seize arhat," pp. 250ff, 267–268ff; *Fa yüan chu lin* (Forest of pearls in the garden of the law), pp. 609.c.6–611.a.14, 610.b.17; *Ching pin-t'ou-lu fa ching* (Method for inviting Pindola) *T.* 32, no. 1689, 784.c.7–8; T'ang, *Han wei liang-chin nan-pei-ch'ao fo-chiao shih,* p. 219.

39. This was either a supernatural manifestation or a very old, white scar

left from burning the character onto the skin. A photograph of a monk with a freshly burned character for Buddha on his chest appears in Prip-Møller, *Chinese Buddhist Monasteries,* p. 322.

40. Barbarians, probably the T'o-pa Wei.

41. The phrase "as the *Classic of History* says" does not specifically appear in the text. Chinese writings are full of allusions to the classics whose contents became a stock source for phrases and sentences, much as the King James Version of the Bible and the works of Shakespeare are now stock sources for the English language. The reference has been added in the translation simply to point out a little more explicitly to the English-speaking reader that the indigenous tradition underlies much of this Buddhist material. The quotation comes from the *Classic of History,* part 5, *The Books of Chou,* book 1, "The Great Declaration," part 2, where the complete quotation is "I have heard that for the good man doing good, one day is not enough; and for the wicked man doing evil, one day is also not enough."

42. Fa-yin and Seng-shen. Fa-yin has no separate biography but is mentioned in the table of contents to *Kao seng chuan* as appearing in the biography of Seng-shen, whose biography is in *Kao seng chuan* 9:399.c. In fact, Fa-yin's name does not appear in Seng-shen's biography and perhaps has accidently been dropped out at some point in the transmission of the text. Both monks appear in the table of contents to the *Meisōden-shō* (Ming seng chuan ch'ao) of Pao-ch'ang but are not extant.

43. Wen-hsüan. See biography 39, chap. 3 n. 10.

44. Seng-tsung and Fa-yüan. See biography 42 for Seng-tsung. The text does not supply the full name of the monks. Although this is common practice, it nevertheless sometimes creates ambiguity, and this is true in the case of the monk Yüan who is tentatively identified as Fa-yüan whose biography appears in *Kao seng chuan* 8:376.c.

45. Seng-shen and Fa-yin. See biography 43, n. 42.

46. Samantabhadra (universal sage) is the name of a great bodhisattva who appears in the *Flower of the Law Scripture* and who is depicted as riding on a six-tusked white elephant.

47. T'an-ch'i and Fa-yüan. The title masters of exegesis does not appear in the biography. The two monks are classed in that category in *Kao seng chuan.* Fa-yüan is the same monk as mentioned in biography 44. T'an-chi is mentioned briefly in the biography of T'an-pin in *Kao seng chuan* 7:373.b.6; and also has a partially extant biography in Pao-ch'ang's *Meisōden-shō* (Ming seng chuan ch'ao).

48. Wen-hui and Wen-hsüan; see above, biography 39, chap. 3 n. 10.

49. *Vimalakīrti,* see biography 9, chap. 1 n. 73.

50. Ch'ing-ho, present-day Hopei Province, Ch'ing-ho county. See map.

51. This is probably not the same nun as in biography 35.

52. Huai River; see map.

53. Hui-ming (d. ca. 498). He may or may not be the same Hui-ming in *Kao seng chuan* 11:400.b.4.

54. Wen-hui and Wen-hsüan; see above, biography 39, chap. 3 n. 10.

55. This is probably the White Mountain that was close to the capital Chien-k'ang.

56. The text says eighteenth night, but this is most likely an error because the woman who is the subject of biography 47 also burned herself alive at the same time as T'an-chien, and her biography says the eighth night, and also because the numinous or spiritually propitious night for the act would be the eighth and not the eighteenth. See introduction.

57. Chin-ling, in present-day Chiangsu Province, Wu-chin County. See map.

58. Reading *Sheng* in conformity with the Sung, Yüan, and Ming editions. These are the ways of (1) the arhat or hearer, who gains enlightenment after hearing the Buddhist teaching preached; (2) the solitary Buddha who becomes a Buddha through his own efforts without hearing the teaching from others; and (3) the bodhisattva who follows the bodhisattva path and use his accomplishments to teach and to help others.

59. Lü-ch'iu district, in present-day Shantung Province, Chin-hsiang County. See map.

60. Ching Province, generally including present-day Hupei, Honan, and Shensi provinces.

61. Chiang-ling, see map.

62. Visualizing the Buddha in one's presence: literally reads *pan-chou* (san-mei ching), or *Pratyutpanna-samādhi-sūtra* (The practice of constant meditation scripture), *T.* 13, no. 418. It describes a ninety-day ceaseless practice. See also *T.* 13, nos. 417, 419. The summer of austerities of mind and body could refer to this ninety-day practice. The text had been translated at a very early date, sometime between A.D. 167 and 186. See Oda, *Bukkyō-daijiten,* p. 1435 and Mochizuki, *Bukkyō-daijiten,* pp. 2569, 4215.

63. Shen Yu-chih (*Sung chu,* chap. 74; *Nan Shih,* chap. 37).

64. Wang Hsiao-i (*Nan ch'i shu,* chap. 22; *Nan shih,* chap. 42).

65. Provinces of Ching and Shan, included the general region of Hupei, Honan, and the central portion of Shensi.

66. They are food, clothing, bedding, and medicine or, shelter, clothing, food, and medicine.

67. Master of Meditation Hsüan-ch'ang. His biography is in *Kao seng chuan* 8:377.a. No dates for his birth or death are recorded. He was a soothsayer and magician, among other things.

68. Literally *a-li,* a transliteration of the Sanskrit word *ārya,* meaning "sage" or "wise one."

69. Spells, or *dhāranī*, were not to harm or help someone but were for developing, within the practice of meditation, a supernatural power for retaining the good effects of the practice, such as never forgetting any of the Buddhist teachings that were once learned.

70. Despite the same last name, there is no reason to assume that the nun and the scholar were related.

71. Ch'ien-t'ang, in present-day Chechiang Province, Hang Chou city. See map.

72. The five classics are the *Book of Changes, Book of Odes, Book of History, Book of Rites,* and *Spring and Autumn Annals.*

73. Mud Mountain. T'u Shan in Chechiang Province, Shao-hsing County.

74. Hui-chi (biography in *Kao seng chuan* 8:379.a). When he was a young man just freshly received into the monastic community, he became a peripatetic scholar, traveling around to inquire of various masters the meanings of the many Buddhist scriptures. Later, he was famous in his own right for his knowledge of the scriptures.

75. Chinese Buddhists traditionally accepted either the eighth or the fifteenth day of the second month as the day of the Buddha's final nirvana. Also see introduction.

76. P'i-ling, in southern Chiangsu Province, Wu-chin County.

77. Sun Yü, perhaps the Sun Yü mentioned in *Chin shu,* chap. 20.

78. Yü Province, covered the present-day territory of Anhui Province, western section, and the eastern section of Honan Province.

79. Nun Kuang—not the same person as in biography 25.

80. Emperor Wen of the Sung dynasty. See biography 34, chap. 2 n. 119.

81. Gunavarman. See biography 14, chap. 2 n. 6.

82. I-k'ang. The prince was not named as the grand general until the sixteenth year of *yüan-chia* (439), but in traditional Chinese biographical writing the usual practice was to refer to individuals by their latest or highest titles, regardless of anachronisms (*Sung shu,* chap. 68; *Nan shih,* chap. 13).

83. Kingdom Convent, read *kuo* in place of *yüan* from the Sung, Yüan, and Ming editions and in conformity with the reading in *Sung shu,* chap. 69.

84. Sanghavarman; see biography 14, chap. 2 n. 10.

85. The nuns T'an-lan and Fa-ching were involved in a political intrigue. Fa-ching is mentioned in *Sung shu,* chap. 69, because of the intrigues.

86. K'ung Hsi-hsien, son of K'ung Mo-chih. K'ung Hsi-hsien, his fellow conspirators, and many members of his family were executed in the twenty-second year of the *yüan-chia* (445). The punishment of a criminal usually meant punishment of the whole family (*Sung shu,* chaps. 69, 93; *Nan shih,* chap. 33).

87. Yen region, in present-day Chechiang Province, Sheng County.

88. Ch'en-liu, in present-day Honan Province, Ch'en-liu County. See map.

89. A textual variant reads Prospering of Ch'i Convent, but from biography 65 we know that the name of the convent was Brightness of Ch'i.

4. The Liang Dynasty

1. Pao-ch'ang excerpted this biography from a much longer original written by the scholar Shen Yüeh (441–513) and found in the Chinese Buddhist canon in *Kuang hung ming chi* (The extended collection making known the illustrious). Some details have been added to the present translation from the longer biography found in *T.* 52, no. 2103, chap. 23, 270.b.7. The longer version is reproduced with slight variations in *Ku chin t'u shu chi ch'eng* (Complete collection of books and records ancient and modern), vol. 506, chap. 203, the section on nuns.

2. Wu-shih in An-ting. Tentatively located in present-day northern Shensi Province. See map.

3. Lung-ch'uan County, in present-day Kuangtung Province. See map.

4. *Nirvāna Scripture, T.* 12, no. 374, 11:432.c.13ff. See biography 42, chap. 3 n. 30, and bibliography, *Great Final Nirvāna Scripture.*

5. The five fundamental precepts: abstention from harming living beings, from wrong or false speech, from wrong sexual actions, from theft, and from intoxicating substances.

6. Twenty-nine years old: the basic text reads nineteen; the Sung, Yüan, and Ming editions, and Shen Yüeh's version in *Kuang hung ming chi* (The extended collection making known the illustrious) read twenty-nine.

7. Master of the Law Yao, otherwise unknown. Two monks with the second syllable Yao as part of their names are noted in the table of contents to Pao-ch'ang, *Ming seng chuan* (Lives of famous monks), 14:5, Hui-yao of Sung, and Hui-yao of Ch'i. Their biographies are no longer extant.

8. Master of the Law Yao could have lectured on any of these three texts, but the first is most likely: *Sarvāstivāda Monastic Rules in Ten Recitations, T.* 23, no. 1435, *Shih sung lü* (Sarvāstivāda-vinaya), translated by Punyatara, Dharmaruci, and Kumārajīva; *T.* 23, no. 1436, *Shih sung pi-ch'iu po-lo-t'i-mo-ch'a chieh pen* (Sarvāstivāda-prātimoksha-sūtra), translated by Kumārajīva; *T.* 23, no. 1437, *Shih sung pi-ch'iu-ni po-lo-t'i-mo-ch'a chieh pen* (Sarvāstivāda-bhikshunī-prātimoksha-sūtra), translated by Fa-hsien. *T.* 23, no. 1437 gives the rules and regulations for nuns. See *Répertoire,* p. 123.

9. Fa-ying: biography in *Kao seng chuan* 11:402.a.6, where it states specifically that he edited the monastic texts on which he lectured to Ching-hsiu.

10. The metaphor is changed for the translation. In the text the Buddha is a rope, and his teachings are the strands or skeins emanating from it and gradually fraying and coming to an end.

11. *Mānatta* ceremony: see appendix B.

12. Gunavarman: see biography 14, chap. 2 n. 6.

13. Emperor Ming of Sung (439–465–472). See biography 34, chap. 2 n. 121.

14. The Dragon Kings, one of the eight classes of spirits found in Indian cosmology, were often benevolent toward those who practice Buddhism, protecting them against malevolent spirits or supporting and encouraging them in their efforts as we see in the case of Ching-hsiu.

15. The term *Holy Monk* can also be translated as arhat, about which see biography 47, chap. 3 n. 58, on "three types of Buddhist paths." For Pindola, see below, and notes to biography 42, chap. 3 n. 38.

16. See biography 47, chap. 3 n. 58, on "three types of Buddhist paths."

17. According to Shen Yüeh's biography of Ching-hsiu in *Kuang hung ming chi* (The extended collection making known the illustrious), all the other monks and nuns imitated this change of color, thus establishing what became the traditional color for monastic robes in China.

18. This lake is a mythological lake in the Himalayas.

19. Two-day assembly; other editions say twenty-day assembly.

20. In the Chinese Buddhist canon there is a scripture, *Ch'ing pin-t'ou-lu fa* (Method for inviting Pindola), that is a brief treatise on the proper way to invite the presence of the Holy Monk Pindola, in *T.* 32, no. 1689. Also see biography 42, chap. 3 n. 38.

21. Ch'i heir apparent Wen-hui and prince of Ching-ling Wen-hsüan. See biography 34, chap. 2 nn. 119, 120.

22. Tushita Heaven is ruled over by Bodhisattva Maitreya. See introduction.

23. T'ai-shan Nan-ch'eng, in present-day Shantung Province, Fei County. See map.

24. *Flower of the Law Scripture* chanted seven times comes to a total of approximately 500,000 words at a minimum. To chant the text seven times in a day and a night would require chanting approximately 20,800 words per hour, or 347 words per minute, or 5.7 words per second. See introduction.

25. Sung Wen-ti and Hsiao Wu-ti. See biography 34, nn. 119, 120.

26. Emperor Wu (*Nan ch'i shu,* chap. 40; *Nan shih,* chap. 44).

27. Ch'eng-tu, present-day Ch'eng-tu in Ssuch'uan Province. See map.

28. Kālayashas (biography in *Kao seng chuan* 3:343.c.11). See biography 31, chap. 2 n. 110.

29. I Province. This does not appear in the text, but it was in the territory of Shu Province, the present-day Ssuch'uan Province.

30. Chen Fa-ch'ung (*Sung shu,* chap. 78; *Nan shih,* chap. 70).

31. A hearer is a follower of the Disciples' Vehicle and therefore naturally exhibits a darker ray from the point of view of the Great Vehicle.

32. Revelation of doctrine is a sign of holiness. Presumably she would have

been taught by the Buddha himself. At that time the Taoists were receiving great amounts of revealed scriptures. See Needham, *Science and Civilisation* 2:157–158; Strickmann, "On the Alchemy," in *Facets of Taoism,* p.187; *Ch'u san-tsang chi chi* (Collected notes), chap. 5, 40.b, gives notice that from 499 to 505 a young girl living in Green Garden Convent chanted texts as they were revealed to her in a trance. These texts are listed in the section of *i,* or "suspect" texts.

33. Prince of Lin-ch'uan. See biography 61, chap. 4 n. 77.

34. Nan-yen, in present-day Chiangsu Province, to the north of the capital.

35. Shan, in northern China, north of the territory of western Ch'u.

36. Southern Ch'u, which cannot be placed with certainty. It probably refers to somewhere in the Huai River valley, between that river and the Yangtze River, especially Hupei Province.

37. A pagoda and a temple. On the origin of this phrase see *Kuang hung ming chi* (The extended collection making known the illustrious), T. 52, no. 2103, *chüan* II.101.c.1–4. This indicates the building built to house the Buddha's relics where one could offer flowers and respect.

38. Chang Chün (*Nan ch'i shu,* chap. 32; *Nan shih,* chap. 31).

39. Chang Chün's father, Chang Tai (413–483), was the better known of the two. He was the governor of I Province between 473 and 477 (*Nan ch'i shu,* chap. 32; *Nan shih,* chap. 31).

40. Liu Chün (*Nan ch'i shu,* chap. 37; *Nan shih,* chap. 39).

41. Prince of Hsüan-wu of Liang, (d. 500). This prince was Hsiao I, elder brother of Emperor Wu (464–502–549), founder of the Liang dynasty. He met death by treachery in the year 500 and was given his offices and titles posthumously, that of prince of Hsüan-wu being bestowed in 502 (*Liang shu,* chap. 23; *Nan shih,* chap. 51).

42. The purpose of this episode is to demonstrate T'an-hui's ability to rise to meet impossible demands. The text in this section, beginning "he sent a maidservant" and ending "without additional help," not only has alternate readings from different editions but also omits any subjects, leaving only verbs and objects. Therefore, although the most logical progression of events has been conjectured, any translation must be tentative.

43. This phrase is taken from the *Vimalakīrti's Preaching Scripture,* a scripture extremely popular in China, and refers to the bodhisattva's inexhaustible store of merit, but in this biography we see the term linked to economic resources. Emperor Wu of Liang established the economic institution of the Inexhaustible Treasury to handle the goods and money donated by the faithful to religious institutions. Such great surpluses were built up that the treasuries became major centers of capital accumulation that in turn could be used to finance further religious activities and also be used to make loans. These inexhaustible treasuries became very large and important in the T'ang dynasty

(618–907). See Ch'en, *Buddhism in China,* pp. 264–267; *Vimalakīrti's Preaching Scripture, T.* 14, no. 475, chap. two, 550.b.10. For their development, see Gernet, *Aspects économiques,* pp. 205–212.

44. Illegitimate because it was non-Chinese.

45. Nun Feng. This biography has been translated in *Buddhist Texts through the Ages,* pp. 293–295.

46. Kao-ch'ang, a central Asian kingdom in present-day Hsinchiang Province, T'u-lu-fan County. See map.

47. This practice, together with the burning of an arm or of one's whole body in honor of the Buddha, was inspired by the *Flower of the Law Scripture,* a Buddhist scripture immensely popular in China (see bibliography under *Flower of the Law Scripture* for *Miao fa lien hua ching,* 53.b–54.a; and *Cheng fa hua ching,* 125.b–126.a). A photograph of this type of mutilation in honor of the Buddha appears in Prip-Møller, *Chinese Buddhist Monasteries,* p. 322. The origins of the sacrifice by fire are difficult to trace. It is not originally a Buddhist phenomenon. One theory about its appearance in the *Flower of the Law Scripture* is that that part of the scripture was composed to exhort greater faith in the face of troubles. Another is that it is a vivid way to describe the yogic experience of heat and ecstasy. See, e.g., Eliade *Myths, Dreams, and Mysteries,* pp. 146–149. Also in the biography of the monk Fa-hsien in *Kao seng Fa Hsien chuan (T.* 51, no. 2085, 862.a.13–20) we read of the death of Ānanda whose body was spontaneously consumed by fire while he was in the "fire-ray" *samādhi.* Afterward he divided the remains into two parts and distributed them. Also see *A Record of Buddhistic Kingdoms,* pp. 75–77. The possibility of influence of Middle Eastern fire cults cannot be overlooked.

48. This is another example of the remarkable speed with which some of the nuns were able to chant scriptures.

49. A partial biography of Fa-hui appears in Pao-ch'ang's *Meisōden-shō* (Lives of famous monks). In that biography we learn that Fa-hui, in his youth, enjoyed hunting, archery, drinking, and singing and that he was married, his wife being the most beautiful woman in the country. But he got into an unpleasant scrape and fled to the country of Kucha. Once there, he was apparently converted and wanted to become a Buddhist monk, but he had no money to buy monastic robes. A foreigner had died, and Fa-hui followed the family to the graveyard. After they had left, he wanted to take the dead man's clothing, which was of excellent quality, but first had to struggle with the ghost. He overcame the ghost, stole the clothing, sold it, and used the money to buy monastic robes. He progressed well in the monastic life and eventually returned to Kao-ch'ang, where he earned much respect and became the chaplain of the nuns. The account of his trip back to Kucha to see the monk Chih-yüeh is essentially the same as in Nun Feng's biography, with this addition:

when Chih-yüeh offers him the wine, Fa-hui also thinks to himself that he has been living a pure life for a long time, a reference of course to his profligate youth that he had left behind. Fa-hui's own biography finishes up by saying that after his return to Kao-ch'ang he was very influential in the whole region, spreading the Buddhist religion very successfully, and that everyone looked up to him (*Meisōden-shō,* chap. 25).

50. *Āchārya* is a Sanskrit word meaning master or teacher.

51. Chih-yüeh, known only in this biography and in the biography of Fa-hui in Pao-ch'ang's *Meisōden-shō* (Lives of famous monks).

52. The third fruit *(anāgāmin)* is that of never again being reborn on earth, but rather in a heaven from whence one can reach final enlightenment.

53. This story has the flavor of the later masters of the Ch'an, or Zen, sect, with their unorthodox teaching methods that included, at times, deliberately breaking one or more of the precepts. The actual verbal exchange between Chih-yüeh and Fa-hui is also full of the flavor of Ch'an. When Chih-yüeh asks, "Have you got it?" Fa-hui does not have to ask what it is he is supposed to have.

54. A textual variant gives the reading "five gates of meditation," which could also be the title of a text, the *Five Gates of Meditation Scripture,* translated by Buddhamitra and Dharmamitra in the capital during the early Sung dynasty (420–479) (*T.* 15, no. 619). The five gates in the scripture are watching one's breath, observing the impurity of all things, cultivating compassion for all living beings, contemplating the causes of dependent arising, and keeping in mind, or calling upon, the Buddha. Another list of five, from the *Vimalakīrti's Preaching Scripture,* is meditating on impermanence, suffering, emptiness, non-ego, and the calm cessation of nirvana (*T.* 14, no. 475, chap. 1, 541.a.15–16).

55. According to a textual variant, the first named (Hui-yin) could also be Ssu-yin. Fa-ying is not the same Fa-ying whose biography appears in *Kao seng chuan* 11:402.a.6.

56. Yung-shih, in present-day Chiangsu Province, Li-ying County. See map.

57. Emperor Wen of Sung. See biography 30, chap. 2 n. 105.

58. Prince of Hsiang-tung, eleventh son of Emperor Wen (*Sung shu,* chap. 8; *Nan shih,* chap. 3).

59. *Flower of the Law Scripture.* See biography 5, chap. 1 n. 53; and biography 7, chap. 1 n. 63; and bibliography.

60. Chü-lu, in present-day Hopei Province, P'ing-hsiang County.

61. These activities carried out by the little girl are described in the *Flower of the Law Scripture,* which says that, even if a child piles up sand to make little Buddhist pagodas, that child has already attained to the Buddhist path, or

if such a one carves or paints images of the Buddha, thereby accumulating merit, he has attained the Buddhist path. See *Flower of the Law Scripture* (Miao fa lien hua ching), pp. 8.c.23–25, 9.a.5–8.

62. She seems to have done this on first entering the monastic life as a tribute to her parents.

63. Ch'i heir apparent, Wen-hui. The text says literally Emperor Wen of Ch'i, but it was a title bestowed on him posthumously (*Nan ch'i shu,* chap. 21; *Nan shih,* chap. 4).

64. The four necessities are food, clothing, medicine, and bedding; or food, clothing, medicine, and shelter.

65. *Discourse on the Completion of Reality* (Ch'eng shih lun) (Satyasiddhi-shāstra?), trans. Kumārajīva, *T.* 32, no. 1646; *Discourse on the Abhidharma* (P'i-t'an). In *T.* there are three volumes of Abhidharma texts, vols. 27, 28, 29. *Great Final Nirvāna Scripture* (see biography 42, chap. 3 n. 30); and the *Flower Garland Scripture* (Hua-yen ching) (Avatamsaka-sūtra), in *T.* 9, no. 278; and *T.* 10. These texts are difficult philosophical and doctrinal texts, and the nun Ching-hsing, able to discourse on them, reveals her own intelligence and education. Her grasping the essential when first hearing the topic echoes Confucius (*Lun yü,* book 7, maxim 8): "If I hold up one corner and a man cannot come up with the other three, I do not continue the lesson" (trans. Waley in *The Analects of Confucius,* p. 124).

66. Hsiao Tzu-liang, Ch'i Ching-ling Wen Hsüan Wang (*Nan ch'i shu,* chap. 40; *Nan shih,* chaps. 5, 44). See also biography 39, chap. 3 n. 10.

67. Seng-tsung and Pao-liang. Their biographies are in *Kao seng chuan* 8:379.c., 381.c., respectively. They are classified among the "monks who explicate the meaning of the scriptures."

68. This is probably the meaning. There is a slight possibility, however, that it means he was selecting a suitable candidate for the position of *seng-lu* (recorder of the assembly) an administrative office of Chinese origin designed to keep track of the assemblies and their activities within a certain region. This office was established during the Yao Ch'in dynasty (384–417) by imperial decree. See Mochizuki, *Bukkyō-daijiten,* 3124.a.

69. *Emperor* probably refers to Emperor Wu (464–502–549) of the Liang dynasty.

70. The five sectarian divisions most likely refers to the schools of the Dharmaguptaka, Sarvāstivāda, Mahīshāsaka, Kāshyapīya or Mahāsāmghika, and Vātsīputrīya. These divisions of the Disciples' Vehicle Buddhism provided the books of monastic rules on which early Chinese Buddhist monasticism was based. Buddhism in China was Mahāyāna or Great Vehicle Buddhism, but, although doctrinally Mahāyāna, depended at this time on the monastic codes of the Disciples' Vehicle. The approach was eclectic. Thus Ling-yü would study all texts of monastic codes available to her. By about A.D. 500, the

major texts had been translated and were generally although not necessarily universally available.

71. Shao-ling prince (*Sung shu,* chap. 90; *Nan shih,* chap. 14).

72. This emperor is Hou-fei, posthumously degraded to the title prince of Ts'ang-wu, who died in 477 at the age of fifteen, stabbed to death by a group of men fed up with his decadence and cruelty that had terrorized all within his reach. This peculiar way of referring to him may indicate the original biographer's repugnance for the emperor's despicable, degenerate character (*Nan shih,* chap. 3).

73. This is the first mention of the complete title of the translation done by Kumārajīva (350–409) in Ch'ang-an in north China.

74. *Shrīmālā Scripture,* see biography 41, chap. 3 n. 25, and bibliography, *Shrīmālā-devī-simhanāda-sūtra; Vimalakīrti Scripture,* see biography 9, chap. 1 n. 73, and bibliography, *Vimalakīrti's Preaching Scripture.*

75. *Sarvāstivāda Monastic Rules in Ten Recitations.* See biography 52, chap. 4 n. 8.

76. Fa-yin and Seng-shen, in *Kao seng chuan* 11:399.c.; 14:421.b.15. Fa-yin is listed in the table of contents of *Kao seng chuan* as a subbiography attached to Seng-shen's, but the text itself does not mention him.

77. Lady Chang was the wife of the prince of Ch'ang-sha, Tao-lien (368–422), a younger brother of Emperor Wu (367–422) of Sung. The prince of Lin-ch'uan, Liu I-ch'ing (403–444), was the second son of the prince of Ch'ang-sha and was adopted as heir by the prince of Lin-ch'uan, Tao-kuei (370–412), another younger brother of Emperor Wu. Lady Chang would have been quite elderly at the time she wanted to give up her residence. Liu I-ch'ing is traditionally ascribed the authorship of a work known as *Shih-shuo hsin-yü* (A new account of tales of the world), described in the bibliography (*Sung shu,* chap. 51; *Nan shih,* chap. 13).

78. See biography 39, chap. 3 n. 10.

79. It must be remembered that Shih Pao-ch'ang, the biographer, compiled the biographies at the request of Emperor Wu, founder of the Liang dynasty.

80. *Great Final Nirvāna Scripture;* see biography 42, chap. 3 n. 30. *Flower of the Law Scripture;* see biography 5, chap. 1 n. 53; *Ten-Stages Scripture* (Shih ti ching) (Dashabhūmika-sūtra); there are several texts in the Buddhist canon, in *T.* 10, and the only one using the title *Shih ti ching* was not translated until much later. The extant texts of the time of the nuns are called *Shih chu ching.* The biography clearly says *Shih ti. Shih ti* could also refer to chap. 22 of the *Flower Garland Scripture* (Ta fang kuang hua yen ching). See *Répertoire,* pp. 37–38.

81. *Mother of Monasticism Scripture, T.* 24, no. 1463, reading *mu* instead of *hai* in conformity with the Sung, Yüan, and Ming editions; and *Répertoire,* p. 125.

82. Ch'ing Province, in present-day central eastern Shantung Province. See map.

83. Garlic and onions. See biography 31, chap. 2 n. 108.

84. *Great Final Nirvāna Scripture* (see biography 42, chap. 3 n. 30); *Flower of the Law Scripture* (see biography 5, chap. 1 n. 53).

85. *Discourse on the Completion of Reality* (Ch'eng shih lun) (Satyasiddhi-shāstra), *T.* 32, no. 1646; *Great Final Nirvāna Scripture* (see n. 84 above).

86. All except T'an-chi have biographies in *Kao seng chuan.* A partial biography of T'an-chi appears in Pao-ch'ang's *Meisōden-shō* (Lives of famous monks) in which the only specific date given is that in the year 458 the emperor requested him to live in the capital. The biography also states that he is the author of a work titled *A Treatise on the Seven Schools.* T'an-pin (biography in *Kao seng chuan* 7:373.a), and Hui-tz'u (biography in *Kao seng chuan* 8:379.b), are both specifically credited with expertise in one or more of the scriptures mentioned above. Seng-jou (biography in *Kao seng chuan* 8:378.c), although not so credited with a specific scripture, is listed among the monks known for their skill in explaining the scriptures.

87. T'an-pin (biography in *Kao seng chuan* 7:373.a.16); T'an-chi is probably the same one who appears as a subbiography in T'an-pin's biography. His is one of the few extant biographies in Pao-ch'ang's *Meisōden-shō* (Lives of famous monks), chap. 16; Seng-jou (431–494) (biography in *Kao seng chuan* 7:378.c.4); Hui-tz'u (434–490) (biography in *Kao seng chuan* 8:397.b.23).

88. *Shrīmālā Scripture* (see biography 41, chap. 3 n. 25).

89. *Infinite Life Scripture* (Wu liang shou ching) (Sukhāvatīvyūha), *T.* 12, no. 360, attributed to Sanghavarman. The biography gives the exact title of the Sanghavarman translation. There are other related texts. See *Répertoire,* p. 46.

90. Wen-hsüan of Ch'i (see biography 39, chap. 3 n. 10).

91. The name of the convent is uncertain because in all major editions it has been given two different names.

92. Cassia Park is tentatively identified as the Cassia Park founded in the time of Emperor Ta of the Wu dynasty (222–252) and located on the south face of the Falling Star Mountain in the capital district.

93. Kuei-chi (see biography 20, chap. 2 n. 53).

94. *Flower of the Law Scripture* (See biography 5, chap. 1 n. 53).

95. Suggesting her holiness and possibly her equivalence with a bodhisattva or a Buddha.

96. Omitting the *four* in conformity with the Sung, Yüan, and Ming editions. Twenty is a common age for taking up the life of a nun.

97. Seng-jou (see biography 63, chap. 4 n. 87).

98. Reading Hui-chi instead of Hui-ch'i in conformity with the Sung, Yüan, and Ming editions. His biography is in *Kao seng chuan* 8:379.a.3.

99. *Sarvāstivāda Monastic Rules in Ten Recitations.* See biography 52, chap. 4 n. 8.

100. Hui-hsi appears in the table of contents to Pao-ch'ang's *Meisōden-shō* (Lives of famous monks) (Ming seng chuan ch'ao), chap. 17.

101. Shan-yin County, in present-day Chechiang Province, Shao-hsing County.

102. Ying-ch'uan, present-day Honan Province, central region.

103. Chou Ying, in addition to his literary efforts, was also a very devout and pious Buddhist layman. He had built his own retreat on Bell Mountain, living like a monk even though he had a wife. He wrote a *Treatise on the Three Schools* (San tsung lun), and *Rhyme Tables of the Four Tones* (*Nan ch'i shu,* chap. 41; *Nan shih,* chap. 34).

104. Ju-nan, in present-day Honan Province, Ju-nan County.

105. Hsiao Chao-chou was the son of the prince of Ching-ling, Hsiao Tzu-liang (460–494), who was the second son of Emperor Wu (440–483–493) of the Ch'i dynasty (*Nan ch'i shu,* chap. 40; *Nan shih,* chap. 44).

106. Hsiao Yüan-chien was the son of Ch'ang, the fourth younger brother of Emperor Wu (464–502–549) of the Liang dynasty. Yüan-chien was the administrator of Kuei-chi some time between 504 and 514, and he died in 519 (*Liang shu,* chap. 23).

Appendix A

1. See introduction, n. 1.

2. *Kao seng chuan* (Lives of eminent monks), by Hui-chiao (497–554), *T.* 50, no. 2059. See Zürcher, *Buddhist Conquest,* p. 10; Wright, "Biography and Hagiography."

3. Biography in *Kao seng chuan* 402.c. See Link, "Shih Seng-yu and His Writings," for a detailed study of the book and its author.

4. *Ch'u san-tsang chi chi, T.* 55, no. 2145.

5. Biography in *Hsü kao seng chuan* (Further lives of eminent monks), by Tao-hsüan (596–667), *T.* 50, no. 2060, *chüan* I.426.b, and especially 427.b.28; See Wright, "Biography and Hagiography," for a comparison between Pao-ch'ang and Hui-chiao as biographers. Pao-ch'ang is partial to the famous, Hui-chiao to the eminent.

6. Wright, "Biography and Hagiography," p. 410, n. 3. The extracts from the *Meisōden-shō* are preserved in Kasuga Reichi, "Jōdokyō-shiryō to shite no meisōden shishishō meisōden-yōbun chō narabi ni mirokunyorai kannōshō dai shi shoin no meisōden ni tsuite," *Shūgaku Kenkyū* 12 (1936): 53–118; also in *Zoku-zōkyō,* Tokyo, 1905–1922, ser. 2, part 2z, case 7, vol. 1; reprinted, Taipei: Shin Wen Feng, 1977, vol. 134.

7. *Li tai san pao chi* (Records of the three treasures through the ages), by Fei

Ch'ang-fang (A.D. 597) (*T.* 49, no. 2034, chap. 11.99.b.), gives a record of the years in which Pao-ch'ang and others were ordered by Emperor Wu of Liang to write various works such as Pao-ch'ang's *Chung ching mu lu* (A catalogue of all Buddhist works), which was originally the work of another monk, Seng Shao, whose catalogue was unsatisfactory to the emperor. Pao-ch'ang's biography in *Hsü kao seng chuan* (Further lives of eminent monks) says (426.c.21ff) that the emperor ordered Pao-ch'ang to complete the catalogue, which he did in four *chüan*. See Tsai, Review of *Biographies of Buddhist Nuns,* p. 89; *Li tai san pao chi,* (99.b.3ff) says that Seng-shao had selected from Seng-yu's catalogue, the *Ch'u san-tsang chi chi,* (*T.* 55, no. 2145), but see also *Fa yüan chu lin,* (1021.b.23–25); and *Li tai san pao chi* (99.b.1–3).

    8. *K'ai-yüan shih chiao lu, T.* 55, no. 2154, chap. 6.536.c.28.

    9. *K'ai-yüan shih chiao lu lüeh ch'u, T.* 55, no. 2155, 746.b.6. These two catalogues were both compiled by the monk Chih-sheng (biography in *Sung kao seng chuan* [Sung dynasty biographies of eminent monks]), *T.* 50, 733.c.26, in the eighteenth year of the *k'ai-yüan* reign period (730) of Emperor Hsüan Tsang (r. 712–756) of the T'ang dynasty.

    10. *Fa yüan chu lin, T.* 53, no. 2122.

    11. Ibid., p. 1021.b.26–c.7. "The emperor commanded that the nine titles in 122 *chüan* be compiled by Pao-ch'ang and others."

    12. *Li tai san pao chi, T.* 49, 99.b.5–21.

    13. Ibid., p. 45.a.10.

    14. See Mochizuki, *Bukkyō-daijiten,* who gives the date 517.

    15. E.g., *K'ai-yüan shih chiao lu, T.* 55, no. 2154, p. 536.c.28; and *K'ai-yüan shih chiao lu lüeh ch'u, T.* 55, no. 2155, pp. 746.b.6.

    16. Wright, "Biography and Hagiography," p. 418; T'ang Yung-t'ung, *Han wei liang-chin nan-pei-ch'ao fo-chiao shih* (History of Buddhism in the Wei, Chin, and Southern and Northern dynasties), p. 579, says it was compiled at the beginning of the *chien-yüan* reign period (479–482) of the Ch'i dynasty (479–502). These fragments have been brought together by Lu Hsün in *Ku hsiao-shuo kou ch'en* (A study of ancient fiction).

    17. *Fa yüan chu lin, T.* 53, 526.b.17.

    18. (1) *Lives* 936.b.11; (2) *Ming hsiang chi* as quoted in *Fa yüan chu lin,* 616.b.5; (3) *Chin nan-ching ssu chi* as quoted in *Fa yüan chu lin,* 526.b.17; (4) *Fo tsu t'ung chi* (Thorough record of the Buddha's lineage) 340.b.29ff.

    19. (1) *Lives* 937.c.24; (2) *Ming hsiang chi* as quoted in *Fa yüan chu lin,* 407.b.15; (3) *Chi shen chou san pao kan t'ung lu, T.* 52, 418.b.7–12.

    20. (1) *Lives* 938.c.16; (2) *Ming hsiang chi* as quoted in *Fa yüan chu lin,* 400.a.9.

    21. (1) *Lives* 941.c.25; (2) *Ming hsiang chi* as quoted in *Fa yüan chu lin,* 304.a.24, 453.b.12.

22. (1) *Lives* 945.a.7; (2) *Kuang hung ming chi,* 270.b.7; and (3) *Ku chin t'u shu chi ch'eng,* vol. 506, pp. 10b–11a.

23. *Kuang hung ming chi,* 357.b.8–15.

24. Shen Yüeh (441–513) styled Hsiu-wen, poet and author of a *Chin shu* (History of the Chin dynasty), now lost; *Sung shu* (History of the [Liu] Sung dynasty), and other secular works. He also wrote essays on Buddhist topics, many collected in the *KHMC*. He served in official positions during the Sung (420–479) and Ch'i (479–502) dynasties.

25. Tao-hsüan (596–667) worked in the north. His biography is found in *Sung kao seng chuan* (The Sung dynasty biographies of eminent monks), *T.* 50, no. 2061, 790.b.

26. Rogers, *Chronicle,* pp. 3–4.

27. In *Han shu i wen chih* (Bibliography in the history of the Former Han dynasty), chap. 30, it is listed as Liu Hsiang's work.

28. Biography of Liu Hsiang in *Han shu* (History of the Former Han dynasty), chap. 36.

29. O'Hara, *Position of Women,* p. 6 n. 18.

30. *T.* 24, no. 1478, 948.b.29ff.

31. She associates with rulers of countries and meddles in politics. See *Mahāprajāpatī, T.* 24, 947.c.20ff.

CHINESE CHARACTER GLOSSARY OF NAMES, TERMS, AND TITLES

Abhidharma　　毗曇
administrator　　太守, 維那
Amita Buddha　　阿彌陀佛
Amitābha Buddha　　無量光佛
Amitāyus Buddha　　無量壽佛
An-ting　　安定
Ārya　　阿梨
Bamboo Garden Convent　　竹圍寺
Bamboo Grove Convent　　竹林寺
Bare Plank Mountain　　白板山
Beckoning Clarity Convent　　招明寺
Bibliography in the History of the Han Dynasty　　漢書藝文志
Black River　　烏江
Bodhi Convent　　菩提寺
Bodhisattva Kuan-shih-yin Scripture　　觀世音經
Brightness of Ch'i Convent in Ch'ien-t'ang　　錢塘齊明寺
Buddhayashas　　佛陀耶舍
Built-by-the-Multitude Convent　　衆造寺
Bukkyō-daijiten　　佛教大辭典
Capital Office Convent　　都郎中寺
Cassia Park　　桂林
Ch'ang-an　　長安
Chang Chün　　張峻
Chang, Empress　　章皇后
Chang Mao　　張茂
Chang Pien　　張辯
Ch'ang-shan　　常山
Chang Tai　　張岱
Chang Yüan of Wu Commandery　　吳郡張援
Chao Chen　　趙珍
Chao Ch'u-ssu　　趙處思 or Chao Ch'ien-en 趙虔恩
Chao Commandery　　趙郡
Chao-kuo Chün-jen　　趙國均仁
Ch'ao Pien　　超辯
Ch'ao-t'ing　　潮亭
Chaturdesha Monastery　　招提寺
Ch'en Commandery　　陳郡
Ch'en Fa-ch'ung　　甄法崇
Ch'en Liu　　陳留
Cheng fa hua ching　　正法華經

Ch'eng shih lun　　成實論
Ch'eng-tu　　成都
Chi Commandery　　汲郡
Chi-nan　　濟南
Chi Province　　冀州
Chi shen chou san pao kan t'ung lu　　集神州三寶感通錄
Chiang-hsia prince, I-kung　　江夏王義恭
Chiang-ling　　江陵
Chiang, Madame　　江氏
Ch'iao Commandery　　譙郡
Chieh-jen　　戒忍尼
chieh-mo　　羯磨
Chieh yin yüan ching　　戒因緣經
ch'ien　　遷
Chien-k'ang　　建康
Ch'ien-t'ang　　錢塘
Chien-wen, emperor of Ch'i　　簡文帝
Chih-ch'ien　　支謙
Chih-shan　　智山
Chih-sheng　　智昇
Chih-yüeh　　直月
Chin-ling　　金陵
Chin-ling　　晉陵
Chin nan ching ssu chi　　晉南京寺記
Chin shu　　晉書
Ching-ai　　淨哀
Ching and Ch'u　　荊楚
Ching and Sha　　荊陝
Ching-ch'eng　　靜稱
Ch'ing-ho　　清河
ching hsing　　經行
Ching-lien　　淨練尼
Ching lü i hsiang　　經律異相
Ch'ing pin-t'ou-lo fa　　請賓頭盧法
Ch'ing Province　　青州
Ching Province　　荊州
ching-sheh　　精舍
ch'ing-shui　　清水
Ching-tu　　淨度尼
Ching-yao　　淨曜尼
Ch'iu Wen-chiang　　仇文姜
Chou Sheh　　周捨
Chou shu i chi　　周書異記
Chou Yung of Ju-nan　　汝南周顒
Ch'ü An-yüan　　曲安遠
Ch'u, Empress　　褚氏
Chü-jung County　　句容縣

Chu-ko Village Convent in Liang Commandery 　　梁郡築戈村寺
Chu, Lady 　　竺夫人
Chü-lu 　　鉅鹿
Chu Fa-hu 　　竺法護
Chu Fo-nien 　　竺佛念
Chu Fo-t'u-teng 　　竺佛圖澄
Ch'u san-tsang chi chi 　　出三藏記集
Chu Shih-hsing 　　朱士行
Chu tzu chi ch'eng 　　諸子集成
Chu wei-mo-chieh ching 　　注維摩詰經
Chuan *Hung-jen* 　　傳弘仁
Chuang Tzu 　　莊子
Chūgoku-bukkyō-tsūshi 　　中國佛教通史
Chung ching mu lu 　　衆經目錄
Chung-hsing Village 　　中興里
Chung-kuo ku chin ti ming ta tz'u tien 　　中國古今地名大辭典
Classic of History 　　書經
Collected Goodness Convent 　　集善寺
*Collected Notes on the Translation of the Buddhist Scriptures into
　　Chinese* 　　出三藏記集
Collected Records of the Responses to the Three Treasures in China 　　集神
州三寶感通錄
commander of the garrison 　　鎮
commandery administrator 　　郡守
Commentary to the Vimalakīrti Scripture 　　注維摩詰經
Complete Collection of Books and Records Ancient and Modern 　　古今圖
書集成
Condensed T'ang K'ai-yüan *Reign Period Catalogue of Buddhist
　　Writings* 　　開元釋教錄略出
Cowherd Convent 　　牛牧寺
Crown Prince's grand secretariat of the right 　　太子舍人
Dharma 　　曇摩
Dharmaguptaka Nuns' Monastic Rules 　　四分比丘尼戒本
Dharmaguptaka vinaya 　　四分律
Dharmarakṣa 　　竺法護
Dictionary of Chinese Place Names Ancient and Modern 　　古今地名大辭典
director of conventual affairs in the capital 　　京邑都維那
Disciples' Vehicle 　　小乘
Discourse on Abhidharma 　　毗曇
Discourse on the Completion of Reality 　　成實論
Eastern Convent of Lo-yang 　　洛陽城東寺
Eastern Green Garden Convent 　　東青園寺
Ekottarāgama 　　增一阿含經
Eminent Dais Monastery 　　高座寺
Eminent Monks 　　高僧傳
Empress Dowager Convent 　　太后寺
Empress Ho Convent 　　何后寺

Establishing Blessings Convent　建福寺
Establishing Peace Convent　建安寺
Establishing Splendor Convent　建熙精舍
Eternal Peace Convent　永安寺
Eternal Quietude Convent in Shu Commandery　蜀郡永康寺
Exalted Sanctity Convent　崇聖寺
Expanding Nation Convent of Nan-p'i　南皮張國寺
Extended Collection Making Known the Illustrious　廣弘明集
fa (dharma)　法
Fa-ch'eng　法成
Fa-chi　法濟
Fa-chin　法進
Fa-ching　法淨尼
Fa-hu　法護尼
Fa-hui　法慧
Fa-lin　法林
Fa-shih　法始
Fa-shih　法施尼
Fa-ts'ai　法綵
Fa-tsang　法藏
Fa-yen　法延
Fa-yin　法隱
Fa-ying　法穎
Fa-yü　法育
Fa-yu　法祐
Fa-yüan　法瑗
Fa yüan chu lin　法苑珠林
Falling Star Mountain　落星山
Fan County　繁縣
Fan-hsien　范先 or Fan-K'ao 范蕘
Fang kuang ching　方廣經
Field of Blessings Convent　福田寺
Five Gates of Meditation Scripture　五門禪經要用法
Flower Garland Convent　華嚴寺
Flower Garland Scripture　大方廣佛華嚴經
Flower Grove Convent　華林寺
Flower of the Law Scripture　法華經
　(a) *Lotus Flower of the Wonderful Law*　妙法蓮華經
　(b) *Flower of the True Law*　正法華經
Fo-t'o-yeh-sheh　佛陀耶舍
Fo tsu t'ung chi　佛祖統記
Fo-t'u-teng　佛圖澄
Forest of Pearls in the Garden of the Law　法苑珠林
Former Ch'in dynasty　前秦
Foundation for Meditation Convent　禪基寺
Founding of Wisdom Convent　建賢寺
Fu Chien (nephew)　符堅

Fu Chien (uncle)　　符健
Fu-liu County　　扶柳縣
Fuh clan　　傅氏
Further Lives of Eminent Monks　　續高僧傳
general of the cavalry　　驃騎
Gold Flower Monastery　　金花寺
governor　　刺史
grand secretariat of the right　　太子舍人
grand tutor, Tao-tzu, prince of Kuei-chi　　太傅會稽王道子
Grass Hall Monastery　　草堂寺
Great Final Nirvāna Scripture　　大般涅槃經
　(*a*) by T'an-wu-ch'an　　曇無讖
　(*b*) by Hui-yen　　慧嚴
　(*c*) by Fa-hsien　　法顯(大般泥洹經)
Great Mysterious Terrace Convent　　太玄臺寺
Great Perfection of Wisdom Treatise　　大智度論
Great Storehouse of Scripture　　大藏經
Great Sung Dynasty Compact History of the Buddhist Assemblies　　大宋僧
　史略
Great Vehicle　　大乘
Green Garden Convent　　青園寺
Grove of Concentration Monastery　　定林寺
Grove of the Way Monastery　　道林寺
Gunavarman　　求那跋摩
hai and *mu*　　海母
Han dynasty　　漢
Han fa pen nei chuan　　漢法本內傳
Han shu　　漢書
Han shu i wen chih　　漢書藝文志
Han wei liang-chin nan-pei ch'ao fo chiao shih　　漢魏兩晉南北朝佛敎史
Hedge Garden Monastery　　枳園寺
*Hidden Account of the Origin of the [Buddhist] Law in the Han
　Dynasty*　　漢法本內傳
Hirakawa, Akira　　平川彰
History of the Chin Dynasty　　晉書
History of the Latter Han Dynasty　　後漢書
History of the Southern Ch'i Dynasty　　南齊書
History of the Southern Dynasties　　南史
History of the Sung Dynasty　　宋書
History of the Wei Dynasty　　魏書
Ho Ch'ung　　何充
Ho-nei　　河內
Holy Monk (Pindola)　　聖僧
Hou han shu　　後漢書
Hsi-p'ing　　西平
Hsiang-kuo　　襄國
Hsiao Chao-chou, Ch'i dynasty prince of Pa-ling　　齊巴陵王蕭照冑

Hsiao Ch'eng-chih　　蕭承之

Hsiao I, the Ch'i grand general of the army and grand marshal, the prince of
　Yü-chang　　齊太尉大司馬豫章王蕭嶷

Hsiao p'in pan-jo-po-lo-mi ching　　小品般若波羅蜜經

Hsiao Tzu-liang, the Ch'i prince of Ching-ling, Wen Hsüan　　齊竟陵文宣王
　蕭子良

Hsiao-wu, emperor of Chin　　孝武

Hsiao-wu, emperor of Sung　　孝武

[Hsiao] Yüan-chien, prince of Heng-yang of Liang　　梁衡陽王元簡

Hsieh Chih　　解直

Hsiu-wu in Chi Commandery　　汲郡修武

Hsü Ch'ung　　徐忡

Hsü kao seng chuan　　續高僧傳

Hsüan-ch'ang　　玄暢

Hsüan-ch'ü　　玄趣

Hsüan-wu, prince of Liang　　梁宣武王

Hsüan yen chi　　宣驗記

Hsün-yang Commandery　　尋陽郡

Hua hu ching　　化胡經

Hua-kuang　　花光尼

Hua yen　　華嚴

Hua yen ching　　華嚴經

Huai-nan　　淮南

Huai Seng-chen　　懷僧珍

Huan Hsüan　　桓玄

Huang-fu Ta　　皇甫達

Huang Hsiu-i　　黃修儀

Hui-ch'ao　　慧超

Hui-chi　　惠基

Hui-chi　　慧基

Hui-chih　　慧智

Hui-ch'ih　　慧持

Hui-hsi　　惠熙

Hui-hsing　　慧形

Hui-kao　　惠高尼

Hui-li　　慧力

Hui-ling　　慧令

Hui-ming　　慧明

Hui-su　　慧宿

Hui-ts'ung　　慧聰尼

Hui-tzu　　慧孜

Hui-yin　　惠隱 or Ssu-yin 思隱

Hui-yin　　慧音尼

Hui-yüan　　慧遠

Hung-nung　　弘農

I Chou　　益州

I-k'ang, grand general of the army, [prince of P'eng-ch'eng] of Sung　　宋大
　將軍義康

I Li　　儀禮

Imperial Encyclopedia, or Complete Collection of Books and Records Ancient and Modern　　古今圖書集成

Increasing Joy Convent　　延興寺

Infinite Life Scripture　　無量壽經

Jeta Grove Convent　　祇洹寺

Jōdokyō-shiryō to shite no Meisōden-shijishō Meisōden-yōbunshō narabi ni Miroku-nyōrai kannōshō dai-yon shoin no Meisōden ni tsuite　　淨土教史料としての名僧傳指示抄名僧傳要文抄并に彌勒如來感應抄第四所引の名僧傳に就いて

Joyful Peace Convent　　樂安寺

ju-lai (thus come)　　如來

K'ai-yüan shih chiao lu　　開元釋教錄

K'ai-yüan shih chiao lu lüeh ch'u　　開元釋教錄略出

Kālayashas　　畺良耶舍

K'ang, emperor of Chin　　康

Kao seng chuan　　高僧傳

Kao-ch'ang　　高昌

Kao-p'ing　　高平

Kasuga Reichi　　春日禮智

Keng ch'u hsiao p'in　　更出小品

Kingdom Convent　　王國寺

Ku chin t'u shu chi cheng　　古今圖書集成

Ku hsiao-shuo kou ch'en　　古小説鉤沈

Ku-su Mountain　　姑蘇山

Kuan-shih-yin Scripture　　觀世音經

Kuang-ching　　光淨

Kuang hung ming chi　　廣弘明集

Kuang-ling　　廣陵

Kuang, nun　　光尼

Kuang Province　　廣州

Kuang tsan ching　　光讚經

Kuei-chi　　會稽

Kumārajīva　　鳩摩羅什

K'ung Hsi-hsien　　孔熙先

K'ung Mo　　孔默 or K'ung Mo-chien 孔默兼

Kuo Hsia　　郭洽

Lan-ling　　蘭陵

Lao-tzu　　老子

Lao-tzu tao teh ching　　老子道德經

Larger Perfection of Wisdom Scripture　　摩訶般若波羅蜜經

Latter Chao　　後趙

Le lie-sien tchouan　　列仙傳

Li chi　　禮記

Li tai san pao chi　　歷代三寶記

Li-yang　　歷陽

Liang Ch'ou　　梁疇

Liang Commandery　　梁郡

Liang shu　　梁書
Liang Ts'an-chih　　梁粲之
Lieh nü chuan　　列女傳
Lin-ch'uan, prince of　　臨川王
Ling-hui　　令惠尼
Ling-nan　　嶺南
Ling-yin Mountain　　靈隱山
Lion's Roar of Queen Shrīmālā　　勝鬘師子吼一乘大方便方廣經
Liu Chün　　劉悛
Liu Hsiang　　劉向
Liu I-ch'ing, prince of Lin-ch'uan　　臨川王劉義慶
Liu Liang　　劉亮
Lives of Eminent Monks　　高僧傳
Lives of Famous Monks　　名僧傳
Lives of Illustrious Women　　列女傳
Lo-yang　　雒陽 or 洛陽
Lo-yang ch'ieh-lan chi　　洛陽伽藍記
Lotus Flower of the Wonderful Law　　妙法蓮華經
Lou-fan in Yen-men　　雁門婁煩
Lu An-hsün　　路安苟
lü and *ying*　　律穎
Lu Hsün　　魯迅
Luminous Blessings Convent　　景福寺
Lun yü cheng i　　論語正義
Lung-ch'uan County　　龍川縣
Ma, Mr.　　馬先生
Mahāprajāpatī Scripture　　大愛道比丘尼經
Mahāsānghika Rites and Rules Book　　僧祇尼羯磨
Maitreya　　彌勒
marquis of Tu-hsiang　　都鄉侯
Meditation Grove Convent　　禪林寺
Meditation of visualizing the Buddha in one's presence　　般舟(三昧)
Meisōden-shō　　名僧傳抄
Meng Ford　　孟津
Meng I　　孟顗
Meng-tzu cheng i　　孟子正義
Method for Inviting Pindola　　請賓頭盧法
Mi-sha-se pu ho hsi wu fen lü　　彌沙塞部和醯五分律
Miao fa lien-hua ching　　妙法蓮華經
Ming, emperor of Chin　　明帝
Ming, emperor of Sung　　明帝
Ming hsiang chi　　冥祥記
Ming seng chuan　　名僧傳
Ming seng chuan ch'ao　　名僧傳抄
minister of public works　　司空
Mo-ha-seng-shih pi-ch'iu-ni chieh pen　　摩訶僧祇比丘尼戒本
Mo-ho pan-jo po-lo-mi ching　　摩訶般若波羅蜜經

Mo-ling　　秣陵 (another name for Chien-k'ang　建康)
Mochizuki Shinkō　　望月信享
Mother of Monasticism Scripture (of the Saravāstivāda sect)　　(十誦)毗
　尼母經
Mu, emperor of Chin　　穆
Mud Mountain　　塗山
Nan-ch'ang princess of Sung　　宋南昌公主
Nan ch'i shu　　南齊書
Nan shih　　南史
Nan-t'i　　難提
Nan-yang　　南陽
Nan-yen　　南兗
New Grove Convent　　新林寺
Nirvāna Scripture (see *Great Final Nirvāna Scripture*)
North Chang Monastery　　北張寺
North Peak Convent　　北岳寺
Northern and southern dynasties　　南北朝
Northern Everlasting Peace Convent　　北永安寺
Origin of Monastic Rules Scripture　　鼻奈耶, 戒因緣經
Ou, master of the law　　偶法師
Pai, nun　　白尼
Pan chou (san-mei) ching　　般舟三昧經
P'an-yü　　番禺
Pao-ch'ang　　寶唱
Pao-liang　　寶亮
Pao-ying　　寶英
Pao-ying　　寶嬰尼
Pao-yung　　寶顒尼
Peak Mountain Convent　　頂山寺
Pei-ti　　北地
P'eng-ch'eng　　彭城
P'eng-ch'eng Monastery　　彭城寺
Pi-ch'iu-ni chuan　　比丘尼傳
P'i-ling　　毗陵
Pi-nai-yeh (Vinaya)　　鼻奈耶
P'i-ni mu ching　　毗尼母經
p'i-t'an　　毗曇
Pindola　　賓頭盧
P'o-hai　　勃海
P'o-kang Canal　　破綱
Po-p'ing　　博平
Pottery Office Monastery　　瓦官寺
Practice of Constant Meditation Scripture　　般舟三昧經
provincial magistrate　　州牧
P'u men p'in　　普門品
P'u-hsien (Samantabhadra)　　普賢
P'u-lien　　普練

pu shu chih jen   卜術之人

P'u-yao   普要尼

Pure Talk   清談

Records of Monasteries and Convents in Lo-yang   洛陽伽藍記

Records of Mysterious Omens   冥祥記

Records of the Strange in the Book of Chou   周書異記

rector of the assembly   僧局

rector of the assembly in the capital   都邑僧正

Reflecting Brightness Convent   照明精舍

Ritsuzō-no-kenkyū   律藏の研究

Rituals for Entering Monastic Life   羯磨

Rituals for Entering the Monastic Life of the Dharmaguptaka Sect   四分比
   丘尼羯磨法

Samādhi   定

Sangha   僧伽

Sanghavarman   僧伽跋摩

Sarvāstivāda Monastic Rules in Ten Recitations   十誦律

   (*a*) translated by Kumārjīva et al.   鳩摩羅什

   (*b*) translated by Fa-hsien   法顯

Scripture on the Conversion of the Barbarians   化胡經

Scripture on the Origins of Monastic Rules   戒因緣經

Selections from the Lives of Famous Monks   名僧傳抄

Seng-chao   僧肇

Seng-ch'ao   僧超

Seng-chien   僧建

Seng-chih   僧志尼

Seng-hua   僧化尼

Seng-lü   僧律

Seng-lu   僧錄

Seng-mao   僧茂尼

Seng-pien   僧辯

Seng-shen   僧審

Seng-tsung   僧宗

Seng-yao   僧要

Seng-yüan   僧遠

Seng-yüan   僧瑗尼

Seven Tallies in a Cloud Satchel   雲笈七籤

Shan region   陝

Shan-yin County   山陰縣

Shantung   山東

Shan-yang   山陽

Shao-ling, prince of Sung   宋邵陵王

Shen Yu-chih   沈攸之

Shen Yüeh of Wu-hsing County, vice president of the department of the imperial grand secretariat   中書侍郎吳興沈約

Sheng-man shih-tzu hou i sheng ta fang pien fang kuang ching   勝鬘師子吼
   一乘大方便方廣經

Shih-chia-mo-ni　　釋迦牟尼
Shih Hu, Emperor　　石虎
Shih Lo, Emperor　　石勒
Shih Pao-ch'ang　　釋寶唱
Shih sung lü　　十誦律
Shih sung pi-ch'iu po-lo-t'i-mu-ch'a chieh pen　　十誦比丘波羅提木叉戒本
Shih ti ching　　十地經
Shou-leng-yen san-mei ching　　首楞嚴三昧經
Shrīmālā-devī-simhanāda-sūtra　　勝鬘師子吼一乘大方便方廣經
Shu Ching　　書經
Shu Commandery　　蜀郡
Shūgaku Kenkyū　　宗學研究
Shūrangama Scripture　　首楞嚴三昧經
sifted and weeded　　沙簡
Simple Tranquility Convent　　簡靜寺
Site of the Way Monastery　　道場寺
Six Prohibitions Monastery　　六重寺
Small Vehicle　　小乘
Smaller Perfection of Wisdom Scripture　　小品般若波羅蜜經
Solitude Convent of Liang　　梁閑居寺
Southern Chin-ling Convent　　南晉陵寺
southern Ch'u　　南楚
Southern Establishing Joy Convent　　南建興寺
Southern Eternal Peace Convent　　南永安寺
Southern Grove Monastery　　南林寺
Southern Peace Convent　　南安寺
Spiritual Root Monastery　　靈根寺
Splendidly Adorned Monastery　　莊嚴寺
Ssu fen pi-ch'iu-ni chieh-mo fa　　四分比丘尼羯磨法
Ssu fen pi-ch'iu-ni chieh pen　　四分比丘尼戒本
Ssu Province　　司州
Ssu-li Province　　司隸州
Ssu-ma Lung　　司馬隆
Ssu-River　　泗
Stone Top Hill　　石頭崗
Study of Ancient Fiction　　古小説鉤沈
Sun Yü　　孫毓
Sung Dynasty Biographies of Eminent Monks　　宋高僧傳
Sung kao seng chuan　　宋高僧傳
Sung shu　　宋書
swallowing the breath　　服氣
Ta-ai-tao pi-ch'iu-ni ching　　大愛道比丘尼經
Ta chih tu lun　　大智度論
Ta pan nieh-p'an ching　　大般涅槃經
Ta-po　　大秫 or T'ai-mo 太秫
Ta-shih-chih (Mahāsthāmaprāpta)　　大勢至
Ta sung seng shih lüeh　　大宋僧史略

Ta tsang ching　大藏經
T'ai-p'ing yü lan　太平御覽
T'ai shan　泰山
T'ai-shan nan-ch'eng　泰山南城
Taishō-shinshū-daizōkyō　大正新修大藏經
T'an-cheng　曇整
T'an-chih　曇芝
T'an-jui　曇叡
T'an-lan　曇覽尼
T'an-lo　曇羅
T'an-mo-chieh-to　曇摩羯多
T'an-pin　曇斌
T'an-tsung　曇宗
Tan-yang　丹陽
T'an-yin　曇寅
T'ang K'ai-yüan *Reign Period Catalogue of Buddhist Writings*　開元釋教
　錄
T'ang Seng-chih　唐僧智
tao　道
Tao-an　道安
Tao-ch'ang　道場
Tao-chao　道照尼
Tao-hsüan　道宣
Tao-lien, Ching prince of Ch'ang-sha of Sung　長沙景王道憐
Tao-shih　道世
Tao teh ching　道德經
Taoist master of pure water　清水道師
Te-sheng　德盛尼
Ten-Stages Scripture　十地經(十地品)
Tessara　鐵薩羅
Thorough Record of the Buddha's Lineage　佛祖統記
Three-Story Convent of Chiang-ling　江陵三層寺
Ti Mountain Convent　邸山寺 or 底山寺
T'ien Hung-liang　田宏梁
Ting-yin neighborhood　定陰里
Tsang, Madame　臧氏
Ts'en Shuai　岑率
Tseng-ch'eng in Tung-kuan　東官曾成
Tseng i a-han ching　增一阿含經
Tsukamoto Zenryū　塚本善隆
Tu and Sheng mountains　嶀山,嵊山
T'u-lu-fan County (Turfan)　吐魯番縣
Tu Pa　杜霸
Tun-huang　敦煌
Tung-ch'ien　東遷
Tung-hsiang in Shan-yang　山陽東鄉
Tung-huan　東莞

T'ung-kung Lane　　通恭巷
Tushita Heaven　　兜率天
Undersecretary of the provincial forces　　外兵郎
Undersecretary of the Yellow Gate　　黃門侍郎
Universal Gate chapter　　普門品
Universal Wisdom Convent　　普賢寺
Upper Grove of Concentration Monastery　　上定林寺
Venerating Seclusion Convent　　崇隱寺
Vimalakīrti's Preaching Scripture　　維摩詰所説經
　(a) translated by Kumārājīva　　鳩摩羅什(維摩詰所説經)
　(b) translated by Chih-ch'ien　　支謙(維摩詰經)
Vinaya　鼻奈耶
Voice of the Teaching Convent　　法音寺
Wang Ch'en　　王忱
Wang Kung　　王恭
Wang Lun of Lang-yeh, palace attendant　　南齊侍中瑯琊王倫
Wang, Madame, mother of the eldest son (Lang) of the prince of Chiang-hsia　　江夏王世子(朗)母王氏
Wang P'u-yang　　王濮陽
Wang Tao-chi　　王道寄
Wei Lang　　韋朗
Wei-mo-chieh ching　　維摩詰經
Wei-mo-chieh so shuo ching　　維摩詰所説經
Wei Shou　　魏收
Wei shu　　魏書
Wen, emperor of Sung　　宋文皇帝
Wen-hsüan, minister of education, the prince of Ching-ling of Ch'i　　司徒竟陵文宣王
Wen-hui, heir apparent of Ch'i　　齊文惠帝
West Convent of Ssu Province　　司州西寺
Western Green Garden Convent　　西青園寺
Western Paradise　　極樂, 安養西方
White Mountain　　白山
Wonderful Appearance Convent　　妙相尼寺
Wu Commandery　　吳郡
Wu County South Convent　　吳縣南寺
Wu, emperor of Liang　　武梁皇帝
Wu-hsing Commandery　　吳興郡
Wu liang shou ching　　無量壽經
Wu men ch'an ching yao yung fa　　五門禪經要用法
Wu-shih in An-ting　　安定烏氏
Wu-wei Commandery　　武威郡
Yang Ling-pien　　楊令辯
Yang Mi　　羊彌
Yangtze River　　江
Yao, master of the law　　曜法師
Yeh　　鄴

Yellow Emperor and Lao-tzu   黃老
Yellow River   河
Yen   剡
Yen-kuan County   鹽官縣
Yen-men   雁門
Yin Chung-k'an   殷仲堪
yin-yuan   因緣
Yü Cave   禹穴
Yü-chang   豫章
Yü-hang   餘杭
Yü, Lang-yeh prince, governor of Yang Province   楊州刺史瑯琊王郁
Yü Province   豫州
Yü P'u   虞溥
Yü-yung of Ying-ch'uan   穎川庾詠
Yüan Chien   阮儉
Yüan, Empress   元皇后
Yüeh-chih   月支，月氏
Yüeh, kingdom of   越
Yüeh Ts'un   樂遵
Yün chi ch'i ch'ien   雲笈七籤
Yung-shih   永世
Zoku-zōkyō   續藏經

BIBLIOGRAPHY

Texts Mentioned or Implied in the Biographies

All bibliographic references to the *Taishō-shinshū-daizōkyō* edition (q.v.) of the Chinese Buddhist canon will be abbreviated *T.*

Bodhisattva Kuan-shih-yin Scripture (Kuan-shih-yin ching). In the *Flower of the Law Scripture.*

Classic of History (Shu ching). In *Shoo-king.* Translated by James Legge. Shanghai Publishing, 1904.

Dharmaguptaka Monastic Rules (Ssu fen pi-ch'iu-ni chieh-pen). Translated by Buddhayashas (408–412), in the north in Ch'ang-an. *T.* 22, no. 1431.

Discourse on Abhidharma (P'i-t'an). There are at least ten different texts that this abbreviated title could represent.

Discourse on the Completion of Reality (Ch'eng shih lun) (Satyasiddhi-shāstra). Translated by Kumārajīva (401–409 or 413), in the north in Ch'ang-an. *T.* 32, no. 1646.

Five Gates of Meditation Scripture (Wu men ch'an ching yao yung fa). Translated by Buddhamitra and Dharmamitra (424–442), in the south in Chien-k'ang. *T.* 15, no. 619.

Flower Garland Scripture (Hua-yen ching) (Avatamsaka-sūtra). Translated by Buddhabhadra (408–429), in the north in Ch'ang-an. *T.* 9, no. 278. *The Flower Ornament Scripture: The Avatamsaka-sūtra.* Translated by Thomas Cleary. Boston: Shambala Publications, 1993.

Flower of the Law Scripture: (a) Lotus Flower of the Wonderful Law (Miao fa lien hua ching) (Saddharmapundarīka-sūtra). Translated by Kumārajīva (401–409 or 413), in the north in Ch'ang-an. *T.* 9, no. 262; *(b) Flower of the True Law* (Cheng fa hua ching). Translated by Chu Fa-hu (286), in the north in Ch'ang-an. *T.* 9, no. 263. Translated into English from Kumārajīva's Chinese text by Leon Hurvitz, *Scripture of the Lotus Blossom of the Fine Dharma: The Lotus Sutra.* Columbia University Press, 1976; also translated from Kumārajīva's Chinese text is Burton Watson, *The Lotus Sutra.* New York: Columbia University Press, 1993; and from the Sanskrit by H. Kern, *The Saddharma-pundarīka, or the Lotus of the True Law.* Oxford: Clarendon Press, 1909.

Great Final Nirvāna Scripture (Ta pan nieh-p'an ching) (Mahā-parinirvāna-sūtra): *(a)* Translated by T'an-wu-ch'an (421) in northwest China. *T.* 12, no. 374; *(b)* Translated by Hui-yen (ca. 433) in the south in Chien-k'ang. *T.* 12, no. 375. This is a revision of no. 374; *(c)* (Ta pan ni-yüan ching), translated by Fa-hsien (413–416) in the south in Chien-k'ang. *T.* 12, no. 376.

Infinite Life Scripture (Wu liang shou ching) (Sukhāvatīvyūha-sūtra). Translated by Sanghavarman (252), in the north in Lo-yang. *T.* 12, no. 360. Translated from the Sanskrit by F. Max Müller, *The Larger Sukhāvatī-vyūha*, and *The Smaller Sukhāvatīvyūha*. In *Sacred Books of the East*, vol. 49.

Kuan-shih-yin Scripture. See *Bodhisattva Kuan-shih-yin Scripture*.

Larger Perfection of Wisdom Scripture (Mo-ho pan-jo po-lo-mi ching) (Pañchavimshati-sāhasrikā-prajñāpāramitā-sūtra). Translated by Kumārajīva (401–409 or 413), in the north in Ch'ang-an. *T.* 8, no. 223. Translated from the Sanskrit by E. Conze, *The Large Sutra on the Perfection of Wisdom: With the Divisions of the Abhisamayalankara*. Berkeley, Calif.: Center for South and Southeast Asia Studies, University of California, Berkeley, 1974.

Lion's Roar of Queen Shrīmālā (Sheng-man shih-tzu hou i sheng ta fang pien fang kuang ching) (Shrīmālā-simhanāda-sūtra). Translated by Gunabhadra (443–468), in the south in Chien-k'ang. *T.* 12, no. 353. Translated into English, *The Lion's Roar of Queen Śrīmālā*, by Alex and Hideko Wayman. Columbia University Press: New York, 1974.

Lun yü (Lun yü cheng i) (Correct interpretation of the Analects). In *Chu tzu chi ch'eng* (Complete collection of all the philosophers), 8 vols. Peking: Chung-hua Publishing, 1954. For translations see Sources, Reference Works, and Readings.

Mencius (Meng-tzu cheng i) (Correct interpretation of Mencius). In *Chu tzu chi ch'eng* (Complete collection of all the philosophers), 8 vols. Peking: Chung-hua Publishing, 1954. For translations see Sources, Reference Works, and Readings.

Mother of Monasticism Scripture (P'i-ni mu ching) (Vinayamātrkā). Translator unknown (350–431). *T.* 24, no. 1463.

Origin of Monastic Rules Scripture (Chieh yin-yüan ching) (alternate name: *Vinaya* [Pi-nai-yeh]). Translated by Chu Fo-nien (ca. 385), in the north in Ch'ang-an. *T.* 24, no. 1464.

Practice of Constant Meditation Scripture (Pan chou [san-mei] ching). *T.* 13, no. 418. See also *T.* 13, nos. 417, 419.

Rituals for Entering the Monastic Life (of the Dharmaguptaka sect) (Chieh-mo, Ssu fen pi-ch'iu-ni chieh-mo fa). Translated by Gunavarman (431), in the south in Chien-k'ang. *T.* 22, no. 1434.

Sarvāstivāda Monastic Rules in Ten Recitations (Shih sung lü). Translated by Punyatara, Dharmaruci, and Kumārajīva (ca. 406–410), in the north in Ch'ang-an. *T.* 23, no. 1435.

Shrīmālā-devī-simhanāda-sūtra (Sheng-man shih-tzu hou i sheng ta fang pien fang kuang ching) (Shrīmālā Scripture). See *Lion's Roar of Queen Srīmālā.*

Shūrangama Scripture (Shou-leng-yen san-mei ching) (Shūrangama [samādhi] sūtra). Translated by Kumārajīva (401–409 or 413), in the north in Ch'ang-an. *T.* 15, no. 642. Translated from Chinese as *The Shurangama Sutra.* 7 vols. Commentary by Hsüan Hua. City of Ten Thousand Buddhas, Talmage, CA: Buddhist Text Translation Society and the International Institute for the Translation of Buddhist Texts, 1977–1980.

Smaller Perfection of Wisdom Scripture (Hsiao p'in pan-jo po-lo-mi ching) (Astasāhasrikā-prajñāpāramitā-sūtra). Translated by Kumārajīva (401–409 or 413). *T.* 8, no. 227. Translated from the Sanskrit by E. Conze, *The Perfection of Wisdom in 8,000 Lines and Its Verse Summary.* Wheel series no. 1. San Francisco: Four Seasons Foundation, 1973.

Ten-Stages Scripture (Shih ti ching) (Dashabhūmika-sūtra). This abbreviated title probably refers to chap. 22 in the *Flower Garland Scripture.*

Universal Gate Chapter. Chapter in the *Flower of the Law.*

Vimalakīrti's Preaching Scripture (Vimalakīrti-nirdesha-sūtra): *(a) Vimalakīrti Scripture* (Wei-mo-chieh ching). Translated by Chih Ch'ien (220–252), in the south in Chien-k'ang. *T.* 14, no. 474; *(b) Vimalakīrti's Preaching Scripture* (Wei-mo-chieh so shuo ching). Translated by Kumārajīva (401–409 or 413), in the north in Ch'ang-an. *T.* 14, no. 475. Translated from Kumārajīva's Chinese text into English by Charles Luk, *The Vimalakīrti Nirdesa Sutra.* Boston: Shambala Publications, 1990.

Sources, Reference Works, and Readings

An asterisk marks the more easily available works that may be of further interest to the reader.

Biographies of Buddhist Nuns: Pao-chang's Pi-chiu-ni chuan. Translated by Li Jung-hsi. Ōsaka: Tohokai, 1981. See also Tsai, Kathryn. "Review of *Biographies of Buddhist Nuns, Pao-chang's Pi-chiu-ni chuan,*" translated by Li Jung-hsi, *Cahiers d'Extrême-Asie* 1 (1989): 87–101. Mr. Li's translation is adequate, except for the sections where references to sources other than the biographies themselves, such as the Chinese Buddhist scriptures, the dynastic histories, or important secondary sources were necessary to understand the text. His introduction, however, was written under political circumstances that apparently constrained him to make statements that, although not contradicting the official ideology, were quite contrary to what was evident in the biographies themselves. Although of interest, the book is for all practical purposes unobtainable in the United States.

*Blofeld, John E. *The Wheel of Life: The Autobiography of a Western Buddhist.* Boston: Shambala Publications, 1988. Mr. Blofeld is an accurate and eloquent observer. This account of his sojourn in China before World War II gives us a vicarious experience of things that are no more.

Buddhist Texts through the Ages. Edited by Edward Conze. New York: Harper & Row, 1964. Contains selections from the whole range of Buddhist scriptures. It includes Arthur Waley's translation of biographies 1, 27, and 55.

*Chen-hua. *In Search of the Dharma: Memoires of a Modern Chinese Buddhist Pilgrim.* Edited by Chün-fang Yü and translated by Denis C. Mair. Albany: State University of New York Press, 1992. A lively, readable account of a modern Chinese Buddhist pilgrim.

*Ch'en, Kenneth. "Anti-Buddhist Propaganda during the Nan-ch'ao." *Harvard Journal of Asiatic Studies* 15(1952): 166–192. The period covered by this article is exactly the same as that covered by *Lives of the Nuns.* Ch'en translates many arguments offered by both Taoists and Confucians against the foreign religion of Buddhism, as well as the responses by Buddhist apologists.

*———. *Buddhism in China: A Historical Survey.* Princeton, N.J.: Princeton University Press, 1964. Ch'en's valuable book has something on every aspect of Buddhism in China and also includes an excellent bibliography.

*———. *The Transformation of Chinese Buddhism.* Princeton, N.J.: Princeton University Press, 1973. An overview of cultural aspects of Buddhism in China.

Chi shen chou san pao kan t'ung lu (Collection of records of miracles wrought in China by faith in the Three Treasures). Compiled by Tao-hsüan (596–667). T. 52, no. 2106.

Chin shu (History of the Chin dynasty). 10 vols. Compiled by Fang Hsüan-ling (578–648) and others. Peking: Chung-hua Publishing, 1974.

Ch'u san-tsang chi chi (Collected notes on the translation of the Buddhist scriptures into Chinese). By Seng-yu (ca. 515). T. 55, no. 2145.

Chu wei-mo-chieh ching (Commentary to the Vimalakīrti). By Seng-chao (374–414). T. 35, no. 1775.

Chuang Tzu. *Complete Works of Chuang Tzu.* Translated by Burton Watson. New York and London: Columbia University Press, 1968.

Chung-kuo ku chin ti ming ta tz'u tien (Dictionary of Chinese place names ancient and modern). Compiled by Tsang Li-ho and others. 2d. ed. Hong Kong: Shang-wu Publishing, 1933.

Classic of History. See *Shoo-King* (Shu ching).

Collected Notes on the Translation of the Buddhist Scriptures into Chinese. See *Ch'u san-tsang chi chi.*

Commentary to the Vimalakīrti. See *Chu wei-mo-chieh ching.*

Confucius. The Analects. Translated by D. C. Lau. New York: Penguin Classics, 1979; and *The Analects of Confucius.* Translated by Arthur Waley. N.Y.: Vintage Books, 1938. Both of these excellent scholarly translations of the *Lun yü,* each with a valuable introduction, are available in convenient editions.

Cullavagga. Vol. 20 in *Sacred Books of the East,* edited by F. Max Müeller. Reprint. Delhi: Motilal Banarsidass, 1965.

de Groot, J. J. M. *The Religious System of China.* 6 vols. Reprint. Taipei: Ch'eng Wen Publishing, 1972.

Demiéville, Paul. "Momies d'Extrême-Orient." *Journal des Savants* (1965): 144–170; reprinted in P. Demiéville, *Choix d'étude sinologiques.* Leiden: E. J. Brill, 1973, pp. 407–432.

des Rotours, Robert. *Traité des fonctionnaires et traité de l'armée, traduits de la nouvelle histoire des T'ang* (chaps. 44–50) vols. 1, 2. Bibliotheque de l'institut des hautes études chinoises, vol. 6. Leiden: E. J. Brill, 1948, 1949.

Dharmaguptaka-bhikshunī-pratimoksha. See *Ssu fen pi-ch'iu-ni chieh pen.*

Dharmaguptaka-vinaya. See *Ssu fen lü*

Dudbridge, Glen. *The Legend of Miao-shan.* London, Oxford Oriental Monographs No.1, Oxford University, 1978.

Ekottarāgama. See *Tseng i a-han ching.*

Eliade, Mircea. *Myths, Dreams, and Mysteries.* New York: Harper Torchbooks, 1967.

———. *Shamanism: Archaic Techniques of Ecstasy* (in French). Translated by Willard R. Trask. Bollingen Series no. 77. Princeton, N.J.: Princeton University Press, 1964.

Eminent Monks. See *Kao seng chuan.*

Ennin's Diary: The Record of a Pilgrimage to China in Search of the Law. Translated by Edwin O. Reischauer. New York: Ronald Press, 1955. This Japanese pilgrim traveled to China just in time to witness the great persecution in the mid-ninth century. Although the time is later than that covered by the biographies of the nuns, it is still valuable for its eye-witness account of Buddhism in medieval China.

Fa yüan chu lin (Forest of pearls in the garden of the law). Compiled by Tao-shih (fl. 656–668). *T.* 53 no. 2122.

Facets of Taoism in Chinese Religion. Edited by Holmes Welch and Anna Seidel. New Haven, Conn.: Yale University Press, 1979.

Fo tsu t'ung chi (Thorough record of the Buddha's lineage). Compiled by Chih-p'an (fl. 1258–1269). *T.* 49 no. 2035.

Forest of Pearls in the Garden of the Law. See *Fa yüan chu lin.*

*Friedman, Lenore. *Meetings with Remarkable Women: Buddhist Teachers in America.* Boston: Shambala Publications, 1987.

Further Lives of Eminent Monks. See *Hsü kao seng chuan.*

Gernet, Jacques. *Les aspects économiques du bouddhisme dans la société chinoise du Vᵉ au Xᵉ siècle.* Paris: École Française d'Extrême Orient, 1956.

————. "Les suicides par le feu chez les bouddhistes chinois du Vᵉ au Xᵉ siècle." *Mélanges publiés par l'Institut des Hautes Études chinoises* 2 (1960): 527–558.

Great Perfection of Wisdom Treatise. See *Ta chih tu lun.*

Great Sung Dynasty Compact History of the Buddhist Assemblies. See *Ta sung seng shih lüeh.*

Han fa pen nei chuan (Hidden account of the origin of the [Buddhist] law in the Han dynasty.) This text was probably forged during the sixth century and no longer exists as a separate work, but parts and summaries exist in other works. See Zürcher, *Buddhist Conquest,* vol. 2, p. 325, n. 23.

Han shu (History of the Former Han dynasty), 12 vols. By Pan Ku (32–92). Peking: Chung-hua Publishing, 1987.

Han shu i wen chih (Bibliography in the history of the Former Han dynasty), Chap. 30 of *Han shu* (q.v.).

*Herrmann, Albert. *Historical and Commercial Atlas of China.* Harvard-Yenching Institute monograph series no. 1. Cambridge, Mass.: Harvard University Press, 1935. This old but still valuable work is excellent for its graphic presentation of the shifting political boundaries of the Northern and Southern dynasties. It also has maps of the ancient capitals of Ch'ang-an, Lo-yang, and Chien-k'ang (Nanjing). The entire atlas is a treat for those who enjoy contemplating history by means of maps.

Hirakawa Akira. *Ritsuzō-no-kenkyū.* Tokyo: Sankibo-Busshorin, 1970.

Historical Atlas of China, The (Chung-kuo li-shih ti-t'u chi). Vol. 4, *The Eastern Jin Dynasty and Sixteen Kingdoms Period, The Southern and Northern Dynasties Period.* Edited by Tan Qixiang. Shanghai: Cartographic Publishing House, 1982. Title and introduction in Chinese and English, maps in Chinese only.

*Horner, I. B. *Women under Primitive Buddhism.* 1930. Reprint. Delhi: Motilal Banarsidass, 1975. This is a study of monastic life for women in the earliest days of Buddhism in India.

Hou han shu (History of the Latter Han dynasty). By Fan Yeh. 12 vols. Peking: Chung-hua Publishing, 1965.

Hsü kao seng chuan (Further lives of eminent monks). By Tao Hsüan (596–667). *T.* 50, no. 2060.

*Jan Yun-hua. "Buddhist Self-Immolation in Medieval China," *History of Religions*, 4, no. 2 (winter 1965): 243–268. This article discusses all kinds of suicides, not only those by fire.

K'ai-yüan shih chiao lu (The T'ang *k'ai-yüan* reign period catalogue of Buddhist writings). By Shih Chih-sheng (ca. 730). T. 5, no. 2154.

K'ai-yüan shih chiao lu lüeh ch'u (The condensed T'ang *k'ai-yüan* reign period catalogue of Buddhist writings). By Shih Chih-sheng (ca. 730). T. 5, no. 2155.

*Kaltenmark, Max. *Lao Tzu and Taoism* (in French). Translated by Robert Greaves. Stanford, Calif.: Stanford University Press, 1969. A popular and erudite introduction to Taoism.

Kao seng chuan (Lives of eminent monks). By Hui-chiao (ca. 530). T. 50, no. 2059.

Kao seng Fa Hsien chuan (Biography of the eminent monk Fa Hsien). T. 51, no. 2085.

Kasuga Reichi, "Jōdokyō-shiryō to shite no meisōden-shishishō meisōden-yōbun chō narabi ni mirokunyorai kannō shō dai shi shōin no meisō-den ni tsuite," *Shūgaku Kenkyū* 12 (1936): 53–118. (The title of this journal has been miscopied as *Shūkyō Kenkyū* in other publications.)

Ku chin t'u shu chi ch'eng (Imperial encyclopedia, or, Complete collection of books and records ancient and modern). Chung-hua Publishing, 1934. Photolithographic reproduction of palace edition, presented to the emperor in 1725.

Kuang hung ming chi (The extended collection making known the illustrious). Compiled by Tao-hsüan (fl. 624–667). T. 52, no. 2103.

Kuang tsan ching (Perfection of wisdom in 25,000 lines; Sanskrit: *Pañchavim-shatisāhasrikā-prajñā-pāramitā*). Translated by Chu Fa-hu (Dharmaraksha) (fl. 265–310) in the north in Chang-an and Lo-yang. T. 8, no. 222.

*Lao tzu tao teh ching. Vol. 3, *Chu tzu chi ch'eng,* Chung-hua Publishing, 1954. Many good translations into English are available.

*Le Lie-sien tchouan: Biographies légendaires des immortals taoïstes de l'antiquité. Translated by Max Kaltenmark. Peking: Université de Paris, Publications du centre d'études sinologiques de Pékin, 1953.

Lévi, S., and E. Chavannes, "Les seize arhat protecteurs de la loi." *Journal Asiatique* 8, series 11, (September–October 1916): 189–304.

Li tai san pao chi (Records of the Three Treasures through the ages). By Fei Ch'ang-fang (597). T. 49, no. 2043.

Liang shu (History of the Liang dynasty). 3 vols. Compiled by Yao Ssu-lien (636). Peking: Chung-hua Publishing, 1973.

Lieh nü chuan (Lives of Illustrious Women). Compiled by Liu Hsiang (77–6 B.C.).

*Link, Arthur E. "Biography of Shih Tao-an." *T'oung Pao* 46(1958): 1–48. A

very scholarly translation of the biography of Shih Tao-an, a man of
exceeding importance in the early history of Buddhism in China.

―――. "Shih Seng-yu and His Writings," *Journal of the American Oriental
Society* 80, no. 1 (January/March 1960): 17–43.

―――. "Taoist antecedents of Tao-an's Ontology," *Symposium on Taoism in
History of Religions* nos. 2, 3 (November 1969–February 1970):
181–215.

*Liu I-ch'ing. *Shih-shuo hsin-yü.* Translated by Richard Mather. *A New
Account of Tales of the World.* Minneapolis: University of Minnesota
Press, 1976. A highly entertaining collection of tales of lives and events
covering roughly the years 120–420, therefore overlapping somewhat
with the *Lives of the Nuns.* The tales are divided by category and for
the most part deal with members of the upper classes.

Lives of Eminent Monks. See *Kao seng chuan.*

Lives of Famous Monks. See *Meisōden-shō.*

Lives of Illustrious Women. See *Lieh nü chuan.*

Lives of the Nuns. See *Pi-ch'iu-ni chuan.*

Lo-yang ch'ieh-lan chi. By Yang Hsüan-chih (532–534). *T.* 51, no. 2092.
Reprinted. Taipei: Shih-chieh Publishing, 1962.

Lu Hsün. *Ku hsiao-shuo kou ch'en* (A study of ancient fiction).
2 vols. Hong Kong: Hsin-yi (New Arts) Publishing, 1967.

Lun yü. See Confucius.

Mahāprajāpatī-sūtra. See *Ta-ai-tao pi-ch'iu-ni ching.*

Mahāsānghika-bhiksunī-prātimoksha. See *Mo-ha-seng-shih pi-ch'iu-ni chieh
pen.*

Mahīshāsaka-vinaya. See *Mi-sha-se pu ho hsi wu fen lü;* and *Mo-ha-seng-shih
pi-ch'iu-ni chieh pen.*

Maspero, Henri. "Les Origins de la communauté bouddhist de Loyang." *Journal Asiatique* 225 (1934): 87–107.

―――. *Le Taoïsme et les religions chinoises.* Paris: Gallimard, 1971.

Meisōden-shō (Ming seng chuan ch'ao) (Selections from the lives of famous
monks). In *Zoku-zōkyō,* ser. 2 (Tokyo: Zōkyō-shoin, 1905–1912),
part 2z, case 7, vol. 1. (Reprint, Taipei: Shin Wen Feng, vol. 134, n.d.)

Mencius. Translated by D. C. Lau. London: Penguin, 1970. An excellent
scholarly translation in a convenient edition. Chinese version in *Chu
tzu chi ch'eng,* vol. 1, Peking: Chung-hua Publishing, 1954.

Method for Inviting Pindola (Ch'ing pin-t'ou-lu fa). Translated by Hui-chien
(457), in the south near Chien-k'ang. *T.* 32, no. 1689.

Mi-sha-se pu ho hsi wu fen lü (Mahīshāsaka-vinaya). Translated by Fo-t'o-
shih and Chu Tao-sheng (early fifth century). *T.* 22, no. 1421.

Ming hsiang chi (Records of mysterious omens). By Wang Yen (ca. 479). The
complete book is no longer extant, but fragments have been brought

together by Lu Hsün in *Ku hsiao-shou kou ch'en* (A study of ancient fiction). 2 vols. Hong Kong: Hsin-i (New Arts) Publishing, 1967.

Ming seng chuan (Lives of famous monks). By Shih Pao-ch'ang. See *Meisō-den-shō.*

Mo-ha-seng-shih pi-ch'iu-ni chieh pen (Mahāsānghika bhikshunī-prātimoksha). Translated by Fa Hsien (ca. 416+). *T.* 22, no. 1427.

Mochizuki Shinkō. *Bukkyō-daijiten* (Encyclopedia of Buddhism). 10 vols. Tokyo: Seikai-shōten, 1968.

Nan ch'i shu (History of the Southern Ch'i dynasty). 3 vols. Compiled by Hsiao Tzu-hsien (489–537). Peking: Chung-hua Publishing, 1972.

Nan shih (History of the Southern dynasties). 6 vols. Compiled by Li Yen-shou (mid-seventh century). Peking: Chung-hua Publishing, 1975.

*Needham, Joseph. *Science and Civilisation in China.* Cambridge: Cambridge University Press, various dates. This series about the history of science in China can be of great interest and use to the general reader who is not necessarily well versed in science. Volumes 1, 2, and 5.2 have much on Chinese history in general and on both Buddhism and Taoism as well as other Chinese philosophical traditions. The bibliographies are exceptionally full.

Ngo Van Xuyet. *Divination magie et politique dans la Chine ancienne.* Paris: Presses Universitaires de France, 1976.

Oda Tokunō. *Bukkyō-daijiten.* Revised ed. Tokyo: Daizō-shuppan, 1969.

*O'Hara, Albert Richard, S. J. *The Position of Women in Early China.* Washington, D.C.: Catholic University of America Press, 1945. Translates and analyzes the *Lieh nü chuan* (Lives of illustrious women), compiled by Liu Hsiang (77–6 B.C.).

*Paul, Diana. *Women in Buddhism.* Berkeley, Calif.: Asian Humanities Press, 1980. A thorough study of the feminine in Buddhism.

Pi-ch'iu-ni chuan (Lives of the nuns). Compiled by Shih Pao-ch'ang (ca. 516), in the south in Chien-k'ang. *T.* 50, no. 2063.

Pi-nai-yeh (Vinaya). Translated by Chu Fo-nien (fl. 365–385) in the north in Ch'ang-an. *T.* 24, no. 1464.

*Prip-Møller, Johannes. *Chinese Buddhist Monasteries: Their Plan and Its Function as a Setting for Buddhist Monastic Life.* 1937. Reprint. 2d ed. Hong Kong: Hong Kong University Press, 1967. The materials for this extraordinary book were collected during the late 1920s and 1930s amid the terrible conditions prevalent at that time in China. Numerous photographs and drawings are enhanced by the discussion in the text. This book, together with Holmes Welch's *Practice of Chinese Buddhism* (see below), present the best picture that we have of the time when Buddhist monastic life in mainland China was viable and thriving.

Psalms of the Sisters (Therīgāthā). Translated by Caroline Rhys Davids. London: Pali Text Society translation series no. 1, Luzac, 1909; 1964. This is a translation of a very early collection of verses supposedly recited by women at the time of their enlightenment. It is the only other Buddhist canonical work (it is found in the Pali canon) that can compare with the Chinese *Lives of the Nuns*. It is not biographical in the historical sense but rather in the realm of the heart and spirit and complements the *Lives* very well.

Record of Buddhistic Kingdoms, A: Being an account by the Chinese monk Fa-hien of his travels in India and Ceylon (A.D. 399–414) in search of the Buddhist books of discipline. Translated and annotated with a Corean recension of the Chinese text by James Legge. New York: Paragon Book Reprint Corp., and Dover Publications, Inc., 1965.

Record of Monasteries and Convents in Lo-yang, A. See *Lo-yang ch'ieh-lan chi.*

Records of Mysterious Omens. See *Ming hsiang chi.*

Répertoire du canon bouddhique Sino-Japonais, édition de Taishō (Catalogue of the Sino-Japanese Buddhist canon of the Taishō edition). Supplement to Hōbōgirin. 2d ed., rev. and enl. Edited by Paul Demiéville, Hubert Durt, and Anna Seidel. Paris: Adrien-maisonneuve, 1978.

Robinson, Richard H. *Early Mādhyamika in India and China.* Madison: University of Wisconsin Press, 1967.

*Robinson, Richard H., and Willard Johnson. *The Buddhist Religion.* 3d ed. Belmont, Calif.: Wadsworth Publishing, 1982. A general historical introduction to Buddhism from its beginning to the present day.

Rogers, Michael C., trans. *The Chronicle of Fu Chien: A Case of Exemplar History.* Chinese Dynastic Histories translation no. 10. Berkeley and Los Angeles: University of California Press, 1968.

*Seidel, Anna. "Chronicle of Taoist Studies in the West 1950–1990." *Cahiers d'Extrême-Asie* 5 (1989–1990): 233–347. A scholarly treat for the specialist.

Selections from the Lives of Famous Monks. See *Meisōden-shō.*

Seng-chao. *Chu wei-mo-chieh ching* (Commentary to the Vimalakīrti scripture). *T.* 38, no. 1775.

Seven Tallies in a Cloud Satchel. See *Yün chi ch'i ch'ien.*

Shih Pao-ch'ang. See *Meisōden-shō.*

Shoo-king. Translated by James Legge. Shanghai: Shanghai Publishing, 1904. Includes Chinese text.

Soper, Alexander. "Literary Evidence for Early Buddhist Art in China." *Artibus Asiae.* Suppl. 19. 1959.

Ssu fen lü (Dharmaguptaka-vinaya). Translated by Buddhayashas and Chu Fo-nien (ca. 365), in Ch'ang-an, in the north. *T.* 22, no. 1428.

Ssu fen pi-ch'iu-ni chieh-mo fa (Dharmaguptaka nuns' rites and rules book).

Translated by Gunavarman (431), in the south in Chien-k'ang. *T.* 22, no. 1434.

Ssu fen pi-ch'iu-ni chieh pen (Dharmaguptaka nuns' rule book). Translated by Buddhayashas (ca. 408–412), in Ch'ang-an, in the north. *T.* 22, no. 1431.

Stein, R. A. "Remarques sur les mouvements du Taoïsme politico-religieux au IIᵉ siècle ap. J.-C." *T'oung Pao* 50 (1963): 1–78.

Study of Ancient Fiction. See Lu Hsün. *Ku hsiao-shuo kou ch'en.*

Sung kao seng chuan (The Sung dynasty biographies of eminent monks). Compiled by Ts'an-ning (919–1001). *T.* 50, no. 2061.

Sung shu (History of the Sung dynasty). 8 vols. Compiled by Shen Yüeh (441–513). Peking: Chung-hua Publishing, 1974.

Symposium on Taoism. In *History of Religions.* 9, nos. 2, 3 (November 1969/February 1970): 107–255.

Ta-ai-tao pi-ch'iu-ni ching (The scripture of Mahāprajāpatī's vinaya). (412–439) Anonymous. *T.* 24, no. 1478.

Ta chih tu lun (Great perfection of wisdom treatise). By Nāgārjuna. Translated into Chinese by Kumārajīva. *T.* 25, no. 1509, and into French by E. Lamotte, *Le Traité de la grande vertu de Sagesse de Nāgārjuna.* Vol. 1. Louvain: Publications Universitaires, 1949; reprinted 1966.

Ta sung seng shih lüeh (Great Sung dynasty compact history of the Buddhist assemblies). Compiled by Ts'an-ning (997). *T.* 54, no. 2126.

T'ai-p'ing yü lan (The *T'ai-p'ing* encyclopedia). Compiled by Li Fang et al. in the mid-tenth century. Reprint. Taipei: Ta-hua Publishing, 1980.

Taishō-shinshū-daizōkyō (Chinese Buddhist canon newly edited in the Taishō era [1912–1925]). 55 vols. Edited by Takakusu Junjirō, Watanabe Kaigyoku, and Ono Gemmyō, Tokyo: Taisho Issai-kyō kanko kwai, 1924–1929.

T'ang Yung-t'ung, *Han wei liang-chin nan-pei-ch'ao fo-chiao shih* (History of Buddhism in the Han, Wei, Chin, and southern and northern dynasties). Peking, Chung-hua Publishing, 1955.

*Teachings of the Compassionate Buddha. Edited with commentary by E. A. Burtt. New York: Mentor Books, 1959. Pocket-sized selection of texts from all types of Buddhism.

*Thompson, Laurence G. *The Chinese Way in Religion.* Encino and Belmont, Calif.: Dickenson Publishing, 1973. This volume reprints the diary, first published in 1923, of a modern Chinese woman who decides to become a Buddhist nun.

———. *Chinese Religion: An introduction.* 2d ed. Encino and Belmont, Calif.: Dickenson Publishing Co., 1975.

Thorough Record of the Buddha's Lineage. See *Fo tsu t'ung chi.*

*Tsai, Kathryn. "The Chinese Buddhist Monastic Order for Women: The First Two Centuries." *Historical Reflections/Réflexions Historiques* 8, no. 3 (fall 1981): 1–20. A very technical version of the present introduction to the biographies of the nuns.

Tseng i a-han ching. Translated by T'i-ho (Gautama Sanghadeva) [ca. 383–398], in both north and south. *T.* 2, no. 125.

Tsukamoto Zenryū. *Chūgoku bukkyō tsūshi* (History of Chinese Buddhism). Tokyo: Suzuki-gakujitsu zaidan, 1968.

*Van Gulik, Robert. *Sexual Life in Ancient China: A Preliminary Survey of Chinese Sex and Society from ca. 1500 B.C. till 1644 A.D.* Leiden: E. J. Brill, 1961. This valuable book provides much information about the life that Buddhist nuns left behind.

Watson, Burton. *The Complete Works of Chuang Tzu.* New York: Columbia University Press, 1968

Waley, Arthur F. *The Analects of Confucius.* See Confucius.

Wei shu (History of the Wei dynasty). 8 vols. Compiled by Wei Shou (551). Peking: Hsin-hua Publishing, 1974.

*Welch, Holmes. *Taoism: The Parting of the Way.* Rev. ed. Boston: Beacon Press, 1966. A well-written overview of Taoism.

*———. *The Practice of Chinese Buddhism, 1900–1950.* Cambridge, Mass.: Harvard University Press, 1967. Welch interviewed many monks who had fled from mainland China after the communist takeover and, using their testimony, reconstructed general patterns of life in Chinese Buddhist monasteries. It is a very valuable book that stands together with *Chinese Buddhist Monasteries* by Johannes Prip-Møller (see above).

*Wright, Arthur F. "Biography of the Nun An Ling-shou." *Harvard Journal of Asiatic Studies* 15(1952): 193–196. Another version of biography 2.

*———. *Buddhism in Chinese History.* Stanford, Calif.: Stanford University Press, 1959. A short introductory book.

*———. "Fo-t'u-teng: A Biography." *Harvard Journal of Asiatic Studies* 11(1948): 321–371. A very scholarly translation of Fo-t'u-teng's biography with introduction and annotation that gives a good picture of the times.

———. "Biography and Hagiography: Hui-chiao's Lives of Eminent Monks." *Silver Jubilee Volume of Jimbunkagakukenkyushō (Zinbunkagakukenkyusyō)*, pp. 383–432. Kyoto: Jimbun Kagaku Kenkyūsyo, 1954. A good study of the *Kao seng chuan* and its sources but hard to find.

Yün chi ch'i ch'ien (Seven tallies in a cloud satchel). 3 vols. Taipei: Tzu-yu Publishing, 1978. A Sung-dynasty collection (ca. 1025) of major Taoist writings.

Zoku-zōkyō, ser. 2. Tokyo: Zōkyō-shoin, 1905–1912. See also *Meisōden-shō.*

*Zürcher, Erik. *The Buddhist Conquest of China: The Spread and Adaptation of Buddhism in Early Medieval China.* 2 vols. Leiden: E. J. Brill, 1959. A solid work of the history of the period.

INDEX

Persons and Place Names

Ānanda, Buddha's disciple, 133 n. 92

Central Asia: and importance in spread of Buddhism, 117 n. 13
Chang, Empress (Madame Ho), 26
Chang, Lady, mother of prince of Lin-ch'uan, 101
Chang Chün, 94
Chang Pien, governor of Yü-chang, 39
Chang Tai, governor of I Province, 71
Ch'ang-an: convents in, 6; sacked by nomads, 3
Ch'ao-ming, nun, 83–84
Ch'ao-pien, Master of the Law, 59
Chen Fa-ch'ung, governor of I Province, 92
Chiang, Madame, wife of Wang Lu: composed eulogy, 73
Chieh-jen, nun, 101
Chien-wen, emperor of Chin, 30
Chih-hsien, nun, 21–23
Chih-shan, monk of Kashmir, 18
Chih-sheng, nun, 73–76
Chih-yüeh, monk, 95–96
Ching-ai, nun, 58
Ching-ch'eng, nun, 48, 55–56
Ching-chien, nun: as first Chinese Buddhist nun, 5, 17–19, 21, 62
Ching-hsien, nun, 97–98
Ching-hsing, nun, 99–100
Ching-hsiu, nun, 10, 87–91, 101; as Master of Meditation, 88; sources and versions of, 109
Ching-hui, nun, 78–79
Ching-kuei, nun, 80–81; and asceticism expressed in suicide by fire, 16
Ching-lien, nun, 78
Ching-yüan, nun, 98, 99
Chou Ying, scholar, 106, 151 n. 103

Ch'u, Empress, consort of K'ang, 28
Ch'ü An-yüan, fortune-teller, 31
Convent: Bamboo Garden, 61, 86, 99; Bamboo Grove in Lo-yang, 18; Bamboo Grove in Tung-hsiang of Shan-yang, 55; Beckoning Clarity, 106; Black River, 30; Brightness of Ch'i, 72, 84, 86, 105; Built by the Multitude, 70; Capital Office, 95; Central, 51; Chu-ko Village, 45, 46; Collected Goodness, 82, 97; Cowherd, 39; Eastern, 29; Eastern Green Garden, 78, 86, 97; Empress Dowager, 41; Empress Ho, 26, 35, 100; Establishing Blessings, 25, 27, 38, 40–41, 71, 74; Establishing Peace, 62, 69; Establishing Splendor, 44; Eternal Blessings, 63; Eternal Peace, 50, 58; Eternal Sanctity, 70; Expanding Nation, 44; Field of Blessings, 82; Flower Garland, 72; Flower Grove, 76; Foundation for Meditation, 76; Founding of Wisdom, 21; Great Mysterious Terrace, 42, 56; Green Garden, 58, 77, 88, 89; Increasing Joy, 28; Jeta Grove, 41; Joyful Peace, 103; Kingdom, 85; Luminous Blessings, 36, 53, 59, 62; Meditation Grove, 89, 91, 97, 101; New Grove, 31; North Peak, 23; Northern Everlasting Peace, 26; Peak Mountain, 105; Reflecting Brightness on White Mountain, 86; Saman-tabhadra, 78; Simple Tranquility, 33; Solitude, 102; South, 48; Southern Chin-ling, 100; Southern Eternal Peace, 68, 85; Southern Peace, 43; Three-story, 60, 81; Ti Mountain, 104; Universal Wisdom, 62, 64; Venerating Seclusion, 84; Voice of the Teaching, 79, 80, 84; West, 21; Western, 69;

General Subjects

www.ingramcontent.com/pod-product-compliance
Lightning Source LLC
Chambersburg PA
CBHW020458100426
42812CB00024B/2703